CW01511817

Move Slow and Upgrade

For far too long, tech titans peddled promises of disruptive innovation – fabricating benefits and minimizing harms. The promise of quick and easy fixes overpowered a growing chorus of critical voices, driving a sea of private and public investments into increasingly dangerous, misguided, and doomed forms of disruption, with the public paying the price. But what's the alternative? Upgrades – evidence-based, incremental change. Instead of continuing to invest in untested, high-risk innovations, constantly chasing outsized returns, upgraders seek a more proven path to proportional progress. This book dives deep into some of the most disastrous innovations of recent years – the metaverse, cryptocurrency, home surveillance, Covid-19, online proctoring, AI, and cybersecurity – while highlighting some of the unsung upgraders pushing real progress each day. Timely and corrective, *Move Slow and Upgrade* pushes us past the baseless promises of innovation, toward realistic hope.

EVAN SELINGER is a Professor of Philosophy at Rochester Institute of Technology. His research focuses on the ethical and privacy dimensions of emerging technology. Selinger's previous Cambridge University Press books include the co-authored *Re-Engineering Humanity* and co-edited *The Cambridge Handbook of Consumer Privacy*. He is a contributing writer at *The Boston Globe*.

ALBERT FOX CAHN is the Surveillance Technology Oversight Project's founder and Executive Director. He has served as Practitioner-in-Residence at NYU Law School's Information Law Institute and a fellow at the Harvard Kennedy School's Carr Center for Human Rights Policy, Yale Law School's Information Society Project, Ashoka, and TED.

"In this wise and timely book, Evan Selinger and Albert Fox Cahn offer an incisive critique of the 'move fast and break things' ideology of innovation that has done such harm to society in recent years. But they do something more: they provide a practical alternative, an approach to technological progress that aims not to disrupt people's lives but to make them richer and more fulfilling."

Nicholas Carr, author of *Superbloom* and *The Shallows*

"Selinger and Cahn have written a tour de force – a stirring indictment of many of the techno-utopian promises that have never fully come to fruition. *Move Slow and Upgrade* provides an urgent blueprint for policy-makers and citizens alike to thoughtfully and collectively improve our society."

Cyrus Farivar, author of *Habeas Data*

"We find ourselves at a moment where technological hype dominates narratives about who we are, who we should be, and what is possible. In this landscape, *Move Slow and Upgrade* is a crucial text, for layperson and expert alike, to help us understand how we got here and how to recognize innovation boosterism. Perhaps most importantly, through detailed case studies, the book shows us that another way is possible – that carefully upgrading rather than recklessly innovating is the key to addressing the problems we face as a society. *Move Slow and Upgrade* will be a foundational text at the intersection of tech and public policy for years to come."

Chris Gilliard, Co-director of The Critical Internet Studies Institute

"'Move fast and break things' has left us with a society that is collectively winded and flat broke. In *Move Slow and Upgrade*, Selinger and Cahn take stock of all the destruction and folly and then point us towards a better way. Their upgrader approach is a better way to build software products, companies, and ultimately, society."

Dave Karpf, Associate Professor of Media and Public Affairs, George Washington University

"Selinger and Cahn make a compelling and riveting case for what seems like it would be the most boring of arguments: that we should be more contemplative and recursive in how we deploy new innovations. It's an overdue, sharp, and thoughtful rebuke to tired but dominant theory driving technological development and markets. *Move Slow and Upgrade* isn't just the perfect title, it's a mantra we should shout from the rooftops."

Kate Klonick, Associate Professor, St. John's Law School

"*Move Slow and Upgrade* is a book at once cuttingly critical and wise. Selinger and Cahn take no prisoners in their debunking of fads like the metaverse and trends like AI job interviews. But they are also keenly aware of the many ways technology properly bounded and understood can make our lives better. They make incrementalism exciting in this fast-paced, enjoyable, and deeply edifying read."

Frank Pasquale, Professor of Law, Cornell Tech
and Cornell Law School

"With a sure hand and clear voice, Selinger and Cahn share a revolutionary new approach to the automated age: patient, mindful, and deliberately incremental development. In an age when our leading technologists seek to crash the systems by which we live, here's a hopeful and actionable path to a human-centered future."

Douglas Rushkoff, author of *Team Human* and *Survival of the Richest*

"An inciteful response to the culture of innovation at all costs, and to the many ways many innovators misunderstand technological change."

Bruce Schneier, author of *A Hacker's Mind*

"*Move Slow and Upgrade* is the perfect book for our high-tech moment: an ode to the joys and power of carefully and meticulously improving our high-tech systems, instead of lunging for the latest shiny toy. It's also a fun read – crammed with fascinating stories. Read it and upgrade yourself."

Clive Thompson, author of *Coders: The Making of a New Tribe
and the Remaking of the World*

Evan Selinger
Albert Fox Cahn

Move
Slow and
Upgrade

The Power of
Incremental Innovation

CAMBRIDGE
UNIVERSITY PRESS

CAMBRIDGE
UNIVERSITY PRESS

Shaftesbury Road, Cambridge CB2 8EA, United Kingdom

One Liberty Plaza, 20th Floor, New York, NY 10006, USA

477 Williamstown Road, Port Melbourne, VIC 3207, Australia

314–321, 3rd Floor, Plot 3, Splendor Forum, Jasola District Centre, New Delhi – 110025, India

103 Penang Road, #05–06/07, Visioncrest Commercial, Singapore 238467

Cambridge University Press is part of Cambridge University Press & Assessment, a department of the University of Cambridge.

We share the University's mission to contribute to society through the pursuit of education, learning and research at the highest international levels of excellence.

www.cambridge.org
Information on this title: www.cambridge.org/9781009466578

DOI: 10.1017/9781009466592

When citing this work, please include a reference to the DOI 10.1017/ 9781009466592

First published 2026

Printed in the United Kingdom by CPI Group Ltd, Croydon CR0 4YY

A catalogue record for this publication is available from the British Library

A Cataloging-in-Publication data record for this book is available from the Library of Congress

ISBN 978-1-009-46657-8 Hardback

For EU product safety concerns, contact us at Calle de José Abascal, 56, 1°, 28003 Madrid, Spain, or email eugpsr@cambridge.org

For those who do the hard work, walk the long path, even as others seek shortcuts.

Contents

Foreword

Justin Hendrix, CEO and Editor of Tech Policy Press

If you are ever invited to write the foreword to a non-fiction book that describes phenomena in the recent past, one thing you may observe in your reading is how the assumptions and assertions in the text have aged in the few short months since the authors put down their pens or entered their last keystroke before sending the final draft to the publisher. One of the dangers any author faces is that events will overtake them and that their words will seem, at best, stale or feeble or, at worst, plain wrong. The inverse of this danger is the possibility that events will reinforce the author's conclusions.

The book you are holding is an example of the latter scenario. While Selinger and Cahn completed their work just after the November 2024 US election, from my temporal vantage, only three months into 2025, many of their conclusions speak directly to the events of recent weeks. As the world's richest man – a technologist who, perhaps more than any other person, is the archetype of the disruptive innovator – proceeds to wage a "war on bureaucracy" in his bid to purportedly reduce the size of the US federal government and increase its efficiency, the dangers of setting disruptive "innovation" as the North Star have never been more apparent. Elon Musk's chaotic project to install artificial intelligence in place of institutions, to pool data once kept in silos out of fears over the despotic power that might come from combining it, and to make government ever more reliant on a handful of big technology firms has put these dangers in stark relief.

This book gives us the tools to evaluate such dangers and more. Yet it primarily offers us an alternative to the Silicon Valley brand of innovation that has produced them. The authors urge the reader to adopt an "upgrade mentality" rather than the "innovation mentality" or the "casino mentality" favored by so many of today's technologists and capitalists. The upgrade mentality does not mean deference to or preference for the status quo, but it is a rejection of the solutionist approach of today's technology industry. Rather than putting our faith entirely in the next technological marvel, Selinger and Cahn propose an "evidence-based, sustainable pathway to progress that addresses our society's most intractable issues."

It is not that there is no room for disruptive innovation. The authors do not argue for stopping the advancement of new technologies. Instead, they call for more care and judiciousness in their application. "Wisdom," they write, "requires admitting that innovation's shortcomings have not been widely enough acknowledged, and a combination of arrogance and ignorance has led to tremendous overinvestment in it." The internet, they argue, may be one example: it is dawning on many that the version of the internet we have arrived at a quarter way into this century may present more obstacles to human progress than it does advantages.

This caution seems particularly necessary when government leaders worldwide appear eager to collaborate with the tech elite to invest heavily in the development and adoption of artificial intelligence. On some level, who can blame the politicians? With democracy in decline and trust in institutions plumbing new lows, the magic elixir on sale from firms such as Google, Microsoft, Meta, and OpenAI must have an intoxicating aroma to politicians desperate to solve complex, interconnected problems that are increasingly beyond their control. But the promise of artificial intelligence, as sold by figures such as Elon Musk and OpenAI CEO Sam Altman, goes beyond solving today's challenges. In the near term, we are told, tech firms will achieve artificial general intelligence – the ultimate innovation. Our economies, our politics, and the very nature of our existence are poised for disruption, they say. The challenge of separating hype from reality when it comes to artificial intelligence is a test for the authors' focus on "effective and responsible upgrades that address genuine problems." Yet the path forward through the marketing haze is in some ways straightforward: prize evidence, prize outcomes, prize humanity.

The core argument is that those who adopt the upgrade mentality "begin the process of sustainable change-making with a focus on what changes are needed, whereas innovators too often start by asking what solutions can be readily offered." Centering technology and innovation for the sake of it "perverts the entire process, sending companies and countries alike chasing after changes that won't serve their interests at all." The authors are encouraging us to adopt a more humane, mature approach. This may be a generational project; as the effects of climate change, inequality, and geopolitical conflict bear down on people over what appear to be quite difficult years ahead, the necessary wisdom may come through more suffering that is, on balance, exacerbated rather than alleviated by technology.

At a time when speed is mistaken for progress and novelty is prized over good judgment, it can be hard to see through the fog of meme coins and metaverses and Musk. Yet it's possible to imagine, as Selinger and Cahn do, a more just and sustainable future ahead. Let this book guide your path.

CHAPTER ONE

Introduction

THE INNOVATION TRAP

Imagine you're driving down a wintery road, sheltered from the elements in your sleek, new car. Outside the snow makes the roads slick and the temperature arctic, but inside an array of heaters, massagers, and air fragrance systems keep you insulated from the elements. But then, all of a sudden, your visibility starts to fade, and the windshield quickly fogs up. For generations, car owners would have solved the problem with a simple turn of the knob or push of the button. Muscle memory would have guided your hand to the right place without even taking your eyes off the road. But now cars have gotten too innovative.[1] Scrolling through pages of options on the cutting-edge touchscreen control, you search in a panic as the visibility drops, taking your eyes off the cars in front of you in the process. We're constantly told that technological innovation is the road to a better future. But all too often, the sudden changes it brings about are a figurative (or even literal) car wreck.[2]

Or a submarine disaster – like the Titan, the carbon fiber death trap whose makers proudly declared, "innovation is outside of an already accepted system."[3] The predicable calamity came in the summer of 2023 when OceanGate's Titan submersible imploded, killing four people, including Stockton Rush, the company's CEO, while traveling to see the fabled wreckage of the Titanic. In the aftermath, Karl Stanley, one of Rush's friends, described the vessel as a "mousetrap for billionaires" that was destined for tragedy.[4] One didn't need to wait until after the disaster to see the dangers. Rush had been warned that his disruption would be deadly long before the cut-rate craft made its first trip to the Titanic.[5] Unfortunately, far too often, warnings like these go unheeded.

Many of us were taught Aesop's fable of the tortoise and the hare, but far fewer of us truly learned the lesson, especially when it comes to technology. The speedy hare zips off, but it is so overconfident that it loses focus and takes a nap. When the smugly sleeping sprinter wakes up, the tenacious tortoise has won the race. The moral is so simple we teach it to toddlers. Yet the message continues to elude so many of those who hold power in the United States. CEOs, politicians, celebrities, seasoned and burgeoning entrepreneurs, and even non-profit leaders all wax poetically about speedy, hare-like innovations. Indeed, as we're writing this chapter and Donald Trump is about to start his second term as president, Elon Musk is urging Republicans to wage a "war on bureaucracy" by embracing the disruptive entrepreneur's approach to politics.[6]

While innovation has many upsides, it has also played a crucial role in transforming the United States into a "risk society."[7] The lessons we draw from our country's misadventures are instructive for those wrestling with technology around the world. Although the United States is a relatively young country, it's a global superpower, and the technologies it develops, the norms it cultivates, and the risks it generates have far-reaching impacts. Like many countries, the United States' dwindling social safety net increasingly leaves individuals stuck fending this risk for themselves.

UPGRADES: A BETTER PATH TO CHANGE

Crucially, not every form of innovation drives these risks. Innovation comes in many flavors, more than an ice cream shop's worth. Gradual innovation, or what we are calling "*upgrades*," is like incrementally improving water quality through decades of environmental regulation. In contrast, discontinuous innovation is like trying to clean up a lake by adding a new, invasive species. When we are being critical of innovation in this book, we are talking about the kind that is disruptive (fractures the status quo) and discontinuous (happens abruptly at once). As a shorthand, we'll frequently refer to it simply as "innovation."

To make our case, we will consider many aspects of technology, but also look beyond its technical dimensions to examine the language, values, ideologies, and practices surrounding it – what innovation scholars Lee Vinsel and Andrew L. Russell call "innovation-speak."[8] Venture capitalists and Big Tech use innovation-speak to channel our desires and drive the fear of missing out, painting a utopian picture of tomorrow while down-playing how their innovations have failed in the past. While their sales pitch has been seductive, it is thankfully possible to see through the false promises. Our main goal in this book is to give you the critical thinking skills needed to spot the recurring patterns fueling tech and innovation hype – skills that can help you avoid being misled and better approach many pressing problems. We are inviting you to embrace the upgrade mentality and accept its underlying ethos, which promotes the virtues of incrementalism.[9]

Of course, we're not the first to critique the American obsession with innovation, pushing back against grand-gesture technological utopians who believe that harnessing paradigm-shifting technology is the key to social progress. But existing critiques of innovation tend to fall short. They mostly finger-wave without providing alternatives, identify neglected and ailing infrastructure without offering a new way forward beyond maintenance, provide short-term-oriented options for tweaking the status quo, or offer unrealistic proposals for tearing down longstanding institutions as the predicate to progress. By contrast, upgrades allow us to build an evidence-based, sustainable pathway to progress that addresses our society's most intractable issues.

In *Move Slow and Upgrade*, we'll explain how upgrades often get you where you need to be quicker than if you aim for fast and radical innovations. The key difference between innovation and upgrades might be surprising. It's a realistic type of hope. Innovations are adopted in the hope that untested, unproven changes will provide outsized returns. By contrast, upgrades seek a more reliable return, one that's proportional to the investment. Innovations are driven by best-case scenarios, with advocates often oversimplifying complex situations while downplaying or ignoring a range of risks, including unknown and unquantifiable ones. Alternatively, upgrades are guided by the median case, taking into account more realistic considerations of the costs and benefits of change. With upgrades, therefore, you often know what you'll get. Innovations are when we use a dollar to buy a lottery ticket; upgrades are when we put a dollar in the bank. If Americans turn their backs on the lottery of breakthrough innovation, it may feel deflating, losing the promise of quick fixes and instantaneous success. But by focusing our companies, governments, and communities on upgrading our future, we can make better investments. Turning to key case studies of innovation failure and upgrade success, we can bring an alternative narrative into the foreground, turning the tide on decades of innovation obsession.

INNOVATION HOPE AND HYPE

Unfortunately, too often, our hopes and dreams are being placed on innovation – revolutionary products we're told will help society blaze ahead. Tech executives treat ChatGPT and other AI tools like magic, saying they'll not just help do our work, but make human beings ourselves smarter and healthier. And yet the technology also threatens to inundate the public with algorithmically generated disinformation. Voters will struggle to understand what news stories are real, just as teachers will fight to tell which essays are written by a human student. And like so many innovations before it, the flurry of activity surrounding ChatGPT gets problem-solving backward. Instead of investing in technology to tackle the things that matter most to us, we're being told that the problems ChatGPT "solves" should be prioritized. If you had asked the public a few years ago what issues were most pressing for all of us, few would have answered that it took human beings too long to write content. But now we're being sold on the idea that accelerated content creation is the best path to a better world.

Unfortunately, it seems we're still stuck in a vision of social progress expressed in Mark Zuckerberg's infamous mantra, "move fast and break things." Tech CEOs yearn for a revolutionary product that will change how we live and work, just like Mark Zuckerberg, Jeff Bezos, Steve Jobs, Larry Page, and Sergey Brin did. Policymakers hope transformative innovation will drive economic growth and help us do everything from avoiding global warming to achieving widespread flourishing. Individuals chase the innovation dream because that's what they're taught from early on. What's the best way to get rich and change the world? Create the killer app! When history books compress timelines to provide the big picture, they often teach students that innovation drives history and that innovators are historic figures. Indeed, teachers have long been given material that describes US history as a triumph of the pioneering ethos – a tenacious willingness to explore new places and try new things. As a result, they emphasize a continuity between the frontier days, when covered wagons crossed the prairies, and the present, where startups strive to make their mark. Anchored in this through line, America is characterized as fundamentally an enterprising country where people work hard, take risks, and push past setbacks. We've reached a point where, in certain parts of the country, teachers could be fired for pointing out how this narrative ignores the human cost borne by indigenous and enslaved peoples. Such a perspective, we're told, threatens America's unparalleled greatness.

The media – legacy and newer forms – routinely amplifies the same bias of celebrating, if not worshipping innovation, while propping up the fairy tale of instantaneous transformation. Disruption is a better, in the sense of being more sensational, story to cover than incremental change because it's more dramatic and exciting than the essential-but-more-ordinary upgrade work that's easy to take for granted. Jeff Bezos is so famous that he's a household name. But how much do you really know about the daily jobs performed by your friends and family who are scientists and engineers? How much do you even want to know?

We're living in a deeply fearful time, and fear is a powerful driver of the innovation trap. In the United States and elsewhere, many are profoundly anxious about pressing social problems, from crime to the economy and global warming. Such fear goes hand-in-hand with skepticism. Americans have become deeply skeptical about our ability to put aside partisanship, tribalism, and short-term interests to work together to promote the common good. With distrust of politicians, experts, and institutions rampant, imaginations have atrophied, and a great deal of hope rests on technology saving us.

We understand why people see things this way. Some progress will indeed require great creative leaps forward. Not only do we need bold visionaries with brave proposals, but it would be hyperbole to say innovation must always lead to more harm than good. For example, as we'll discuss in our chapter on the Covid-19 pandemic, it's better to live in world where novel vaccines offer some protection from dangerous viruses than to not have the option of vaccination at all.

But the thing is, society needs both disruptive innovation and incremental upgrades to be wisely developed and used appropriately. Wisdom requires admitting that innovation's shortcomings have not been widely enough acknowledged, and a combination of arrogance and ignorance

has led to tremendous overinvestment in it. The desire for techno-fixes –
a yearning to fix social problems by creating the right gadget or algorithm
that can bypass socially contentious issues and reduce our maladies to
engineering problems – left an indelible imprint on the American psyche
even though it was popularized during the 1960s (a golden age of optimism about technology's promise), though it has a long history of pushback, and though technology critics have become increasingly vocal of
their shortcomings.[10]

Technologies, whether artificial intelligence, quantum computing, or
the next big thing, don't exist in a vacuum. They're deeply intertwined
with the society that creates and uses them, which is why scholars who
critically study technology embrace the concept "sociotechnical
systems."[11] When we uncritically cheer for the next high-tech savior as
a cure-all, we miss the forest for the trees – the intricate, interconnected
web of social and technical factors that shape us and our world. While
high-tech tools can have great potential, they will never be magic wands
that make inequalities disappear or conjure widespread prosperity. How
technologies are created and deployed depends on social, political, economic, and institutional factors. In our market-driven society where an
increasing amount of responsibility for the public good involves the
private sector, the products that tech giants describe as solutions too
often are unconstrained – due, in no small part, to their intense lobbying –
by strong regulations. Consequently, they're often only well-suited to
maximize shareholder wealth, reinforce privilege, and benefit the powerful without coming close to leveling the playing field or avoiding disproportionately harming the most vulnerable among us. The irony is that
while today's tech industry often blames the government for being inefficient (Musk has even successfully lobbied to co-lead a new Department of
Government Efficiency) and portrays the private sector as the key to our
salvation, the current state of technology owes a tremendous debt to the
government for investing so much in scientific research and development
in the past.[12]

Consider the internet. It may be a case of the innovation mentality
doing more harm than good. "Move fast and break things" has become
a widely shared mantra for conducting massive social experi-
ments with the newest devices and services, while leaving others like civil
rights organizations, like the one founded and run by one of us, to deal

with the nightmare results of shattering longstanding norms. If you want to break things quickly, it might mean you think that caring about social and institutional goods that have been built up slowly, often with a lot of care and thought, is something that only small-minded people do. It's also a way to say that those who care about justice and want to hear from a wide range of people, especially the disadvantaged, before shaking things up with technology are too cautious. And it's a way to flatter the excessively bold and overly brash – telling them their ambition of destroying all traces of tradition is noble, not arrogant.

At the center of it all are the venture capitalists who are funding innovation because they're looking for the biggest possible return on their investment, not lasting social change. When executives craft pitch decks, they're thinking of the next funding round, not the foreseeable social effects. They are someone else's problem – externalities others will have to pay for. Tragically, even compliance teams can contribute to the problem by focusing on weak checklist measures rather than efforts that can truly limit social harm.

While it is tempting to wave fingers at others, there is more than enough blame to go around. Frankly, the public shares some of the responsibility. Sure, there are skeptics, there has been a techlash (which includes bipartisan distrust of Big Tech), and there is plenty of ambivalence (a love-hate relationship with devices like mobile phones).[13] But, in the end, rather than meaningfully pushing back against overstatements and outlandish promises about what tech can do, most of us remain all too willing to initially suspend our disbelief. Again and again, convenience trumps conviction. And when the promises fail, the mumbling, groaning, and Congressional hearings don't do much. Apart from outright acts of blatant fraud, there rarely are real consequences for those who gave us false hope in the beginning. And so, the interconnected factors that give rise to this situation have created endless incentives to keep gambling on the next unproven technology and the one after that. Private equity's casino mentality permeates the public sphere.

And this brings us back to the problem of fear – more specifically, the issue of what we should be afraid of. While being too timid and overly cautious gives fear too much power, it's no coincidence that the disruptive spirit of moving fast and breaking things has proven conducive to causing large-scale harm. It's caused accidents, incentivized companies to roll out defective products, shattered stable and dependable norms, strained slow-moving regulation, and overwhelmed the public. These days, there's great concern that privacy is dead and democracy is dying – all thanks to tech companies changing things too dramatically, too quickly. Since upgrades pose less risk, create less uncertainty, and are easier to control, they give us less to be afraid of.

Since each and every one of us is impacted by the innovation debate and the ways that it reshapes public infrastructure, it's crucial that this book is accessible far outside the walls of academia. For years, as aspects of innovation theory have been debated in the scholarly literature, innovation practices have accelerated ahead, with the public paying the price for each new misguided innovation. Rather than rooting this book in obscure theoretical debates or ephemeral definitional questions, we focus on case studies that can help any reader start to re-examine the forces that truly shape our society. You may not walk away from these case studies with a doctorate in upgrading, but you'll begin to see how to avoid falling for the same innovation promises that have misled so many, so often. The insights that you'll develop here should help you see things more clearly and make better decisions, and not just right now. You'll be better prepared to deal with new technologies and new ways of using current ones.

INNOVATION FAILS: UPGRADES PREVAIL

To show how upgrading is a risk-informed route forward to a better future, we – a Philosophy Professor and lawyer who founded and is the Executive Director of the non-profit organization Surveillance Technology Oversight Project (S.T.O.P.) – proceed as follows.

Chapter 2, "Zuckerberg's Mythological Metaverse," shows how when the emperor of innovation isn't wearing any clothes, upgraders can still see the naked truth of the situation. Zuckerberg promised a metaverse, a new digital reality, that would transform human connection, interaction, and commerce. But this handwavy conception of the future lacked any clear vision, let alone consumer demand. Upgraders were able to spot the folly long before it became one of the largest corporate boondoggles in modern commerce, a shorthand for corporate disfunction. In contrast to the unbridled enthusiasm of innovators, upgraders would have started with the question of why the public would ever want this product in the first place. Instead, Meta tried to sway public opinion with overly rosy futuristic promises, trying to move the market to meet their innovation, rather than solving problems that actually mattered to the public. Like other innovations, the metaverse shows how tech companies ignore the fundamentals of human behavior and social change, dooming their grand visions.

In Chapter 3, "The Crypto Con," we dive deep into the beating heart of cryptocurrency, the paradoxical technology that has made early adherents billions, while adding nothing of real value to society. By any measure, crypto has failed at its stated goal: creating a better financial system. Looking to Bitcoin, we show how the core innovation – a distributed encrypted database – makes a terrible payment system, with slow, expensive, uncorrectable transactions. But crypto enthusiasts ignore more than a decade of failure, doubling down on grandiose claims about solving everything from financial inclusion to corporate governance while ignoring the far easier, low-tech solutions to these very real needs. We include an interview with an early supporter of the massive cryptocurrency Ethereum, who came to see how crypto became "just a tool for the wealthy to become wealthier" rather than fulfilling its promise of financial inclusion for the world's 1.7 billion unbanked people.

Innovations not only fail to solve crucial problems: sometimes they are the problem itself. In Chapter 4, "Home Security Upgrades," we explain why Ring doorbell exemplify the threat of home surveillance innovation. The billion-dollar Amazon subsidiary sold millions of Americans on the promise of security via surveillance without any credible evidence that its system works. But rather than encouraging people to adopt proven security upgrades, such as better locks and secure package drops, Ring wins customers by making its digital innovation seem essential amid a climate of rising fear. By fighting against boring yet effective alternatives, Ring's anxiety-inducing features have further normalized intensive networked surveillance and helped turn innocuous neighborly interactions into potential threats.

Chapter 5, "The Failed Promise of Covid Innovation," presents the pandemic as a crucial case study of how innovative thinking let us down at a time of great vulnerability. Simply put, the early days of massive fatalities made Covid-19 a health crisis. But those days also can be seen as a powerful lens for understanding high-tech failure. From contact tracing apps to thermal imaging cameras and digital vaccine passports, there was a fever pitch of government and corporate enthusiasm for innovative solutionism that was predestined to be unreliable and, thus, in context, dangerous. While we acknowledge remarkable breakthroughs like the rapid development of mRNA vaccines, we also make the case that additional effective responses could have come from upgrading existing systems rather than trying to do things entirely new.

Chapter 6, "Moving Fast and Breaking Schools with Remote Proctoring," looks at the failures of educational innovation during the Covid-19 crisis. As schools scrambled to adapt to remote learning, remote proctoring technologies rapidly expanded. They implemented surveillance systems that violated student privacy and disproportionately harmed vulnerable students. Despite claims of maintaining academic integrity, remote proctoring created a stressful, punitive environment that prioritized monitoring over genuine educational support while failing to do nearly enough to address the inequalities at the heart of accessing and using digital resources. Sadly, the rush to innovate missed crucial opportunities to upgrade core educational infrastructure and truly support students during a time of unprecedented challenge. As if this wasn't bad enough, some schools continue to use remote proctoring software. A pandemic problem has thus become the new normal.

In Chapter 7, "Upgrades in the Age of Generative AI," we consider the hype around generative AI tools, like ChatGPT, and explain how the razzle-dazzle has captured the public's imagination, even as the technology hasn't come close to being artificial general intelligence – the goal companies like OpenAI aspire for. While tech giants race to develop generative AI products, we emphasize that they currently are sophisticated pattern-matching systems that simulate intelligence without truly understanding it. Analyzing both negative (political campaigns) and positive (the possibility of helping doctors communicate more empathetically over patient portals) examples, we offer recommendations for spotting uses of generative AI to avoid and how technological upgrades can be carefully and ethically integrated into communication systems to improve human welfare.

Chapter 8, "Upgrading Hiring," explains why there has been so much enthusiasm for integrating AI into multiple dimensions of the hiring process, from resume screening to interview bots, despite these endeavors being marred by fundamental flaws, including, in some cases, integrating bias, unreliable pseudoscientific methods, and dehumanizing interactions. In addition to analyzing the incentives that have motivated companies to use flawed, innovative tools, we provide a road map for how to develop and use responsible AI upgrades in the hiring.

In Chapter 9, "Cybersecurity: The Land of the True Upgraders," we argue that cybersecurity professionals embody the ideal of the careful, systematic upgrading that *Move Slow and Upgrade* has been advocating for. Unlike the flashy innovations that we've criticized in earlier chapters, cybersecurity professionals focus on making small, proven improvements through such practices as privacy by design and zero-trust architecture. Recognizing that no single change can solve complex problems, they layer multiple safeguards while acknowledging that human behavior – from falling for scams to knowingly taking risks – is often the main vulnerability. By discussing how cybersecurity teams do quality work, we aim to offer important lessons about how other industries might benefit from adopting an upgrading mindset.

In Chapter 10, "The Upgrader's Mindset," we conclude with an overview of the broader themes seen throughout this work, showcasing the tell-tale signs of innovation failure. These patterns go to the core of our work, lessons learned from past innovations that can help us to avoid repeating similar mistakes in the future. No one, not even the cagiest upgrader, is going to be able to predict every new technology that will succeed or flop. But with this mindset, you can avoid some of the more obvious traps that investors, politicians, and the public continue to fall for, while valuing the evidence-based alternatives we so often neglect.

CHAPTER TWO

Zuckerberg's Mythological Metaverse

Few innovation mirages are as enticing to technology companies as the "metaverse," the vision of an all-encompassing digital platform that is so immersive that it rivals our physical world in what we consider "real." Long fodder for science fiction, the term has increasingly become the investment thesis for some of the world's largest companies, even if few of them can agree what technologies would be needed to make this high-tech fantasy a reality. In recent years, Mark Zuckerberg became one of the concept's strongest proponents,[1] promoting the platform as a pathway to unprecedented connection and fulfillment. He even renamed the company to signal his commitment. However, the reality of the metaverse hasn't caught up with the rhetoric. The world we're getting is different than the one we were promised.

Many Zuckerberg watchers felt a sense of déjà vu when they heard the metaverse was now his company's top priority in 2021. Zuckerberg's arguments for the ill-defined digital home of the future rehashed many tropes of early social media promotion. He promised an innovative world where connectivity brought us together across borders and ideologies. He envisioned a technological bridge to a harmonious human family. These same promises accompanied Facebook's own meteoric rise beginning in 2004, even though the world has now seen social media's utopian allure tarnished by the reality of disinformation, tribalism, and hate speech. Internet speech hasn't freed our loftiest impulses. Instead, it unshackled our basest instincts.

The connectivity of the metaverse, we're told, will somehow be different. But it wasn't just Zuckerberg's tired techno optimism sales pitch that should have put the public on notice. His metaverse promotion was rife with many red flags: lofty and ill-defined goals, unrealistic timelines for success, measuring progress in terms of money spent (not solutions found), and a lack of evidence that the breakthrough would solve what anyone else considered a problem. These are the warning signs of a dangerous innovation.

THE RISE AND FALL OF METAVERSE HYPE

Are you still a bit unsure about what the "metaverse" means? You're not alone. The term itself has been around for decades, dating back to the classic speculative fiction novel *Snow Crash* by Neal Stephenson. But it is as ill-defined as it is enticing.[2] When Nick Clegg, Meta's president of global affairs, tried to actually define the "metaverse," his vague 8,000 word digression left readers with the impression that the metaverse was nearly every form of technology.[3] Typically, commentators use the term to refer to a mix of virtual reality and augmented reality technologies that could replace the traditional screen and keyboard interfaces we use today. But it can also encompass much more.

Virtual reality users don a headset that uses a pair of stereoscopic displays to create the illusion of a fully immersive, 360-degree, simulated world. Traditionally, the technology has been used most often for computer games, but recent efforts have promoted the use of social media and other apps on the platform. Augmented reality is similar, but rather than showing a user a fully simulated world, augmented reality headsets show users an image of their immediate environment, projecting simulated objects on top of it. An augmented reality user at home might look out at their living room and see all their real-world furniture, along with animated objects that interact with that space. Imagine seeing your sofa and watching a photo-realistic Mickey Mouse trying to hide underneath. Of course, the capabilities of these technologies are quite limited today compared to the metaverse innovation hype.

In 2021, the tech world witnessed a momentous shift as Facebook boldly rebranded as Meta. The move raised eyebrows and stirred curiosity because one of the world's richest and most powerful tech companies – one that has weathered ongoing controversy and scandal – pivoted away from its historically lucrative focus on social media to something even more innovative: an "embodied internet" that could offer unparalleled experiences.[4] This was a crucial year for the metaverse hype cycle.

Zuckerberg's 2021 "Founder Letter" oozed enthusiasm, pledging unwavering dedication to make the metaverse a reality. "We are at the beginning of the next chapter for the internet, and it's the next chapter for our company too ... The metaverse can enable better social experiences than anything that exists today, and we will dedicate our energy to helping achieve its potential."[5] Given the high hopes for digital technology at the beginning of the Covid-19 pandemic and Zuckerberg's business savvy and willingness to invest billions of dollars into metaverse research and development (along with considerable effort from companies like Microsoft, Google, Apple, Amazon, Nvidia, Unity, Snap, and Roblox), it's not surprising that companies scrambled to develop metaverse strategies and people were clamoring to buy virtual real estate. Amid the fervor for metaverse marketing, Microsoft described its intent to buy Activision Blizzard for nearly $70 billion as a metaverse acquisition rather than an extension of its gaming business.[6]

Metaverse enthusiasts imagine us dating in simulated cafés showing a breathtaking earthrise over the lunar surface. They picture students on immersive field trips to long-destroyed historic sites. They talk about tourists going on vacation to some of the planet's most remote regions, or to worlds only before imagined in fiction. And the sexually adventurous won't think twice about exploring new options, like having mixed-reality orgies with thousands of others.[7] And this is supposedly just the tip of the iceberg. The metaverse's ambiguity allows proponents to promise seemingly everything, claiming we'll all one day want smart specs to see our Metaverse world.[8]

If Mark Zuckerberg focused purely on the existing technology – virtual reality goggles, smart glasses – few would take him seriously. The goofy googles had been around in one form or another for decades, and VR gaming hardly seemed like an earthshattering change. But in contrast, Jim Cramer didn't bat an eyelid when Zuckerberg framed all of his plans in terms of the future capabilities of the metaverse: "We hope to basically get to around a billion people in the metaverse doing hundreds of dollars of commerce, each buying digital goods, digital content, different things to express themselves."[9] The *Wall Street Journal* eagerly declared, "The Metaverse will change the way you work."[10] And more recently, the World Economic Forum predicted the metaverse will "be worth $6–13 trillion by 2030, with global revenues expected to reach $800 billion by 2024."[11]

When writing this chapter, Meta was still broadcasting an optimistic message: "We believe in the future of connection in the metaverse."[12] Indeed, many companies are working hard to infuse "metaverse" innovations with positive connotations and get people to associate it with desirable real-world applications. Restaurant chains like Applebee's promotes "Metaverse Mondays," and Wendy's advertises the "Wendysverse."[13] Coca-Cola even got in on the action with the "innovative taste" of Coca-Cola Zero Sugar Byte, calling the drink "a portal between the digital and physical worlds."[14] Walmart, Disney, Ralph Lauren, Bumble, and Nike also made moves to "claim their own corner of the metaverse."[15]

But even amid the fervor, cracks in the foundation began to appear, raising concerns about the feasibility of Zuckerberg's vision. In 2023, Disney ditched its interactive storytelling team, "which focused on metaverse strategies."[16] Meta's Reality Labs – its core metaverse unit – suffered staggering losses. In 2022, it lost $13.7 billion,[17] and another $3.7 billion in the second quarter of 2023.[18] A month before its second quarter, 2023 earnings report, Meta announced that it would curtail remote work, requiring employees in the office three days a week.[19] While many leading companies had walked back Covid-19-era flexibility, Meta's decision was notable because it showed the limitations of Meta's own Horizon Workrooms, a metaverse product it had pitched as the future of work.[20] One *Bloomberg* writer alleged, "Meta isn't practicing what it preaches."[21] Finally, by 2023, the artificial intelligence boom drove Zuckerberg to stress how important it is for Meta to keep up with developments in AI. A *CNN* headline aptly captured the change in tone, "What metaverse? Meta says its single largest investment is now in 'advancing AI.'"[22]

Zuckerberg hasn't given up, but he is actively working to lower expectations. Now, he frames the metaverse as "a very long-term bet,"[23] where a year earlier he predicted it would go mainstream in the next five to ten years.[24]

Most outside observers agree with the revised assessment. A 2023 Pew Research report found that most experts believe that a "fully-immersive, well-functioning" Metaverse will become an "aspect of daily life for a half billion or more people globally," but not until 2040.[25] Around the same time as the Pew report, Apple announced its own version of the metaverse, the Apple Vision Pro. Metaverse proponents were excited at first that the company that mainstreamed the personal computer and smartphone might be able to do the same for metaverse hardware. But when Apple announced its $3,500 price tag, limiting the technology to only the most affluent purchasers, it became clear that the metaverse would remain a niche product, at least for now.[26]

EVADING REALITY

But why was the hype able to reach such a fever pitch in the first place? Here, we can look at a red flag in plain sight: Meta's decision to rebrand itself with such a bold, future vision – without even having launched a discernible product, let alone a killer app. By focusing on the quasi-mystical metaverse and avoiding discussion about what that term practically means, Meta was able to avoid the hard questions. Questions like: "why exactly do we need this?" And "what exactly *is* this?"

The history of hardware upgrades shows that a new platform will rarely flourish without a killer app, the software that turns a new technology from novelty to necessity. For the early era of personal computers, no application was more transformative than VisiCalc, the first widely adopted spreadsheet program. VisiCalc could save users endless hours of tedious calculations, justifying the purchase price of personal computers not just by individuals, but by companies. Later on, word-processing technology, graphic design tools, and blockbuster video games served the same role for other platforms. In contrast, not only is the hardware of the metaverse ill-defined, but there's absolutely no indication of what the killer app could be. Rather than being given a detailed script, we've been sold more of an incomplete outline for a metaverse movie.

The metaverse, as a term, sounds like an entirely new thing. In truth, it's unclear how many of the innovations that make up the metaverse are superior to mobile phones and desktops today. We can look to both virtual reality and augmented reality.

Virtual reality has had a fringe following for years, but it's generally just a small number of gamers who spend considerable time using the technology. And this is hardly for lack of opportunity. Ivan Sutherland and Bob Sproull debuted their tongue-in-cheek titled "Sword of Damocles" in the 1960s,[27] and numerous other VR headsets have been commercially produced in the years since, all to lackluster (at best) success.

And for many of us, it's easy to see why concrete metaverse innovations failed to find a foothold. What would you do if a colleague invited you to a virtual reality party? Most of us can't just say yes, even if we want to. When one of us was invited to a virtual reality workshop on the metaverse and human rights, frustration ensued. Why? Neither of us has a virtual reality headset. First, we needed to find a friend who could loan one out and further explain how to use it. And we were lucky we had a friend who could. A VR headset and suitably fast computer can cost thousands of dollars, far more than it would cost to travel in-person to give such a talk. Then, we had to log on to a separate virtual reality platform, going through hours of confusing technical and registration tasks just to give a short talk. By contrast, using Zoom often just takes a few mouse clicks.

Once logged on, the effort didn't prove worth it. Using the organizers' chosen social virtual reality platform made interacting with the other participants on a virtual stage far more complicated than exchanging ideas over Zoom or in-person. Moving around felt awkward, and it was hard to get a sense of when you were in a good location to grab someone's attention. And the virtual reality innovations hardly left us feeling more connected. The legless cartoonish avatar was a distraction, not an advantage. Even worse, the virtual reality hardware gave us a headache, which is quite common with the technology. "Virtual reality sickness"[28] is so common and acute that Meta's health and safety warnings advise users to take extended breaks from virtual reality every 30 minutes.[29] Which once again should have flagged to all involved that this technology probably won't be capable of creating the long-term, alternative reality that is imagined.

Certainly, the science and technology behind virtual reality will get better. Headsets will get lighter and feel more comfortable to wear. The software will display better graphics and become easier to use. Systems might become affordable enough to support mass consumption. But we still don't know if most users will be able to comfortably use the technology for extended periods any time soon. And if proponents do solve these core safety issues, it's also a long way away from finding that still-elusive killer app.

There are also related issues for augmented reality. Since you can run augmented reality apps on your phone, it might seem like the technology is an easier onramp to the metaverse. But the most popular apps are video games, and this isn't a revolutionary innovation. Next-level features, however, require special glasses that augment your normal vision with graphics and apps, acting like a smartphone through which you see the world. Some of the most impressive uses of augmented reality that Zuckerberg envisions are improved GPS navigation while walking (no more staring down and possibly getting hit by a car), finding lost objects (because the camera in your glasses will keep track of where you left them and the navigational function will direct you to them), and greatly improving coaching (you can look directly at the food you're preparing while receiving step-by-step cooking instructions).

However, even this vision – of a metaverse-lite – would require expensive hardware, in the form of smart glasses or goggles, like Apple's $3,500 offering. And for such products there are plenty of failed launches that make up a graveyard of techno-optimism. Since the heavily derided Google Glass, smart glasses are widely seen as privacy problems waiting to happen, and they have never been able to approach the popularity of smart phones or even smart watches. Despite this sentiment, Facebook released Ray-Ban Stories – smart glasses that take photos and videos and play music – in 2021.[30] Sales were poor, under 50 percent of the intended mark.[31] Two years later, 90 percent of the people who own the specs appear to have stopped using them. Apparently, even if you're the type of person the sales pitch initially appealed to, you lost interest fast.[32]

So why does Meta think it can spin a wonder out of hardware horror stories? It desperately needed a new wonder.

MARKETING THE GOSPEL OF THE METAVERSE

When Meta speaks of the metaverse, the company invites us into a dream world where we have the freedom to explore without consequence:

> In the metaverse, you'll be able to do almost anything you can imagine . . . In this future, you will be able to teleport instantly as a hologram to be at the office without a commute, at a concert with friends, or in your parents' living room to catch up. This will open up more opportunity no matter where you live. You'll be able to spend more time on what matters to you.[33]

If Meta's rosy optimism sounds familiar, it's because it is a disturbing resuscitation of its now-discredited approach to social media. When Facebook first gained prominence, it promised us new connections as an unalloyed good. Suddenly, more people than ever in more places than ever would wield the power of global connectivity, not just speaking online, but potentially being heard by millions, even billions. Social media was meant to be a way to improve everything from mental health to democracy itself. Yet two decades into the social media era, we see just how naïve those promises were.

Rather than leading to a world where we feel closer together, social media innovation caused greater feelings of isolation. Sustained use of the technology, especially for children and teens, leads to higher rates of depression and even suicidality. Sure, we may be "friends" with hundreds, even thousands of other users, but that doesn't mean we feel meaningfully connected. And even though we are able to see elements of our friends' lives, the highly curated vignettes of Facebook and Instagram have only led to further alienation. We don't see the reality of our friends' lives, just the gleaming self-selected snapshots of success, a promotional peak into lives far more complicated than what many show. And the result is a growing sense of inadequacy, failing to measure up to a truly impossible standard of a good life.

The impact on democracy has been even worse. The optimism of moments like the Arab Spring have long since faded, and with it the hope that social media could transform closed societies into more open, democratic ones. While social media did help fuel protests that led to the downfall of countless strongmen, the postscript to those stories was far uglier than we could imagine. As we write this paragraph, haunting images of mass flooding in Libya fill our TV screens, thousands swept out to sea in a country that hasn't had a stable government since the extrajudicial killing of Muammar Gaddafi in 2011. Gaddafi, an antidemocratic strongman whose forces were accused of war crimes, led the country for more than thirty years. His toppling is emblematic of the larger Arab Spring revolution. His regime systematically violated human rights and international law. And yet in the years since his ouster, Libya has seen civil war, a reduction in the standard of living, and growing instability.

Social media's effects on American democracy have been equally alarming. Rather than promoting a post-partisan era, social media platforms like Facebook have fueled an ideological fracturing, driving the public not just toward increasingly irreconcilable policy preferences, but undermining even our shared universe of facts. The social media age is one of constant ontological uncertainty, when different factions wield different conceptions of reality to advance their priorities and candidates. And that's before getting into scandals like the abuse of the platform by foreign governments and the misuse of social media data by firms like Cambridge Analytica, the British consulting company that collected personal data from millions of Facebook users without their consent, largely for political advertising.

Still, none of these abuses comes close to the harm the platform has inflicted on some of the most vulnerable communities around the world. According to Amnesty International, "Facebook's algorithms were intensifying a storm of hatred against the Rohingya" prior to the 2017 genocide.[34] Facebook also enabled deadly anti-Muslim attacks in India to appease the country's Hindu nationalist prime minister,[35] and as one *Guardian* headline proclaimed: "Facebook 'lets vigilantes in Ethiopia incite ethnic killing.'"[36]

META'S HIDDEN REALITY

Even in its infancy, the metaverse is enabling many of the same abuses seen on social media. Mere months after Meta began its wholesale push for the metaverse, reports began to emerge of how this new digital world was already plagued with harassment and simulated sexual assault.[37] Facebook sought to reassure the public with glossy videos that promised user control in the metaverse, but the accusations of sexual assault and harassment have only grown.[38]

These reports follow the predictable pattern for social media innovations. What we've seen for decades is that it's relatively cheap and easy to bring people together, but it's very hard and expensive to ensure they're safe. Instead of taking a duty of care to ensure that users are affirmatively protected from those doing harm, most platforms prioritize the myth of user control, the claim that with just the right combination of settings and opt-outs, we can choose the digital experience that actually makes us happy. Sadly, for all but the most technically sophisticated users, user control is just spin ... a way to paper over the foreseeable harm such technological innovation causes.

Many social media firms use dark patterns, design features that lure users to spend more time on the platform, thus making social media companies more money. This is the case for design features, algorithms, and privacy features. A striking example of the illusion of "user control" comes from Apple, which in 2021 changed the default settings for its iOS mobile operating system.[39] Prior to the change, apps like Facebook and Instagram collected massive amounts of device data by default. But after the change, users had to affirmatively opt in to share their device ID. Notably, prior to the change, 75 percent of users had shared this data, but after the change, 79 percent now refused.[40] They hadn't had a mass conversion on the question of privacy. Instead, they showed that the choice to opt-out had never really been a meaningful choice at all.

The pattern repeats with harassment, hate speech, and so many of the other harms of social media. Initially, social media companies had minimal controls, and they touted that users could control who they follow, who they see. But even "block" features were slow to arrive, and ineffective against new forms of online harassment. Eventually, social media companies came to admit that the way to protect against harassment and harm in a wide-open online space is the intensive and costly effort of moderating content on a vast scale. But the corporate commitment to addressing content moderation is not up to the monumental challenge of dealing with one piecemeal interaction at a time. Reporting[41] and scholarship[42] show how the internet's gleaming high-tech platforms were built on the backs of low-paid and deeply traumatized moderators, scanning through a seemingly endless torrent of the most vile content imaginable.[43] There is no magic algorithm to solve the question of what speech should be allowed on social media or the metaverse, but there is an army of anonymous human beings making as little as $1.50 per hour to decide what is and isn't abusive.

Meta has failed to clean up the social media environments it has created so that they can approach anything like the bold visions it sold in the 2000s. That's a significant reason why the Facebook brand was worth retiring in favor of Meta. The company wanted to be able to start over fresh, with a new dream on the metaverse. But is there any reason to think that the metaverse will be able to avoid the same challenges that have awaited every other social network?

If anything, as the metaverse makes our digital lives more immersive, the potential for digital harassment is even more destructive. And while Meta and other firms are pouring billions into building out the metaverse technology, it's unclear if they've even begun to think about how to upgrade the tools to moderate user content. Meta has only invested in the status quo of content moderation. Recently, Meta even rejected a shareholder proposal for a third-party evaluation of the platform's "psychological and civil and human rights harms to users" and mitigation strategies.[44] Even worse, internal documents suggest company leaders think that moderation "at any meaningful scale is practically impossible."[45]

But no matter how hard content moderation is on current platforms, it will be much harder in the metaverse.[46] Partly that is because we don't yet know how our analog norms will translate to our digital life. As tech writer Aaron Mak notes:

> [M]oderation is complicated by trying to map the social conventions of the physical world onto virtual reality. If you covered yourself in purple body paint and showed up at an in-person medical conference, you'd probably be asked to leave. At a metaverse medical conference, the other attendees wouldn't even bat an eye. This relaxing of certain social norms leads people to test the bounds of acceptable behavior, and moderators in some cases have to decide what crosses the line.[47]

When Mathew Ball, a venture capitalist and the former global head of Amazon Studios, wrote the popular *The Metaverse: And How It Will Revolutionize Everything*, he suggested we could deal with issues like this by using techno-fixes: "[U]sers may need to give other users explicit levels of permission to interact in a given spaces and platforms will also automatically block certain capabilities ('no touch zones')."[48] Permissions might sound fine in the abstract. But in practice, they are far from a panacea. They're subject to misunderstanding, especially when the familiar and the fantastical collide in virtual worlds. Likewise, policing what virtual bodies can do by blocking undesirable movements and gestures might sound okay on paper. However, gestures often have contextual meanings in practice, and evolving context creates a problematic cat-and-mouse game for identifying what's offensive and harmful, especially in our pluralistic and divided society.

Crucially, conducting enough surveillance to find all possible infractions inevitably will create other problems. By Ball's own account, the metaverse can be so "massively scaled" that, in principle, it can be accessed by "an effectively unlimited number of users."[49] In other words, Facebook's classic problems of dealing with scale and moderation haven't gone away.

And any automated surveillance tools powerful enough to track users this intimately on this large a scale raises chilling concerns around privacy and corporate power. As with any innovation that makes those in power even more powerful, without providing any checks or balances for the public, we should be concerned if the metaverse is becoming a recipe for the dystopia so many authors feared. It's fair to say that Zuckerberg's emphasis on the metaverse looks like a canny play to rebrand away its problems – to pivot to something new so that it doesn't have to address the dilemmas and dangers that Facebook has long presented.

METAVERSE HYPE: A CATALYST FOR FAULTY SOLUTIONS

Metaverse innovation hype is emblematic of innovation exaggerations in the tech sector, where nearly every entity has an incentive to sell the next big thing.[50] Startups need a narrative to promise venture capitalists enormous returns that could justify risky early-stage investments. Consultants justify their cost by convincing clients that their current business practices will soon go obsolete. Additionally, even some respected technology publications, like *CNET*, reportedly pressure employees to "change stories and reviews" to make them more "favorable to advertisers."[51] Dispiritingly, Canadian reporting on AI between 2012 and 2021 "closely reflects business and government interests in AI by praising its future capabilities and under-reporting the power dynamics behind these interests."[52] The metaverse is such a crucial case study, not because it's an outlier, but because it showcases the innovation cycle so many other companies fall victim to.

And the pattern isn't limited to Silicon Valley. In 2023, as enthusiasm for the idea of the metaverse was fading, the University of the Southwest proudly bragged it was testing the instructional capabilities of the metaverse. In a similar spirit, an earlier news release from the University of Kansas Nursing School described its launch of a "Metaversity" – which is "part of Meta's $150 million endeavor to increase access to education and change the way people learn" – as having the "potential to revolutionize nursing education."[53] The innovation hype cycle feedback loop only accelerates once the media are included. A Morehouse College professor running a Black history class in virtual reality prompted NBC News to say the school "made history" by teaching "in the metaverse."[54]

The irrational exuberance and false optimism of innovation booster-ism make it impossible to critically focus the tech discourse on actual problem-solving.[55] Technologies like virtual and augmented reality will continue to develop whether or not people continue to talk about the metaverse. Nonetheless, the term does not appear to be going away any time soon, and the enthusiasm surrounding the metaverse will almost certainly continue to lead people to overestimate the value of initiatives.

It's a strange confluence: a hype cycle around a term – the metaverse – that vastly outstrips the existing technologies' capabilities. Meanwhile, those technologies – virtual and augmented reality – are still searching for real-use cases, despite steady advancement. Both these dynamics are red flags, despite the efforts of boosters to make bold claims that virtual reality, in the words of a viral TED talk, is "the ultimate empathy machine."[56]

This thesis is an update of the claim that fiction helps us understand how other people feel and deepen our empathy.[57] Literature creates connections with characters – links that open us up to new perspectives and help us relate to other people's struggles, limitations, and flaws. And so, the reasoning goes, virtual reality can improve traditional storytelling modes and better expand our moral imaginations through more visceral and interactive presentations. International charities, including Amnesty International, the International Rescue Committee, UNICEF USA, and Médecins Sans Frontières, have assumed this logic is sound; they have integrated virtual reality in their fundraising efforts.[58]

A scientific meta-analysis of "all known studies investigating the rela-tionship between virtual reality and empathy," however, concluded virtual reality "does not create substantive improvements in empathy beyond those that can be achieved with less expensive and less technologically advanced methods."[59] The less expensive methods include reading. The authors come to this conclusion by distinguishing between two types of empathy: emotional and cognitive. Emotional empathy is "fast, auto-matic, and occurs spontaneously."[60] By contrast, cognitive empathy is a more "advanced" mental activity – a "deliberate skill ... that requires attention and effort to decipher the thoughts and feeling of another person."[61] They found virtual reality can improve emotional empathy (feeling for others), but doesn't boost cognitive empathy (thinking about other people's perspectives). Interestingly, they speculate this limitation may occur because virtual reality leaves too little to the imagination. In other words, virtual reality might deprive users of the skillful mental effort required to put themselves in someone else's place.

Innovations are frequently sold to us as a way to improve human nature. But the reality is that technology often just gives us new places and new ways to behave in familiar, if not worse, ways. Creating an empathy machine or an enlightenment engine would make us better people. But when innovators promise that their tools will fundamentally improve how we view the world and treat one another, there is deep reason for skepticism. Especially at a moment of global strife, it's so soothing to envision a technology that can truly bring us together and build a sense of global community. But the truth is that when technology brings us together, we still behave like ourselves.

The sad truth about misguided innovations like the metaverse is that once the idea catches fire, the embers never fully go out. In 2024, the most recent wave of augmented reality revelry came from a company with a genuine history of transforming humanity through technology: Apple. Apple's foray into the metaverse, the Vision Pro, was remarkable for just how unremarkable a change it proved. The pricey headset, which started at $3,500, promised to not just be an augmented reality headset, but to usher in a new age of "spacial computing." Promotional materials promised that users could strap on the astronomically expensive device to "do the things you love in ways never before possible."[62] Apple promised that you could have nothing short of "an infinite canvas that transforms how you use the apps you love."[63] That you could "transform any room into your own personal theater."[64] Yet when I (Albert) tried wearing the device for two weeks, I found it impossible to do even the most basic tasks needed. The Vision Pro tries to answer the question of how you can use a computer without a mouse or keyboard. It answers it poorly. When you mount Apple's personal panopticon to your face, an augmented-reality interface appears, using a dozen cameras to map out your environment. It films everything around you, every piece of furniture, every scrap of paper – Post-it notes, bank statements, health-insurance bills – even your choice of recreational beverage to show you a grainy, digitized copy of your world on a screen. It's like seeing a funhouse version of your home, only with lots of apps layered on top.

Just setting up the headset turned into a nauseating ordeal. Want to navigate an app? Use your hand to click and zoom. Imagine how it would look to someone watching from across the room as you try to hunt and peck letters on a simulated keyboard, constantly cursing in irritation. As I tapped at the imaginary keyboard, it became clear just how little thought Apple gave to one of the most important features of digital life: passwords. Even more stunning was the device's failure to enable even the most rudimentary forms of digital work. As much as I tried, I never found a comfortable way to even write a Microsoft Word document or email while strapped in. When I connected my Apple MacBook to use the display, the lagging cursor constantly threw me off, every disorienting keystroke delayed before it appeared on my simulated screen. Even when I bought a Bluetooth keyboard, I was still able to type out only a couple of short paragraphs before the eye strain became overpowering.

This is a stunning fall from grace for the Cupertino colossus. Apple had long been synonymous with the best aspects of disruptive innovation. Their introduction of the iPod and upgrade path to the iPhone is seen as an inflection point for the overall history of mobile computing. But spacial computing follows the predictable hype path of so many failed metaverse products before it. The Vision Pro is more powerful than its predecessors, with more cameras to record your environment, your family, and your own body than anything that came before. But it still doesn't have a useful app, let alone a killer one. Even with prescription inserts, using the device for more than just a few minutes leaves users nauseated and disoriented. And removing the device to look at your phone to check a text message or call is its own stomach-churning ordeal.

Despite being sold as a mobile device that can be worn nearly anywhere, in truth Vision Pro's greatest weakness may be walking. With Albert's first step he saw the simulated version of his apartment shudder and shake, accelerating the growing motion sickness he felt when seated. From typing, to the two-hour battery life, to motion blurring, and an array of other malfunctions, it became clear that Apple really hadn't worked out so many of the basics we'd need to make this a serious device. If upgraders had a voice at Apple, the company could have clearly avoided the trap that so many other companies fell into before.

First, like so many innovators, Apple solved for the wrong problem. The Vision Pro boasts remarkably clear displays and disturbingly effective cameras, going beyond the clarity and level of tracking any prior headset made possible. But an upgrader would have asked if screen resolution or lack of adequate cameras were a real concern for other headsets. Innovators often look to where they have a comparative advantage, any form of superior technology, and reverse-engineer a product to fit the capability. But upgraders start first by looking at whether that advantage is something that consumers and society want/need. Given the widespread reports of purchasers returning Vision Pros, the answer for Apple is a clear "no."[65]

Next, upgraders would zero in on the main barriers past headsets have had to success. When you look at past complaints about similar devices, many of the same points arise. Users simply find the experience of using the devices physically uncomfortable. For upgraders, that would be a red flag that any innovations that fail to make the headset physically tolerable to use for long periods of time are going to be a distraction, not a solution. Complaints from users like Albert were certainly no surprise to Apple execs. After all, their own safety materials warn users against strapping in to the Vision Pro for more than 20 to 30 minutes.[66]

Third, upgraders would have warned that the Vision Pro still lacks a killer app. Apple made some inroads on this point, unveiling the ability to take and view 3D photos for the first time on any Apple device. But even if there were a clamorous demand for 3D photography, the sheer discomfort and inconvenience of plugging into the Vision Pro to view your photo album makes the app seem dead on arrival, not the new killer. Even worse is the prospect of using the Vision Pro to take photos. Apple's promotional videos shows a young family lovingly filmed in 3D by a Vision Pro at their child's birthday party, the smoke billowing out from the child's birthday cake. Yet if one imagines the scene, it goes from Rockwellian to Orwellian when you imagine the parent who photographed the scene, hidden from their children by their other-worldly goggles, unable to join in eating the cake because their stomach is still too sensitive from their time viewing this milestone through the Vision Pro. It portends a future where you can record your family's most precious moments in ever greater fidelity, but never truly witness them yourself.

Lastly, upgraders would have warned about Apple's tragic misunderstanding of video calls. The Vision Pro makes the people you're speaking to on Facetime or Zoom look great, even larger than life if you want. But they can't see you. Of course, if you were on camera, they would see the strange sight of someone strapped into a headset, unable to make eye contact or other movements. So Apple's innovative solution was to create a deep fake of every user, a simulated version that could join calls from an anodyne CGI setting that could stand in for a second-rate therapist's office. The effect was jarring. This creation fell squarely into the uncanny valley, that disturbing niche of computer-generated human beings that look nauseatingly close to life-like, but not close enough. Once again, upgraders could have warned that this sort of CGI innovation was a mistake, that human beings don't like being asked to treat facsimiles of our friends and family as the real thing, but Apple sadly chose instead to innovate.

CHAPTER THREE

The Crypto Con

When you look at the number of people who are underbanked, or unbanked, in the United States and globally – it's indicative of a system that does not work for everyone ... Cryptocurrencies do provide a potential way to address a number of these issues, making it easier, cheaper, faster and more equitable for people to do what they need to do to manage their financial lives.

Sam Bankman-Fried[1]

Perhaps no technology embodies the hype, excesses, and failures of innovation better than cryptocurrency, the array of poorly understood technologies that have generated unprecedented wealth while consistently failing to deliver on their promise of a better financial world. Backers of cryptocurrencies like Bitcoin and Ethereum have painted their platforms as the solution to nearly everything wrong with the world economy, ranging from financial instability,[2] to financial inclusion,[3] and even inflation.[4] For more than fifteen years, these innovations have been sold to the public as a way to heal all that is wrong with the way our monetary supply works, but the better you understand how the crypto con has unfolded, the better you can understand why so many innovations fail us. And you'll also see that the sort of outlandish claims made above by disgraced crypto tycoon Sam Bankman-Fried aren't rare, but emblematic of the innovation mindset shared by so many.

THE ORIGINS OF CRYPTO

By now, most people have heard 1,000 jargon-filled explanations of the tech, but many remain confused about what it really is. The annoying truth is that when you strip away the hype and self-promotion, crypto's innovation is pretty basic: it's a shared database. That's it. If you walk away from this chapter understanding nothing more, you'll understand the tech far better than most, and better than anyone should have to. The innovation that made crypto so powerful was to share that database across computers, using millions of participants to collectively do the work of tracking transactions, rather than using a single, centrally operated server that one person can control. This distributed database of transactions is called the "blockchain."

I (Albert) first came across this computing approach as a student in suburban Massachusetts. A shy, introverted college kid, I always was eager to geek out on new technology projects. So, I was quick to sign up when I learned about a way to run software on my laptop that could work with countless computers around the country to solve really hard math problems. It was the sort of math that would normally take a very expensive, cutting-edge supercomputer, the type housed in super-cold, ultra-clean labs under lock and key. Using a supercomputer was extraordinarily expensive, even for just a few hours, but by getting lots of users to download part of a math problem, solve it on their computer, and upload the results, you could do the same thing, and the whole undertaking was free.

Just to be clear, I wasn't an early crypto investor who made billions on Bitcoin. Instead, the project I was donating computing time to was an earlier, even geekier effort called SETI@Home,[5] which borrowed my CPU to help search the cosmos for intelligent life. Spoiler alert: we didn't find any. Software to let computers solve math problems together, that's all crypto is at its core.

Roughly a decade after SETI@Home aimed its distributed computing system at the heavens, the first cryptocurrency (Bitcoin) started with an earthlier ambition: printing money. Launching in late 2008, at the depths of the financial crisis, Bitcoin's developers sought to use this same shared computing model to create a distributed ledger to track token transactions across computers, rather than through a single centralized server. That's it.

The software would use encryption to track the tokens as they were traded from one person to another, creating a shared ledger to make sure the same tokens weren't traded more than once.[6] "We have proposed a system for electronic transactions without relying on trust," wrote the secretive creator of Bitcoin.[7] They describe "a peer-to-peer network using proof-of-work to record a public history of transactions that quickly becomes computationally impractical for an attacker to change . . ."[8]

Having virtual currencies on its own was nothing new. Video games like the fantasy role-playing game World of Warcraft and much less fantastical Second Life had had virtual currencies for years.[9] Whether the gold and silver of World of Warcraft or the "Linden Dollars" minted by the owners of Second Life (Linden Labs), video game players like myself had long grown accustomed to the idea that software systems could create virtual money we could use for in-game purchases.[10]

Not only would players collect these virtual currencies for making progress in the game, but they spawned a whole subsidiary economy. So-called "gold farmers" – largely in developing economies – would spend grueling hours playing World of Warcraft to collect virtual gold that they could then sell on third-party ecommerce websites like eBay.[11] But no one argued that virtual World of Warcraft gold would displace the US dollar or UK pound.

Video game companies completely controlled these currencies and could radically revalue them on a whim.[12] And while people could buy and sell these currencies in online exchanges, there was almost no place you could use these virtual currencies outside of the games. Importantly, these video game currencies had none of the elements of a real-world currency: unit of value, unit of account, wide acceptance, easy authentication, and low transaction costs.[13]

So, if something's called a currency, is traded in a small number of places like a currency, but doesn't actually meet the criteria for currency, what is it? Just barter. Bartering goods and services is older than any coin or paper note, and you can always barter a good even if it's not a currency. In fact, you can barter anything. Imagine an idyllically agrarian scenario where you trade an hour plowing a neighbor's field for a few dozen eggs fresh from their henhouse. You're both giving something of value to the other, but neither of those things is truly a currency. You can cook the eggs, you can eat them, but you can't take them to the bank.

Those behind cryptocurrencies have always wanted to claim that their tokens were more like Dollars and Euros than the virtual gold people barter from Warcraft, but the primary difference is just that crypto currencies were decentralized like SETI@Home. Sure, there was no video game company that could change the number of tokens on the market, no single point of failure. To many observers, that on its own isn't enough to replace government-backed currencies.

Still, amid the bank failures and sovereign credit fears of 2008, as so many of the financial institutions that once felt rock solid exploded into molten magma, this argument had an appeal. Why trust institutions to mint money when you can trust math? But the reality is that Bitcoin and the countless cryptocurrencies that followed were largely another video game currency. They do have an interesting breakthrough in encryption, but like so many innovations, those making money from the technology continue to try to sell it as the solution to situations it can't actually address. And after more than fifteen years of crypto capitalism, it's clear that the technology is just a vehicle for speculation.

DIGITAL TULIPS: THE EARLY BOOM

If cryptocurrency innovations have failed as broadly as we claim, why have they made so many people so rich? You might have met friends or family who speak with smug certainty of the promise crypto poses for the future, offering their own success investing in crypto as proof. Sadly, like so many innovations, cryptocurrency was able to generate a huge financial return for investors without ever creating an underlying product that could do the things promised in the first place.

When Bitcoin first launched, the early adherents loved the dream that one day it could displace government-run printing presses as a currency. You could do business in Bitcoin, get paid in Bitcoin, and live an entire financial life on the blockchain.[14] But we've never seen this vision come about. Almost no one is paid in Bitcoin.[15] You can't walk into a store and see prices in Bitcoin.[16] Not only do most shoppers lack any intuitive sense of what Bitcoin's price is, but that price is constantly in flux. And on the rare occasions that people try to make online purchases or donations in cryptocurrency, some part of that transaction has to actually take place in US Dollars or another government-backed currency (so-called "fiat" currencies).[17] The success hasn't been in getting people to use Bitcoin and other cryptocurrencies as a currency. Instead, it's been getting people to *invest* in cryptocurrencies.[18]

Creating a currency is hard, very hard. Creating something that huge numbers of people readily exchange for a recognized unit of value is rare throughout human history, and is almost exclusively the domain of government-backed currencies today. But creating an investment is easy. Almost any object (physical or computer-based) can become a vehicle for speculation, whether the tulip mania of seventeenth-century Netherlands (where the value of the colorful flowers skyrocketed before crashing to Earth),[19] or the more whimsical asset bubbles like the Beanie Baby craze of the 1990s and 2000s.[20]

No one thinks that tulips are about to replace legal tender. Investors never hoped to walk into stores with prices denominated in Savvy The Foxes, Emmett Dinos, or other adorable stuffed collectables. Instead, people were crazed with collecting these assets because they thought that the value would go up. The Beanie Babies and the tulips don't pay interest, they don't have a dividend, they don't have any social utility apart from looking pretty, but in an asset bubble – when lots of people believe that an item will get more valuable in the future – that can become a self-fulfilling prophecy . . . for a time. For those observing an innovation from the outside, you should be wary anytime the pace of investment dramatically exceeds the pace of adoption for a new technology.

Bitcoins and other cryptocurrencies have one feature that makes them appealing for this sort of speculation: there's a fixed supply. As part of the decentralized creation of cryptocurrency, the computer code was written to cap the number of tokens that could be created.[21] This creates a guarantee of scarcity that Bitcoin backers hold up as proof that the currency will gain value with time. But if you had mathematical proof that the number of Beanie Babies would never go up, that wouldn't mean those toys would get more valuable in the future (or have any value at all). In an asset bubble based solely on something's rarity, the bubble only keeps going as long as investors believe someone else will pay more for the toy tomorrow than they pay today.

This is the market mechanic that drove Bitcoin from a few cents in 2010 to more than $65,000 in 2021: pure speculation.[22] This is fundamentally different from the type of growth that we see in assets like stocks and bonds, which generally derive their value from the profitability of the underlying company or debt that's being bought. When investors buy shares in a company, they can look at the value of the money that company is making today and what it's projected to make in the future.[23] They can look for stocks they think will grow as the company grows, or prioritize stocks that pay a dividend, giving investors money back for each share they own. Yes, some shares can swing wildly, and a small number of investors can speculate the same way that cryptocurrency and Beanie Baby owners do. But ultimately that share has a value that can be traced back to the company that issues it.

With cryptocurrency, there are no profits, no dividend, no company, just tokens on a distributed ledger. Crypto falls into the investment category of SWAG, short for Silver, Wine, Art, and Gold.[24] SWAG are things that people can speculate on, buying and selling as the price varies, but which don't generate any income on their own.[25] This doesn't mean that the Bitcoin bubble and other cryptocurrency hype cycles will burst tomorrow – gold has been in a bubble for millennia[26] – it just means that ultimately the only thing keeping the value of cryptocurrency afloat today is the belief it will be worth more tomorrow. Crypto enthusiasts may claim that they trust in the math, but the truth is that their fortunes are resting on nothing more than the power of positive thinking.

Following Bitcoin's success in driving up prices and making investors money, wave after wave of crypto copycats came to try to do the same thing. Like Bitcoin, many of these currencies were exceptionally successful in driving speculation, generating hundreds of billions of dollars in profits for early investors. Some of these currencies, like Ethereum, even began to rival Bitcoin with new computing strategies and product models. But despite all of their different branding, strategies, and financial models, all of these cryptocurrencies essentially rested on the single premise that collective computing was a better model for minting money than turning to governments. The sole difference between these tokens and video game tokens of earlier eras is that the encryption built into the cryptocurrency code would ensure a fixed number of tokens that couldn't be altered in the future and a decentralized way of keeping track of how those tokens are exchanged. No matter how lofty crypto backers' claims are about the value of their technology, for those evaluating it on the outside, the only question that really matters is: does decentralized record keeping and a fixed number of tokens create something valuable for society? Sadly, the answer is almost always no.

NOT THE RIGHT INNOVATION FOR THE PROBLEM

The innovation behind cryptocurrency, the decentralized storage of information across multiple computers, may have some positive social value one day. Already people are experimenting with ways to integrate the strategy into all manner of technologies, and it's hard to know if some of those might eventually make a positive impact. But what is clear is that Bitcoin, Ethereum, and other so-called cryptocurrencies will fail to live up to their name and actually become currency. And even if some of the thousands of newer cryptocurrencies on the market may address some (but not all) of these issues, Bitcoin and Ethereum alone continue to account for 70 percent of the cryptocurrency market at the time of writing.[27]

CREEPING CRYPTO: SLOW TRANSACTION SPEEDS The math behind crypto is compelling. As a child, I (Albert) remember hearing my father, a computer scientist for IBM, talk about the difficulties of creating digital money. He and his co-workers had looked at different ways that you could use encryption to create a decentralized digital currency, "electronic dollars" as I remember them being described at the time. The crude idea in the dial-up era was to use hardware tokens that could exchange encrypted dollar bills offline, using an encryption engine on the device to verify the transaction. The project went nowhere as people understood the difficulty of deploying this system in a way that prevented digital counterfeits. The brilliance of Bitcoin was to do this sort of tracking through a decentralized database that was fully visible to the world and processed (collectively) through donated computing time. The problem is that while Bitcoin solved this one problem, it never figured out the other aspects of a usable currency.

Crypto may be framed as cutting-edge technology, but it feels like out of the Stone Age when measured by the thing that matters most when making a payment: how long it takes. Unlike credit and debit card payments that are processed in a matter of seconds, Bitcoin trades are measured in minutes, hours, or even days. Bitcoin transaction times tend to be around 40 minutes to an hour and a half, but on some extreme days, it can be far worse.[28] For example, on October 1, 2023, the transaction backlog was so bad that it took 25,809 minutes to process Bitcoin transactions . . . over 17 days.[29]

Waiting 17 days for an investment to sell could be frustrating and deeply costly, but if businesses accepted Bitcoin as payment, the impact would be far worse. No modern economy could function with a currency that took so long to process. Even worse, the unpredictability of not knowing day to day how long transactions would take could completely upend any business truly relying on Bitcoin. Like so many innovations, the backers of Bitcoin tried to rush to market with a product that simply couldn't do what was required to succeed. The advancements they made in decentralized record keeping is useless for anyone trying to run a modern business and offer quick, reliable payments.

Of course, crypto backers will be quick to highlight how some more recently developed cryptocurrencies support faster transaction speeds.[30] Still, even the fastest tokens, such as Solana – which can process 65,000 trades per second[31] – still take 10 seconds to process each transaction ... more than three times what it takes for a traditional credit card swipe.[32] And super-speedy Solana accounts for just 3 percent of cryptocurrencies,[33] with the vast majority of crypto wealth held in slower, stodgier, and more unwieldy currencies like Bitcoin and Ethereum.[34]

The lethargy of crypto payments should have been a major red flag to innovation skeptics from the start. All things considered, consumers will very rarely adopt an innovation that's less convenient than the status quo. Customers often switch technologies for greater convenience, and they are sometimes persuaded to adopt a change that's comparably convenient (if it means gaining some other benefit), but they are almost never willing to take a step backward.

"NO BACKSIES": NON-REVERSIBLE PAYMENTS Mistakes happen. Perhaps one of the only universal rules of finance is that irrespective of how people make payments, some of those payments will be wrong. Sometimes users will enter the wrong account number. Sometimes they will send the wrong amount. And sometimes the same payment will be processed multiple times. While this is never a pleasant process, it's something that has been built into the mechanics of banking for decades. That's because bankers and regulators have understood that even the best-run businesses and most diligent individuals will sometimes make a mistake.

In the United States, the dominant electronic money transfer system is Automated Clearing House (ACH), which reportedly processed more than $80 trillion in payments in 2023 alone.[35] Under rules maintained by the National Automated Clearing House Association (NACHA), customers have clear guidance on how transfers can be reversed when they make a mistake.[36] This doesn't mean customers can always get their cash back, but when the wrongful transfer wasn't their fault, they often won't be left high and dry.

And reversibility goes far beyond the United States. The Society for Worldwide Interbank Financial Telecommunications (SWIFT) operates the dominant international interbank transfer network, processing nearly 50 million payments and securities transfers a day. And just like ACH, the system incorporates safeguards to reverse transactions that are clearly made in error.[37]

With Bitcoin, not only is there no regulating body like NACHA or SWIFT to create reversal rules, there's no bank to implement them. Cryptocurrency's radical decentralization makes such protections impossible. Instead, financial transactions are final and at users' own peril. Online message boards are filled with mournful crypto users asking for help after sending funds to the wrong account.[38] While the lack of a way to reverse transactions may be heartbreaking for users, it's a far larger problem for crypto as a whole.

And that's before taking into account the billions lost every year to a growing array of increasingly brazen scams. According to the FBI, in 2023, Americans suffered $5.6 billion in crypto fraud, a 45 percent increase from the prior year.[39] And that's just the losses that have been reported. And because of the lack of reversibility, there's often no way to get that money back. Without this basic safeguard against routine banking errors, there's simply no way to enable the scale of mass adoption needed to make crypto a currency and not just a collectible. Like so many innovations, backers of the tech focused on their technical advancement without looking holistically at the needs of those using the product.

A COSTLY WAY TO PAY Another source of uncertainty for crypto payments is how much it costs to pay with the token. Unlike credit cards, checks, and traditional forms of payment, there is no fixed price for transacting blockchain business. Instead, the fees are set based on the size of your transfer, the level of network demand, and how quickly you want the transaction to go through.[40] This payment, called a "gas fee," is paid out to the computers processing the crypto transaction. Unlike me and the other volunteers who donated our computers to SETI@Home all those years ago, the shared cryptocurrency database only works because people are paid for the time they spend processing transactions.[41] While Bitcoin average transaction costs have typically stayed around a dollar or two, they have surged to more than $100, and the amount can be exponentially higher for those seeking to make large payments quickly.[42]

While this sort of instability may not matter much to an investor who buys and sells crypto a couple of times a year, it could be maddening to the shopper who wants to use crypto as a currency. Imagine if every time you went to the market or mall, you not only had no idea how long it'd take for your payment to process, you had no idea what the eventual fee would be. This lack of certainty flies in the face of what consumers need to actually transact daily business. And the problem is far worse for institutions. For large banks and companies to convert their financial activity to cryptocurrency, it would mean accepting massive volatility in daily transaction costs for thousands, or even millions, of customers.

And Bitcoin doesn't just pose an uncertain economic cost with each payment, but an uncertain environmental impact as well. As of 2023, Bitcoin alone accounted for up to 0.9 percent of global electricity, possibly the same as the entire nation of Australia.[43] Think of it, an entire continent's worth of energy just to power the computers tracking the transactions for a virtual token. For companies facing growing pressure to reduce their carbon footprint, Bitcoin and many other cryptocurrencies are simply too polluting to process.[44] This is especially true given Bitcoin and other cryptocurrency's dependence on electricity from oil, gas, and even coal.[45] If Bitcoin were to grow to the scale needed to sustain large volumes of financial transactions as a currency, and not merely an investment asset, the impact could be catastrophic.

Perhaps the most ironic impediment to cryptocurrency's success as a *currency* is its remarkable success (for the moment) as an *asset*. Many of those who most strongly believe in Bitcoin as the future of payments would never actually pay for a cup of coffee or their new outfit with the token. Why spend a Bitcoin when you can hold onto it and let the price go up? That's the payments paradox. The more people believe in Bitcoin and other tokens as the payments platform of the future, the less likely they will be to actually spend those coins on daily life. And if the true believers did start to transact business in the tokens (rather than just buying and selling them in the hopes of getting rich), the outflows of money from crypto would cause the price to plummet.

The expense of Bitcoin transactions was another early warning sign many missed. Crypto was often cheaper to trade than stocks or bonds when it launched, which helped it gain momentum as an investment. But it is a much more expensive way to conduct many routine financial transactions. Given consumers' aversion to new technologies that are more expensive than the status quo, Bitcoin boosters should have seen that it had much more promise as an investment than a payments platform.

ENDLESS PROMISES

Despite all of the evidence that cryptocurrency is unfit for banking, a growing army of adherents keep putting forward narratives for why the innovation is more than digital tulips. Perhaps these arguments are a way to help fend off long-threatened regulation. Perhaps they're a way to avoid the perception that this is just a runaway asset bubble. Or perhaps people who made extraordinary amounts of wealth want to rationalize that as good for society. Regardless of the reason, not only does cryptocurrency fail to solve real-world problems, it continues to get far more attention than much more effective upgrade alternatives.

UNHELPFUL FOR THE UNBANKED When Sam Bankman-Fried made the utopian cryptocurrency promises that open this chapter, he was a multi-billionaire, founder of the leading cryptocurrency exchange FTX, and one of the most prominent advocates for the mass adoption and legalization of cryptocurrency on the planet. Less than a year later, Bankman-Fried would witness FTX's implosion in one of the largest bankruptcies in US history.[46] Less than a year after that, the one-time wunderkind would find himself convicted of a $10 billion fraud in federal court, counts that would eventually lead to a twenty-five-year sentence.[47]

Bankman-Fried's rise and fall may have been singular in their scale, but his behavior is largely emblematic of the crypto industry as a whole. The crypto kingpin built a fortune by betting on the rise and fall of crypto prices, trading the tokens like digital tulips, all while claiming that one day crypto would actually transform the world in how it was used, not just how it was invested.

One of the most oft-repeated justifications for crypto is to provide a financial onramp to the staggering number of unbanked and underbanked people. According to some of the most recent estimates available from the World Bank, 1.7 billion people around the world don't have bank accounts.[48] While the percentage of people with accounts is much higher in developed economies like the United States, there are still nearly 6 million American households without banking.[49]

Being unbanked is often a regressive tax on the most impoverished communities. It means spending more time and money to do relatively simple tasks, such as cashing a paycheck, paying utilities, or making foreign remittance payments.[50] And predictably this impact isn't uniform. Instead, historically marginalized communities are less likely to have bank accounts, including "lower-income households, less-educated households, Black households, Hispanic households, working-age households with a disability, and single-mother households."[51]

Crypto boosters have used this painful history of financial redlining and inequity to position their product as the key. Cleve Mesidor, founder of National Policy Network of Women of Color in Blockchain (later, the Blockchain Foundation Executive Director), claimed: "When you have been locked out of the system, when you haven't had pathways to create generational wealth, you see this as an opportunity ...."[52] She also claimed that the "possibility of leveraging blockchain and cryptocurrency to help the unbanked is absolutely possible ... This country cannot compete in the global innovation economy without making sure that these people can participate." Mesidor also framed crypto as an alternative financial system free from discrimination.[53]

When larger, more established companies sought to break into the crypto sector, they also rationalized the move with financial inclusion. Facebook launched its ill-fated cryptocurrency effort "Libra" with ample rhetoric about the unbanked. Dante Disparte, head of policy and communications for the Libra Association, claimed the "central goal here really is financial inclusion ... to build a financial ecosystem that can plug in and empower billions of people."[54] When Mark Zuckerberg testified about Libra to the US House Financial Services Committee in 2019, he claimed the "financial industry is stagnant and there is no digital financial architecture to support the innovation we need. I believe this problem can be solved, and Libra can help."

Zuckerberg's sales pitch did little to assuage those in Congress or observing from the sidelines. A particularly prescient piece of pushback came from Mehrsa Baradaran, a professor at University of California Irvine Law. She wrote in the *Washington Post* that for "all their expertise in cutting-edge technology, these innovators have not demonstrated even a rudimentary understanding of the lives of the poor: Tech entrepreneurs usually start with a cool technology and only afterward make claims about helping the marginalized, rather than collecting data about what these communities really need and meeting those needs."[55] As with so many other failed innovations, there were warning signs all along that those developing the technology didn't understand the users they purported to help. Whenever innovators swoop into a market or community where they have no first-hand experience, you should listen with heightened scrutiny.

Look at the reasons unbanked people give for not having accounts, and it's quickly clear why cryptocurrencies and social media payment platforms are a terrible fit for the problem. According to the National Survey of Unbanked and Underbanked Households conducted by the FDIC (America's leading bank regulator), more than a fifth of unbanked households say they simply don't have enough money to open an account. The second leading reason is distrust of banks, and third is fear that using a bank would undermine their privacy.[56] But (as explained in later sections) crypto does almost nothing to address barriers like account minimums, trust, and privacy (despite constant marketing that it does).

But there are numerous upgrades that can directly attack these barriers and create a pathway to financial inclusion for those on the margins. Ever since the Bank Secrecy Act of 1970 and the 2001 USA PATRIOT Act, bank customers have had to provide greater and greater identity proof to open an account.[57] But at a time when 29 million US citizens lack valid photo ID,[58] and millions more undocumented immigrants are ID-less, these verification requirements can be a huge barrier to banking. Rather than turning to an entirely new and unproven cryptocurrency banking system to solve the problem, we could simply follow the lead of Mexico and other countries that have addressed this issue by relaxing the ID verification for some small, new accounts.[59] This upgrade would refine the existing regulations to avoid the unintended consequences of banking rules on low-income households, while still preventing the misuse of high-value accounts for money laundering and other illicit purposes. Additionally, states and municipalities can follow the lead of New York City, which developed its IDNYC card to provide photo ID regardless of immigration status.[60] Working with local credit unions, the city has been able to issue 2.1 million IDs, many going to New Yorkers for whom banking would have been out of reach.

TRUST THE MATH? When Bitcoin was first concocted, distrust of banks was at its core. According to the token's shadowy creator(s): "Banks must be trusted to hold our money and transfer it electronically, but they lend it out in waves of credit bubbles with barely a fraction in reserve. We have to trust them with our privacy, trust them not to let identity thieves drain our accounts."[61] Instead, they argued that what "is needed is an electronic payment system based on cryptographic proof instead of trust, allowing any two willing parties to transact directly with each other without the need for a trusted third party."[62] But things didn't exactly work out that way.

As we discussed above, cryptocurrency systems were slow, expensive, and hard to navigate. So as the value of these tokens boomed and less tech-savvy speculators wanted to get in on the action, a massive market opened up in crypto exchanges.[63] These exchanges provided a user-friendly way to buy and sell crypto without the cumbersome steps of using the formal blockchain. Instead, users could buy and sell with other users on the exchange, with the exchange itself making a market between buyers and sellers. At its height in 2020, nearly a fifth of all Bitcoin and Ethereum tokens were held in these exchanges, but today it's barely a tenth of tokens.[64] And the number of exchanges is declining too.[65] Why? Because Sam Bankman-Fried showed that exchanges were far worse, far less trustworthy than the banks Bitcoin sought to replace.

This is one of the great ironies of cryptocurrency: an innovation intended to make bank runs and financial failures impossible paved the way for one of the largest bank runs in history. This is because as soon as crypto traders move their tokens onto exchanges like FTX, they are no longer trusting the math, they're trusting this institution, a largely unregulated institution in a volatile market seeking to avoid the sorts of regulations that banks face. It's a financial ticking time bomb.

Even worse, Bitcoin enthusiasts fundamentally misunderstand how trust works. The vast majority of people can't trust the math because they simply don't understand the math. Even with our years studying the technology and related encryption issues, the authors of this book could never look at the computer code behind most cryptocurrencies and know if it's secure. We have to defer to cryptographic experts and institutions to tell us what they think of the tech. And with the fantasy that crypto might move from niche investment to actual currency, backers never acknowledge how little the math does for so many to directly prove that the technology is reliable.

As with any other innovation, you should be skeptical whenever those with specialized training or expertise promote products that require the general public to gain that same expertise. People can't use encryption as a substitute for institutions if they don't understand the encryption. Luckily, there are upgrades that can also address the distrust of banks that drove so much crypto adoption.

While relaxing bank ID rules may do little to address trust, there are institutions that can be upgraded to provide trusted banking services. The US Postal Service has long been one of the most trusted institutions in American public life.[66] And even amid the unique stresses of the Covid-19 pandemic, there is some evidence that trust actually increased.[67] And the USPS does a lot more than just deliver the mail. The post office already handles hundreds of thousands of money orders a day, more than 63 million in 2023 alone.[68] It would be a natural upgrade to provide basic banking services to these same customers, setting up the sort of boring checking and savings account traditional banks often disfavor.

Crucially, like the best upgrades, it's already a proven path. Post Offices around the world already offer postal banking, and they have historically been one of the most powerful institutions promoting financial inclusion around the world.[69] When post offices have been allowed to offer banking, the results have often been phenomenal. In the decade after Brazil's post office began offering banking in 2002, more than 10 million accounts were opened.[70] And in Japan, 80 percent of adults hold a postal banking account.[71] While Japan may be an outlier, many other countries report more than 20 or 30 percent of adults as owning a postal banking account.[72] Postal banking may not be as flashy as crypto, it may not make anyone rich, but it can deliver in reality what cryptocurrency has only offered in hype: a path to financial inclusion.

PRETEND PRIVACY Since its inception, Bitcoin and other cryptocurrencies cultivated an air of anonymity. When Maria Bustillos wrote about the still nascent technology for the *New Yorker* in 2013, she said: "Much of what has been written so far about bitcoins has centered on the perceived dangers of their relative anonymity, the irreversibility of transactions, and on the fact that they can be used for money laundering and for criminal dealings."[73] She then went on to describe these fears as a "red herring," since cash is also anonymous.[74] Bustillos was right to frame these arguments as fearmongering, but for the wrong reason ... cryptocurrencies are actually quite easy to track. At the same time that crypto's privacy claims were being touted in prominent outlets, its privacy had been completely eviscerated in the academic literature by a 27-year-old grad student.[75]

Crypto's privacy promises were always undercut by its core innovation, the distributed ledger. When information about every transaction is shared publicly, it actually gets quite hard to keep the identities of those users private. The creators of Bitcoin claimed that the "public can see that someone is sending an amount to someone else, but without information linking the transaction to anyone. This is similar to the level of information released by stock exchanges, where the time and size of individual trades, the 'tape', is made public, but without telling who the parties were."[76]

But in practice, these trades could be connected, their identities revealed. Some of the earliest work in identifying crypto holdings came from Sarah Meiklejohn, a PhD candidate in the Computer Science Department of the University of California San Diego.[77] In 2013, Meiklejohn wasn't able to just identify theoretical shortcoming in Bitcoin's encryption, but to identify one of the largest illicit online businesses on the planet.[78] In the years since, companies have been able to construct entire businesses around amassing massive databases of transactions, trying to map out the identities of everyone buying and selling cryptocurrencies.[79] Companies like Chainanalysis provide consulting services to law enforcement, helping track down the real-world owners of crypto wallets.[80]

Another vulnerability is that when Bitcoin was first dreamed up, its supporters never predicted the role that large exchanges would play as intermediaries. These companies collect huge sums of data about their users, working proactively with law enforcement to screen unwanted transactions.[81] This includes many of the same customer identification requirements that dissuade so many from doing business with traditional banks. If you want to buy or sell small amounts of cryptocurrencies without ever converting that digital asset into hard currencies like dollars or euros, the process can be kept relatively private, but as soon as you want to convert crypto into a currency that can actually be used to pay your bills, you have to go through the same process as any other bank. And when companies have tried to find ways around these rules, federal prosecutors have been quick to swoop in.[82]

Crypto true believers made the classic innovation error of looking at their technology in a vacuum. From the beginning, onlookers could have seen the warning sign that when you make the details of every transaction public, there's no way to truly keep the identities of those participating private. When you look at cryptocurrency in a world where people are conducting multiple transactions with multiple counterparties, where so much data about the rest of our lives is already known and tracked, it's clear why the model falls apart.

The truth is that if we want to have a privacy-preserving way to send money, there's simply nothing better than cash. For those of us who think that the financial system is overly surveilled, the upgrades are clear: loosen regulations on existing financial transactions. It's straightforward to do, and the public can readily understand the costs and benefits. Instead, so many crypto champions choose to peddle their product as the bulwark for financial privacy, completely ignoring how easy it is to truly track.

BLOCKCHAIN BEYOND BANKING Even as crypto promoters struggle to implement the asset's original use case as a currency, an array of even more ambitious plans have been unveiled for how blockchain can be integrated into nearly every aspect of our technological lives. In 2015, Bitcoin had seen wild price swings following its initial 2013 surge.[83] Still, crypto boosterism was so rampant that a trusted outlet like *The Economist* was willing to run a cover story depicting the technology behind Bitcoin as a staggering innovation, "bitcoin's shady image causes people to overlook the extraordinary potential of the 'blockchain', the technology that underpins it. This innovation carries a significance stretching far beyond cryptocurrency . . . Simply put, it is a machine for creating trust."[84] But if you're skeptical about Bitcoin's potential as a currency, you should be downright cynical about the ways the blockchain is marketed for even more complicated tasks.

Around the same time, crypto publications began to write about the virtues of so-called "smart contracts," the idea that everyday computing transactions could be handled with newer cryptocurrencies like Ethereum. Smart contracts aim to create agreements between two parties that aren't just recorded on the blockchain, but which can execute themselves without reliance on a human participant. A "smart contract might automatically transfer ownership of an item when it is fully paid for, upon the passage of a set period of time, or upon the meeting of any other predetermined condition that can be instantiated in computer code."[85] When they work as intended, "smart contracts can be *immediately and automatically* effectuated, without reliance on manual transfer, or the intervention of institutions like courts."[86]

With smart contracts, "moving to the blockchain" became the new high-tech hype version of "moving to the cloud," the ubiquitous pitch from prior years that every application would be better done remotely on a server, rather than a user's end device. "Smart contracts represent a disruptive innovation with a huge potential," wrote *Bitcoin Magazine*'s Giulio Prisco in November of 2015.[87] Prisco prophesized that smart contracts "could soon operate on the Internet of Things (IoT), control objects in the physical world, and power a new decentralized version of the sharing economy." Prisco even believed that smart contracts could let sites like "Uber and Airbnb ... operate in pure P2P mode without centralized management." Sure, some of that is technically possible, but a decade later this use case is no closer to reality, because it still doesn't make business sense.

Crypto backers always talk about a world of decentralization as if it's an unalloyed good, but it's not. Convenience, affordability, and reliability prove to be much more important to customers. Would you rather use a decentralized car key that uses smart payments to check your ownership of the vehicle, or would you rather use something that just works? And as long as decentralized solutions remain slower, more expensive, and less reliable, these types of use cases will remain just as fantastical.

When Austrian car-sharing service Eloop announced it would use smart contracts to share revenue with car owners, it gained global coverage as a cutting-edge innovation.[88] Under the plan, individuals and organizations could gain cryptocurrency tokens as payment for renting out their vehicles.[89] They claimed the approach helped in "fostering deeper engagement with users and providing access to additional liquidity and revenue streams."[90] But the truth is that this car company had simply reinvented the wheel, making the sorts of car-sharing payments that had been routine for decades on centralized systems even more cumbersome. Less than a year after launching the initiative, Eloop was bankrupt.[91]

Not only do crypto supporters ignore the barriers to customer interest, they often ignore when their technologies are likely to stir up unwanted government attention. Perhaps the single most ambitious scheme for the blockchain is a byzantine creation called a Decentralized Autonomous Organization (DAO). It's crucial that you understand that you *don't* need to understand how this works. Writing a detailed explanation of how DAOs operate would be longer than this book, and it'd leave you no better equipped to understand why they fail in the real world. Instead, it's enough to know that DAOs (at their simplest) try to create whole companies that are owned and operated through smart contracts. If that seems confusing to you, you're correct.

Rather than drafting a book-length explanation for why this is a terrible substitute for traditional corporate governance, we can just look at what happens when these innovative entities operate in our existing legal landscape: they get sued, indicted, and shut down. Back in 2017, before the DAO boom first took off, the Securities and Exchange Commission (SEC) was already warning that the approach violated federal law.[92]

It's true that Congress never took any steps to regulate these new blockchain entities, but they didn't have to, since DAO creators had simply reinvented the practice of issuing shares. DAO tokens give a share of ownership in the DAO (just like stock), can be freely bought and sold (like stock), and allow owners to vote on the decisions of the DAO (you guessed it, just like stock). The SEC didn't need a new law because Congress had already required those issuing shares to register offerings with the government after an earlier era of fly-by-night stock offerings helped spark the Great Depression.[93]

Those promoting DAOs don't want to be subject to the same rules that apply to other companies. They argue that the fact they operate via blockchain should make them exempt from a whole host of financial and consumer protection laws that would otherwise apply. But agencies routinely overcome the legal and computational fiction that DAOs are beyond the jurisdiction of the courts. They can be brought to court, and they have lost.[94]

The only thing more chilling than an army of crypto creators forming new entities in clear violation of the law would be if they were permitted to continue with the practice. It may not be clear how any company could benefit from this computerized management structure; it's easy to imagine how these firms could inject massive new forms of financial instability into the market. A mortgage-backed security could just as easily spark another financial crisis, even if it's only issued cryptographically. And many of the novel corporate structures explored seek to roll back a century of protections against manipulative market practices. All of this makes smart contracts feel like a pretty dumb idea.

In the rare cases where lawmakers have backed crypto corporatism, the results have been less than stellar. In July 2021, lawmakers in Wyoming took the extraordinary step of legalizing DAOs as a type of limited liability corporation.[95] The results were problematic. Within months, the SEC swooped in to halt the first Wyoming DAO for violating federal securities law.[96] American CryptoFed allegedly made false and incomplete statements about its effort to launch yet another cryptocurrency through its first-in-the-nation DAO.[97] And when CityDAO used the Wyoming law to buy 40 acres of rugged, rural land for $100,000, the results weren't much better.[98] Within months, project promoters revealed that they hadn't understood zoning regulations that severely restricted development of the parcel.[99] And that was before the project lost nearly $100,000 to hackers, a fate that has frequently beset DAOs.[100]

CRYPTOCURRENCY REGRETS

So many of our friends and family hold regrets about cryptocurrency, bemoaning the fact that they didn't listen to some online stranger who told them to buy tokens when the price was so much lower. People have made titanic fortunes with the technology, even as it struggles to show any broader benefit to the world. Interestingly, some of those who did buy into the tech from the beginning have regrets of their own ... regrets the technology never did what it promised – to actually help people.

When I (Albert) met with Ashley Taylor, I only knew that she had been interested in crypto for many years before becoming disenchanted with the space. But as we sat down for lunch at a laid-back Mediterranean restaurant in Fort Greene, Brooklyn, I had no idea just how early an adopter she had been. Over our lamb hash and brisket, she went on to tell me that she was the first employee of ConsenSys, which was core to the launch of Ethereum. Ethereum is the world's second biggest cryptocurrency, with a market cap at the time of writing close to $300 billion. Still, despite the success of Ethereum, Taylor left ConsenSys after two years to better focus on tools that could meaningfully improve financial access.

Taylor was hopeful that cryptocurrencies like Ethereum could be a curative to a financial world where it felt like a smaller and smaller number of people could actually get ahead and find a pathway to financial stability. "I came to blockchain with a problem that I was already looking at solving . . . economic systems are rewarding fewer and disenfranchised more than even when I started with an original thesis."[101] Originally she had looked at projects around community vouchers that rewarded neighbors for their contributions, but those analog models didn't seem scalable: "a lot of the voucher systems don't scale. They stay small."[102] "So when I saw blockchain, I was like, okay, clearly we move to a world where we're using lots of these like voucher systems."[103]

It was that interest and a New York cryptocurrency meetup that brought Taylor to the NYU Law School classroom where Joseph Lubin was unveiling a new cryptocurrency to an audience of about forty people, apart from Taylor, all men.[104] Lubin (ConsenSys's founder) would go on to earn an estimated $5 billion from his role in the creation of Ethereum.[105]

By most measures, Ethereum has been a fantastic success, but Taylor doesn't think so, because the stated mission of creating a tool for financial inclusion was ultimately drowned out by the desire for a profitable commodity: "looking back on it, [I] understand that they were more interested in . . . crowdfunding infrastructure and that they would be able to invest in that infrastructure."[106]

She continued, "but for what? And that's why the space has continued to suffer, because it fails to answer the problem of what problems in the world does this technology actually solve."[107]

Ultimately, Taylor just doesn't believe that cryptocurrencies were up to the challenge they sought to address. Like so many innovations, they weren't a "complex enough answer to a very, very, very complex problem."[108] In fact, she believes that "if anything, blockchain has just become a tool for the wealthy to become wealthier and extract value from other people."[109] This taps into another classic warning sign of innovation failure: over-simplicity. Many of the most destructive innovations have sought to solve complex interconnected problems through one relatively simple fix. But when an innovation is orders of magnitude simpler than the problem it takes on – encryption as a solution for the instability of a modern, interconnected global economy – it's a clear sign that the technology is likely not up for the job.

CONCLUSION

When one looks at the rapid rise of cryptocurrencies, the billions invested, and the centrality of these tools to the finance discourse, it's easy to think of crypto as unique. But while the scale of crypto's rise is staggering, its failures parallel those of so many other high-tech innovations. Like we've seen throughout this book, those who profit from a new technology are often eager to reverse-engineer explanations for why it can solve whatever problems we face. But not only has crypto utterly failed to provide a usable financial tool (beyond a speculative investment), it continues to distract us from long overdue upgrades we need to the financial system. Until we face those limitations, crypto speculators will continue to make and lose vast fortunes, and the billion and a half unbanked people around the world will continue to be left out in the cold.

CHAPTER FOUR

Home Security Upgrades

SURVEILLANCE VIGILANTISM

What's the right thing to do if you receive someone else's package? Many of us would leave it out with a note to UPS or FedEx. A few unsavory characters might just keep the item. But when one Florida man received a package with a neighbor's medication, he went the extra mile, making sure to deliver the time-sensitive parcel to the right home. In an earlier age, it would have been an unmemorable incident, a moment of neighborly kindness. But in the era of surveillance vigilantism, nothing is so simple.

When Gino Colonacosta and his son, Rocky, received a Ring video doorbell alert of activity at their front door, they had been primed by the surveillance system to treat it as a security threat.[1] They grabbed a pair of .45 caliber handguns and prepared to confront an imagined burglar with deadly force if needed. But there was no burglar outside, just a package. So, they searched further away from the home, eventually finding a woman parked nearby having a phone call in her car.[2] They lowered their guns and instead raised their voices, ordering the woman out of her car.

The driver, however, didn't know anything about the package or the mix-up. Instead, she assumed the two armed men shouting at her wanted to carjack her. She threw her car in reverse and tried to escape. The Colonacostas responded by firing seven shots into the car. They barely missed the driver and instead struck a children's car seat; only by sheer luck was it empty at the time.

The entire incident was an example of the false promise of surveillance technology, especially when it is pitched to everyday citizens. Products like the Ring doorbell camera are marketed as wholesome public safety innovations, allowing individual consumers to take control of their own security and safety. But when one probes the effectiveness of the product, it looks more like a band-aid fix, perfectly adapted to an era of fraying societal bonds. In reality, surveillance innovations like Ring function are more of a public safety *threat* than a public safety solution. As journalist Edward Ongweso Jr. writes, they thrive off a "well-documented pattern of cultivating paranoia."[3] Even as they seek to look outward, they impinge upon our own privacy, both individually and collectively. And, all the while, there's no credible evidence that next-generation consumer surveillance has any public benefit. It's an innovation trap, catering to our collective anxiety.

THE RING INNOVATION

Home security systems are certainly nothing novel in the United States. As early as 1853, Augustus Pope of Massachusetts secured his own security system patent, detailing primitive electromagnetic sensors for doors and windows.[4] A century later, CCTV camera systems were patented by Marie and Albert Van Brittan Brown of Queens, New York.[5] Home alarm systems soon followed that could combine electronic sensors, video, and motion detection.

When the Ring camera was introduced in the early 2010s, its innovations came partly through marketing and partly through its design. Jamie Siminoff and his colleagues first launched Ring to a skeptical reception. Like many earnest startups, Jamie pitched the titular "sharks" of *Shark Tank*, a venture capital reality show where innovators compete for investment from the show's stars. But when they made their 2013 appearance, every one of the investors passed.[6] Flash forward eight years and Ring was selling more than 1.7 million video doorbells per year, roughly a seventh of the overall market, and dwarfing its nearest competitor.[7]

The message on which the company honed in at that time was that their rather standard, affordable camera was instead a breakthrough tech product because it connected users to a broader network. Ring was a "smart" camera that would send notifications and videos to users' devices. To use Siminoff's language from Shark Tank, it's like a "caller ID" for our homes.[8] But rather than just announcing visitors who chose to ring the digital doorbell, the device could alert users anytime it detected motion, whether it was a passing deer, a trick or treater, or (on rare occasion) something more sinister. At the same time, Ring used a national network of law enforcement partnerships to gain access to public safety data and promote a sense of priority for Ring's customers. The company also paired Ring with the Neighbors social media app, fundamentally changing the relationship between purchasers and their surveillance equipment. The combination allowed the company to become synonymous with security, driving sales of sensors, standalone cameras, and other systems. But it was also a ticking time bomb.

By this point, Ring was no longer a standalone startup. It had been purchased in 2018 by Amazon for almost $1 billion.[9] For Amazon, this wasn't just an investment in a promising surveillance company, it was part of a broader effort to shift how Americans think of the type of package theft that so often targeted Amazon's own deliveries.[10] Moreover, the technology neatly plugged into Amazon's growing web of Alexa devices, embedding the company's disembodied AI assistant in nearly every aspect of our homes and offices.[11]

Just as Ring was pitched as a Silicon Valley-style disruption of historical security systems, its user experience followed the logic of modern tech. That is, Ring wasn't designed like most home security systems, to fade into the background until it was needed in an extreme situation. Instead, Ring and its competitors became an active part of one's daily life, a constant source of notifications, and potential threats. They amplified home security. Suddenly, every time someone rang the doorbell or even walked by a Ring owner's home, the owner would receive an alert, priming them to engage more with the platform, and to become ever more vigilant or more fearful. And if this stream of notifications wasn't enough, Ring connected users through its Neighbors app, part community bulletin board, part social media feed. Now, even the most isolated users, who would normally receive the fewest notifications, could be inundated with information about every potential threat in the community. While it's possible to use Ring without the Neighbors app, and vice versa, the vast majority of Ring users participate.

There's both a logic and an irony to Ring's innovations. Ring offered few advances in terms of its actual security technology; the camera and the sensors were not particularly novel. Instead, its major contribution was to bring home security into the realm of social media and Big Tech. This is a logical advance from the perspective of Silicon Valley investors – if you can create a new market in the saturated sector of social media, why not do it? But the irony is that Ring's product then came with many of the downsides of traditional social media: it created a similar dopamine-inducing stream of notifications, which would remind users over and over again about every horrible crime and accident their neighbors report (all without vetting or verification). The effect is not so much to provide the promised peace of mind, but to instill fear and reliance. Users are constantly told why they should be afraid, which encourages them to buy more surveillance equipment. And Ring's partnerships with law enforcement enables policing data to be injected into the system, imbuing the otherwise crowd-sourced platform with the imprimatur of legitimacy, and making customers fear they will miss out on authoritative government data unless they are plugged in to Ring and Neighbors.

THE PRIVATE–PUBLIC SURVEILLANCE STATE

Historically, Americans have exhibited a deep skepticism to many forms of government surveillance. Countries around the world have vocally embraced surveillance in recent decades. British officials embraced closed-circuit cameras as a public safety cure-all, erecting a so-called "Ring of Steel" to monitor seemingly every major street in London. Meanwhile, the Chinese government has become synonymous with surveillance, both for the ubiquitous tracking found throughout major cities, and for the surveillance-fueled genocide of Uyghur Muslims, who were tracked and detained by the millions.[12] American policing surveillance has likewise advanced in the twenty-first century, mirroring many of the same troubling patterns seen in the other surveillance-friendly states. But Americans remain comparatively opposed to surveillance, especially government surveillance of our homes.

At a time of record polarization, in fact, such skepticism remains a rare unifying issue. As of 2023, only 14 percent favored the government "installing surveillance cameras in every household" to decrease "illegal activity."[13] And yet even as American citizens resist state surveillance, *many* have embraced consumer devices like Ring and its competitors, purchasing more than 10 million Ring devices alone.[14] For many, there is no contradiction between the growth of privately owned surveillance systems and nearly unanimous opposition to government home surveillance. But the truth is that law enforcement is intimately intertwined with nearly every aspect of Ring.

This represents a further wrinkle introduced by surveillance innovation: by buying into a network of security cameras, consumers are creeping toward the very type of public surveillance they'd otherwise protest. And at the same time, partnerships between law enforcement and Ring were encouraging public safety to be co-opted by corporate interests.

In 2022, *Politico* reported that nearly 2,200 police departments had agreements with Amazon that let them post alerts and ask for surveillance footage on the Neighbors app.[15] Alarmingly, police departments allowed Ring to script or approve almost all public communications about the technology.[16] Press releases, key talking points, and countless other authoritative government communications were actually being written by employees of a for-profit company that may never have even visited the community where these messages are being posted.[17] Predictably, one of the things Ring fought to control was public statements about these agreements themselves, requiring many to keep the contracts confidential from voters – bypassing basic democratic processes.[18] Only after vocal opposition did the company eventually stop asking for confidentiality and ungagged departments.

The American Civil Liberties Union (ACLU) decried Amazon's influence on law enforcement's speech as a "betrayal of the police department's duty to serve the public first."[19] When a private company can push scripted messages for public officials, it blurs the line between public safety and product promotion. Such arrangements, even when made openly, create a critical conflict of interest.

Perhaps most alarming, however, was the way that Ring officials coached officers to circumvent the Constitution by requesting that residents provide police their recordings, even when police didn't have a warrant.[20] Under the Fourth Amendment, Ring owners have a clear right to say "no" to officers making such requests, but using persuasion, coercion, and the threat of legal process, officers can often avoid the step of getting a warrant.

Because of the product's terms of service, and Amazon's control over users' data, even when Ring owners do invoke their right to refuse, it may not mean much. When Ohio police asked Michael Larkin to hand over Ring footage from his video doorbell, he originally agreed, giving clips of a car that repeatedly drove by.[21] But over the course of a week, the police request expanded, and soon Larkin found himself reviewing a warrant for all the footage from his twenty-one Ring cameras, including those inside the house. With traditional camera systems, Larkin could have refused. But since Larkin (like most users) stored footage on Ring's cloud servers, the footage was the company's to share. When police asked Ring itself to provide the footage, Larkin was left out of the loop, and there was nothing he could do about it.

In 2024, following sustained, national opposition to police footage requests on Neighbors, even Amazon officials saw that the arrangement was indefensible. Police officers can no longer request footage from individual Ring users on the platform. Still, the change doesn't do anything to stop officers from contacting homeowners through other channels or getting a warrant if they refuse.

THE BROKEN RING PROMISE

Technological advancement often comes with tradeoffs. It would be one thing if smart surveillance devices like Ring were offering markedly better security in return for tradeoffs like user paranoia and compromised privacy. But there is no apparent evidence that such innovations are actually providing users the safety they've promised.

Ever since the early days of London's Ring of Steel, researchers have looked for evidence that cameras prevent crime. There is now mild evidence that cameras can be helpful in solving crimes after they occur, but years of evidence indicates that cameras fail at their main task: deterring and preventing crime. Cameras are excellent at capturing photos of the very violence they're supposed to prevent, allowing us to see an ever-growing litany of gruesome images, but they do nothing to intervene.

Ring is in a very similar position. Even as the company depicts itself, in its marketing materials, as fending off a deluge of package thefts, the truth is that the data doesn't support it. To start, Ring has no count of how many package thefts it supposedly deterred.[22] And when independent researchers looked at the question, they found that those who were taking packages generally didn't care whether they were seen. In fact, only "8% took any effort to conceal their identity – even when several observed the camera."[23] The entire economic rationale for Ring is increased security and the deterrence of crimes, but when the *MIT Technology Review* used public crime data to fact-check Ring's claims in 2018, they concluded "the evidence the doorbells slash crime is far shakier than the company would have cities and consumers believe."[24] In fact, "the only study carried out independently of Ring found that neighborhoods without Ring doorbells were actually less likely to suffer break-ins than those with them."[25]

In 2020, *NBC* ran its own inquiry and concluded: "There is little concrete evidence to support the claim ..." that Ring cameras deter crime.[26] In fact, when *NBC* reached out to forty police departments in eight states, it learned that none could provide "data to link the overall drop in property crimes to their deal with Ring."[27] The police departments that had used Ring the longest couldn't even provide anecdotal evidence that Ring deterred crime.[28] The same year, *CNET* found that crime data from Ring's earliest partners showed "minimal impact."[29]

It may seem counterintuitive, but networked systems like Ring can actually get in the way of effective policing. As Lt. Jack Harvey of the Houston Police Department noted, the system makes it easy for the public to inundate cops with "leads" that lead nowhere.[30] The Neighbors app deluges detectives with anonymous, crowd-sourced information on everything from noise complaints to animal control issues.[31] Lam Thuy Vo, a data journalist at *The Markup*, partnered with students from the NY City News Service at CUNY's Craig Newmark Graduate School of Journalism to review Neighbors notifications to the LAPD (Los Angeles Police Department) from July 11 through September 30, 2022. They found that over one-third of the alerts "described non-criminal behavior that had been deemed suspicious by users – like walking by cars to check doors or a stranger ringing someone's doorbell."[32]

This was the all-but-inevitable outcome of Ring's appification innovation. It creates user engagement and data, but this creates an issue we've seen for decades in other areas of policing, defense, and intelligence. Increased data collection, absent adequate analytical capability, simply fails to keep people safer. Today, technology makes it increasingly easy to collect vast quantities of information – whether through distributed surveillance methods like Ring or centralized surveillance endeavors from the National Security Agency. However, our ability to analyze that data is relatively static. And since police attention spans are a limited resource, any time spent reviewing Neighbors tips comes at the expense of reviewing more valuable information. For that matter, Vo found that the pattern only amplifies inequity in public safety, with residents of wealthier neighborhoods posting complaints to Neighbors six times more often than other residents.[33]

THE SURVEILLANCE DOPAMINE KICK

Most customers buy Ring with a noble goal, hoping to protect their homes and families.[34] But the reality of how the product works is far less noble. Like many other habit-forming social media platforms, Ring builds on our neurological response to stimuli and gratification to incentivize behavior that is ultimately harmful. Ring goes beyond what's seen with typical social media platforms, however, because the product leads users toward "intimate new levels of surveillance."[35] Associate Professor Ángel Díaz of the University of Southern California's Gould Law School notes that the app works such that:

> The paranoia of somebody's imagination is making its way into that of other people . . . If you're just passively keeping up with alerts and read them and move on with your day, you get inundated with this fear that your neighborhood is very unsafe, based on unsubstantiated accusations that are oftentimes more reflective of people's own prejudices than anything else.[36]

Ring not only makes it easier than in the past to install and monitor camera systems, the litany of notifications from both cameras and the Neighbors app vies for users' attention, constantly putting their home surveillance state front of mind. Ring creates the illusion of not just safety, but of control, letting users feel like they have great agency over their homes and lives, while simultaneously bombarding users with alerts from Neighbors that reinforce the perception that the world is a deeply dangerous place. It has encouraged people to monitor their neighbors, track their children and visitors, and even pass judgments on housekeepers and babysitters. The normalization of this sort of surveillance can easily extend into other parts of our lives, replacing interpersonal communication and trust with monitoring.

This manufactured anxiety is encouraged because the Neighbors app is designed to grab users' attention by allowing them to receive ongoing safety alerts of nearby incidents. It might have influenced the shooters we discussed at the beginning of the chapter. In fact, apps that have offered similar features to Neighbors also have demonstrated an ability to bring out the worst in people. For example, after a Black man knocked on someone's door in an attempt to discuss real estate, he was reported for being suspicious on the Nextdoor app. The police detained him, even though he had every right to do what he was doing, and even praised the app "for being proactive in keeping the community safe."[37]

But for many people, disproportionately young Black men, such apps can be dangerous, even deadly. When Sally Allwine saw a stranger talking to himself outside her Richland, Washington home, she felt the fear that so many Ring owners feel in similar situations. The man never tried to break into her home; he never attacked her or anyone else. But that night still ended in tragedy. That's because sheriff's deputies saw the footage and responded to the scene, a confrontation ensued, and the man was killed by officers. One man's quirky behavior, seen suspiciously, culminated in his death.[38] Allwine had viewed the situation through the lens that Ring and Neighbors had trained her to use, and she responded as they encouraged. But after seeing her response led to such needless, pointless violence – and after seeing the awful comments other Neighbors users made about the man – she promised never to post again.

When tech writer Max Read tried out Neighbors himself, he found it "terrifically addictive, a wildly engaging hodgepodge of voyeurism, suspicion, unease, and mystery."[39] "Moments you'd never have been aware of without the Ring … a stranger stepping on your stoop, or knocking on your door – mount as evidence of possible danger and urban decay."[40] Separate reporting from *Motherboard* found that a majority of the user-submitted videos it reviewed on Neighbors flagged people of color as "suspicious," with racist language routinely used.[41] To Professor Andrew Ferguson of American University, the results are unsurprising. "Reports of suspicious behavior are coded ways of saying someone does not belong," Ferguson claims, "which in many affluent areas correlates with targeting people of a different race."[42]

In 2020, Ring responded by hiring New York University's Policing Project to audit their service, resulting in new limits that critics claim are largely ineffective. As of 2021, Ring sought to limit racism on the site by requiring posts to be: (1) relevant to local crime and safety; (2) written in a helpful way; and (3) appropriate and safe to share.[43] But it remains unclear how these vague best practices translate into changes in actual user behavior. More impactful measures have also been introduced, giving users the ability to flag harmful content and giving moderators the power to ban harmful users.[44] But these sorts of moderation tools also have their limits. As Ring's consultants at the Policing Project noted: "The very nature of implicit bias makes it difficult to address through content moderation . . . We should not fool ourselves into thinking that profiling and prejudice can be eradicated from social media platforms."[45] All the while, as Vo notes, it's frankly "unclear how much of an effort Ring has made to ensure that people follow these guidelines."[46] And just as Ring has no credible evidence that its innovations prevent crime, it has no credible evidence that its new policies prevent biased abuse of those platforms.

Ring and Neighbors' incentivization of constant surveillance and vigilance are what perceptual psychologist James J. Gibson would call "affordances." Affordances are product designs that make associated actions more appealing, an extension of the premise that you can't separate objects' designs from how we think about using them. Consumer-targeted surveillance devices both legitimize and reinforce suspicion and voyeurism. They make once verboten activities feel like benign, even noble, parts of daily life. And the more widely such technology is adopted, the more homes we see with video doorbells, the more justified we feel in embracing that impulse ourselves.

As we've already seen, when we give ourselves permission to surveil those around us, we don't watch everyone equally. Instead, we see a neighborhood distorted by the constant fearful postings of the Neighbors app and our own bias. We see a world of constant threats, where those who "look out of place" are assumed to be dangers. The cycles of surveillance vigilance and vigilantism inevitably draw us down a dark road to ever greater monitoring, ever more police involvement, and ever more fear. In short, they make us into the opposite of good neighbors.

UPGRADING HOME SECURITY

Like so many heavily hyped innovations, smart surveillance devices like Ring aren't sold with facts, but with flawed intuition and an emotional narrative about the ways technology can fix entrenched problems. Millions of people continue to buy Ring systems and use the Neighbors app despite a lack of evidence that they improve home security. As is so often the case, there are upgrade alternatives – evidence-based solutions that can address these same concerns far more effectively. But as is also often true, these upgrades are overlooked by many because, while they are effective, they are expensive or have more limited upside potential. But even a modest benefit is better than technology that doesn't help at all. And if we can look beyond the innovation trap then we can find the real value of safety upgrades that don't stoke our worst selves or contribute to surveillance creep.

PACKAGE THEFT. Ironically, one of the key drivers of Ring's sales and Neighbors' success is a problem of Amazon's own making: the growing rate of package theft across the United States. Amazon's business model relies on being able to deliver high volumes of packages very efficiently, requiring both flexibility on delivery timing and limited time to wait for recipients to come to the door. Instead, American stoops and doorsteps are now littered with cardboard targets containing everything from high-end jewelry and electronics to shampoo and vitamins. The incentives have made the resulting spike in package thefts all-but inevitable.

Amazon's response has been to not only sell surveillance infrastructure, but to push legislation targeting the newly rebranded crime of "porch piracy," which would make such a crime a felony in many states. But traditional criminal justice theory shows why this approach is quite unlikely to be effective: sentence enhancements are far less likely to deter future crimes than a belief that one has a strong probability to be caught and punished for a violation. Resuscitation of the widely discredited mass incarceration strategies of the 1990s is unlikely to succeed where the first round failed.

Rather than turning to novel technologies to monitor those who take packages and higher criminal penalties in a misguided effort to deter such thefts, we could simply upgrade our capacity to make packages more difficult to steal in the first place. First, Amazon has created this problem by optimizing delivery speed and efficiency over the reliability of delivery. But that's not the only formula. Packages remain unattended in the majority of cases because delivery services make no attempt to figure out whether the recipient is home. By giving recipients an easier option to ensure signature upon delivery, Amazon and other online retailers could dramatically reduce the rate of package theft. Of course, we're not always at home, so this approach could be supplemented by investment in secure package delivery locations that could be used when customers aren't present.

Already, Amazon has begun to slowly expand package lockers at affiliated Whole Foods supermarkets and other high-traffic areas. For customers in more remote areas, without ready access to such a lockbox, there are still numerous options that remain more effective than the myth of surveillance deterrence. Homeowners can install electronic entry systems that provide drivers with a one-time code to access an outbuilding or vestibule to deliver packages. And for those whose homes lack a suitable package delivery space, secure external package drop boxes could solve the issue; the price is comparable to a Ring doorbell, and it's far less than many whole-home surveillance systems.

Lastly, carriers could upgrade their delivery algorithms. They could ensure drivers have time to deliver packages to secure areas and require confirmation that items weren't left outside a dwelling in plain view of a passerby. This measure could help ensure that drivers aren't inadvertently punished for being careful enough to use such a system.[47]

As with most upgrades, these investments are not magical or wildly difficult to achieve; they simply come at a cost to all-out efficiency. Not only is there the capital cost of installing secure delivery infrastructure, but there is also the staffing time of ensuring drivers can use secure drop boxes or redeliver items when a signature isn't possible. As long as we continue to embrace the magical thinking of the innovation mindset, these costs will seem unbearable to delivery companies. By that way of thinking, it's far better to put the burden on us. But that burden means paying for smart home surveillance systems that won't work. Or paying to arrest and imprison those who steal packages despite new draconian laws. And the consequences continue to spread harm.

Upgraders will instead see that the infrastructure alternatives give us a far better, albeit modest, return on the investment. And, more importantly, the burden would be borne by the right people: the companies creating the crisis in the first place.

BREAK-INS. Perhaps no scenario is as frightening to Ring buyers as the thought of a stranger breaking into the home – the horror-movie moment of realizing that someone is forcing their way into your most intimate spaces. Sadly, and predictably, the surveillance safety effect here is again a mirage. Cameras appear well positioned to memorialize such a traumatic moment, but ill-designed to actually prevent it.

Part of the allure of surveillance innovations is that one can have invisible, effortless security, a veritable force field to fend off foes. But the truth is that effective home security upgrades are far more visible. Fortifying entry points to the home with bars and high-security locks may not be as aesthetically pleasing as surveillance solutions, but they actually work, dramatically increasing the time it would take for a burglar to enter the home. Motion-activated entry lights (both inside and outside a dwelling) can make a burglar believe a resident already knows the would-be burglar is there. Additionally, light timers can help convince those planning a break-in that residents are home even when they're away for long vacations. Finally, traditional alarm systems and electron-magnetic window and door sensors can provide much of the peace of mind of video surveillance systems without the harms.

While the efficacy of these measures all vary, past research has found that they typically perform best in combination, with no single measure meaningfully deterring break-ins on its own.[48] As with all upgrades, there are both costs and limitations. Adding physical barriers can alter the aesthetics of a house, and all of these measures can feel somewhat limited in the sense of security that they provide or the level of break-ins they'll prevent. But rather than being reason for concerns, these costs and limitations are the essence of evidence-based decision-making. When one evaluates these matters as an upgrader, the most alarming scenario is when companies claim to offer a cure-all like Ring without identifying relevant harms and limitations. Upgraders learn to apply to technology the rule that we intuitively apply to so much of life: if it seems too good to be true, it probably is.

CHAPTER FIVE

The Failed Promise of Covid Innovation

As we write this, it's estimated that Covid-19 killed 6.65 million people globally. We see the pandemic as a crucial lens for changing the public conversation about technology because the compressed timeline highlights trends that are usually harder to see, because they take longer to play out. In other words, learning from the pandemic doesn't just mean becoming better prepared to face future public health emergencies. It means learning to think more critically about technology itself – being more honest about what problems can be addressed by different types of technologies, and different approaches to technological progress. There are times when technologies can make a world of difference, and there are times to admit that no technology can provide the answers society needs.

Misguided expectations about disruptive innovation are central to this story. Indeed, problems arise when society over-emphasizes game-changing innovation and undervalues less dazzling possibilities, especially incremental shifts. An honest assessment of technology requires admitting that the pandemic was also a time of extreme disappointment. During the darkest days of disease and fear, corporate and elected leaders made grand promises about technology. They rolled out apps to monitor our movements, scanners to measure our temperature, and even wearable devices to view our vital signs. Many of these were invasive, error-prone technologies that promised a return to peace of mind, but ended up wasting billions of dollars and unleashing a lurking surveillance infrastructure, all while failing to make good on their promises.

Covid-19 wasn't unique in inspiring tech opportunists to exploit our hopes and dreams, and that's precisely why it's illustrative. Times of crisis are often when our hopes are most exploitable, and when the cost of temptation is highest. Looking back at years of broken promises, we see a warning about the tactics that will mislead the public in the future if we don't start learning from our mistakes and embracing positive lessons for doing better.

THE VACCINE BREAKTHROUGH

Let's start with Operation Moon Shot – the most remarkable breakthrough that emerged in the wake of the Covid-19 pandemic. Techno-optimists were rightly proud of the warp-speed creation of safe vaccines by companies like Pfizer and Moderna. And it is prime evidence of the power of an innovation mindset. Progress can be hard to judge, but in this case, the evidence is clear. Would you rather live during the fourteenth-century "Black Death" plague, or the 1918–20 flu pandemic, or the global Covid-19 pandemic?[1] The smart answer is that it's far better to be alive today – and medical breakthroughs, including vaccines, are a big reason. The United States is a moonshot culture, which means that taking risks, working hard, and pushing past setbacks are deeply embedded in our cultural DNA. It's these aspects that contributed to the record-breaking path to the Covid vaccine.

Of course, vaccines aren't a silver bullet. Vaccination doesn't make anyone completely immune, and Covid is an evolving virus. And despite the effort to make vaccines widely available, access issues remain within the United States and abroad. Moreover, vaccines, like so many technologies, are highly politicized, which leads to their full potential being unrealized.

Likewise, we need to be careful when using words like "moonshot" or praising risk-taking innovative measures wholesale. We're not faulting Dr. Albert Bourla, Chairman and CEO of Pfizer, for titling his book *Moonshot: Inside Pfizer's Nine-Month Race to Make the Impossible Possible.*[2] But since the idea of a moonshot suggests a radical departure from the norm to make a long shot, it's important to remember the role of longstanding norms and incremental change. For example, public health officials rejected many of the most aggressive and risky proposals for vaccine development, such as challenge trials where volunteers are deliberately infected with Covid.[3] Furthermore, Operation Warp Speed involved incrementally increasing investment in vaccine purchases by having the government agree to pay for production before the completion of trials. And the vaccine production itself relied on techniques that were either repeats of past efforts or marginal improvements on past vaccines.

The vaccines were the first mRNA vaccines ever brought to market, and they were approved for public faster than any predecessors.[4] However, the vaccines' secret to rapid development wasn't some singular break-through, it was decades of incremental upgrades to mRNA technology.[5] In fact, the Pfizer and Moderna vaccines were founded on earlier mRNA vaccines that were developed against Ebola, influenza, and other viruses, but such efforts were never seen by drugmakers as commercially competitive enough to succeed.[6]

So, at once, the Covid-19 vaccines were a realization of innovative technology at its most remarkable, and a product of steady reliable upgrades, brought to bear at the proper moment. It is right to remember both aspects. And it is also important to remember that we lost sight of the balance of upgrade and innovation at many other moments during the fear and chaos of the pandemic.

THE PROBLEM OF SOLUTIONISM

A novel virus was spreading unseen. Reports of new cases made headlines one at a time, then all at once. Almost overnight, our healthcare systems were breaking and hospitals were overrun. We didn't have enough tests, enough masks, enough ventilators. Covid had quickly swamped our limited public health infrastructure, and one of the most vexing issues was that we couldn't even track its spread reliably. Among all the supply-related issues of the day, we were lagging in one of the simplest preventative measures of all – identifying and isolating outbreaks, so that citizens could know where Covid was spreading and protect themselves and others.

When a new infectious disease emerges, disease detectives will try to treat every patient like an open investigation. They're trying to map the contagion, finding its origins and vectors. After they've worked backward to the point of infection, they go forward with notifications to everyone the patient might have exposed, mapping out close contacts and then replicating the process for each new case. But with Covid, the scale of infection quickly escaped the disease detectives' ability to trace it. The traditional public health infrastructure was breaking down and we were working from behind to try to get a handle on how Covid was spreading. We needed a solution. A fast solution. A cheap solution. A high-tech solution.

And so, exposure notifications apps were born. The premise of Covid exposure apps is fairly simple, and that was an immense part of the appeal. If we track everyone you could have potentially exposed over the prior two weeks (the presumed life of a Covid infection), we can notify them as soon as you test positive. This way, we can help people isolate in the first crucial days while awaiting test results (in the days before rapid tests) and even get treatment more quickly if they develop symptoms.

It was alluring, simple to understand, and a prime example of our technological brilliance in action. The problem was just . . . the tech. For all the advancements of smartphones, they actually don't have a way to tell you much about disease transmission. Phones can't monitor the quality of the air we breathe, and they can't detect the viruses on our hands. So instead, app developers turned to distance measurements as a proxy for the risk of infection. Stand within 6 feet of another person for more than 10 minutes, and the app will count that as a close contact.[7]

But unlike human contact tracers, who ask detailed questions and understand the context of potential contacts, all the apps can do is measure distance, or try to. Whether you're indoors or out, masked or unmasked, or even in separate rooms, if you're within 6 feet for 10 minutes, the app will treat it the same way. But, of course, these situations are all completely different. Meanwhile, two people on opposite sides of a wall will be treated as close contacts, while two people on opposite ends of a conference table would not, even if they spend hours in the same unventilated space. These shortcomings mean that Covid apps would be questionable if they were as accurate as claimed. But sadly, they couldn't even meet that low bar.

There's no magical way for cell phones to know how far they are from other nearby devices. To build this capacity onto existing hardware that wasn't designed for the purpose, tech companies and governments had a few routes to choose between. The single most precise way to track device proximity is to have each phone create a constant log of its location using GPS, cellphone towers, and other electronic landmarks. If you upload these logs to a central repository, you can then retrace everyone's movements, taking note of any overlaps. The problem is that this centralized approach is ripe for abuse. The same centralized repository of location records that's collected for Covid-19 can quickly be repurposed by immigration officials, police, or even intelligence agencies. The threat was far from hypothetical. In Singapore, public officials were quick to roll out a Covid detection app, promising that the data would be kept private and only used by public health officials.[8] Within months, officials were already backtracking as police sought to access the data to investigate crime.[9] In Israel, matters were even more dire. Officials quickly not only allowed police to use Covid tracking data, but they even allowed the data to be accessed by intelligence officials.[10] On top of the threats to privacy and civil rights, the tracking didn't work. People were ordered to isolate after exposures they never had, from visiting places where they hadn't been.[11]

US tech firms and the government saw early on that the United States would never accept an Israeli- or Singapore-style contact tracing app. Any app that relied on centralized GPS and cell tower data would be too ominous for a country that was suspicious about every aspect of the pandemic response. But still, the tech giants wanted to believe that their devices and know-how could somehow become the solution, and thus Bluetooth exposure apps were born.

Unlike GPS, which was invented as a tool for finding users' location, Bluetooth was retrofitted for the job. Bluetooth is part of countless electronic devices, a communications protocol that lets devices communicate wirelessly over relatively short distances (around 30 feet). Bluetooth is more agile and energy-efficient than the bulkier Wi-Fi array, and engineers theorized that Bluetooth might be able to do something that GPS data couldn't: it could create a decentralized map of everyone we came near, which could detect potential infection without creating the Orwellian surveillance nightmare. Apple and Google even put aside their historic rivalry to allow their devices to talk to one another for the purposes of exposure tracking apps. But even the backing of these companies couldn't change the fundamental physics at play.

Bluetooth, it turned out, was great for all sorts of everyday tasks, just not measuring distance. Any number of variables, from building materials, to the model of phone you use, to whether you hold your device or have it in your pocket, can distort Bluetooth's distance calculation. Exposure apps were trying to determine whether devices were within 6 feet and nearby for 10 minutes; but that was a level of precision that simply couldn't be achieved.[12]

On top of the technical issues, there was also the problem of convincing citizens to use an app to keep track of exposure. In New York, more than 1 million residents downloaded the app in its first two months. But only 1,000 or so users a week were receiving alerts.[13] Researchers later found that New York Covid patients were less than half as likely than the state overall to even have the application installed.[14] As other states followed, none was able to get a majority of residents to download the software, with many falling below the 15 percent adoption rate that even proponents believe is needed for the software to work.[15] The reversal was even more pronounced in Australia, where the country's health minister not only labeled the $14 million app a colossal waste of money, but went so far as to urge people to delete it.[16] The recommendation came after more than 7 million Australians downloaded the software.[17]

Exposure notification apps were one from among a wave of pandemic-era innovations that exemplify the problem of solutionism. Solutionism is the mistaken belief that we can solve complex dilemmas by treating their core issues as simpler engineering problems. It is doomed to fail for one or more of the following reasons.

- Solutionism does not address the underlying causes of problems.
- Solutionism overestimates technology's effectiveness.
- Solutionism fails to recognize context – the social, political, economic, institutional, and other factors that influence how technologies are used.

Despite these flaws, solutionism is widespread because it meets psychological needs and serves a political purpose. Solutionism is reassuring (action is being taken!) and comforting (technology will solve the problems!). It also draws attention away from businesses, politicians, and others who claim to be making things better when they have no idea how to help or are even actively making things worse.

If leaders had been able to stifle the urge for action and a quick fix, they would have seen well in advance that solutionist technologies like exposure notification apps were doomed to fail. The technological shortcomings were predictable in advance, and the apps ran headlong into their social limitations and privacy flaws. Millions of dollars were spent on the technology, but those who were most at risk of infection were still the least likely to use such apps in the first place. Lower-income individuals are less likely to have smartphones, and far less likely to have the latest models. But the Bluetooth Covid apps performed worse on older devices,[18] they didn't work at all for the oldest smartphones,[19] and they discounted the millions of Americans who lack any smartphone at all.[20]

The privacy oversteps of centralized systems, as used in Israel and Singapore, were apparent from the start. And even the encryption at the heart of Bluetooth apps couldn't withstand the test of time. Google was forced to later admit that it had fallen short of its initial privacy promises, pushing out a fix for a vulnerability that potentially left users' location data compromised.[21]

All the while, the simpler solution for improved contact was right in front of policymakers. It was just a less flashy option for committing millions of dollars of emergency funds: hiring more contact tracers. Some jurisdictions, like Massachusetts, successfully responded to the pandemic by investing in human disease detectives.[22] The Bay State would go on to spend nearly $160 million on contact tracing through the end of 2021.[23] The human contact tracers were low-tech options, but they were reliably able to identify those at risk of contracting the virus, even for lower-income residents without the latest devices.

This fleet of contact tracers helped more than a million people access resources to let them isolate more effectively.[24] And, ultimately, where they ran into shortcomings, it wasn't the need for new types of technologies. Public health officials instead needed updates to relatively rudimentary tools that could track cases, streamline case assignment and management, and back up files. According to *The New York Times'* Sharon LaFraniere: "Decades of underinvestment in public health information systems has crippled efforts to understand the pandemic, stranding crucial data in incompatible data systems so outmoded that information often must be repeatedly typed in by hand."[25] Even as many private health facilities digitized records in recent years, public health officials were often relegated to using fax machines and other primitive tools.[26]

The frustrating reality is that this is exactly where tech companies could have contributed immensely during the Covid crisis. The firms could have helped call centers and government offices upgrade their day-to-day technology. They could have helped migrate legacy databases (some of which run on discontinued computer languages like Cobal) into modern platforms. According to a Senate report on pandemic failures, health departments failed to share information quickly enough about how Covid was spreading because employees "were transcribing information by hand and faxing data."[27] Silicon Valley loves the cheap and easy solution that can scale. And what our public health infrastructure needed was help to upgrade at scale.

Even upgrading something as unglamorous as hospital scheduling technology would have made an enormous difference. Vermont has consistently been a national leader in Covid-19 vaccination, with at least 95 percent of residents receiving at least one shot.[28] While part of their success may stem from the state's political composition, the leading technology driver was its centralized scheduling system for vaccinations.[29] This incremental upgrade to a state health website and vaccine database took far less work than the cutting-edge innovation of contact tracing apps, but it worked far better. In many locations, however, a fractured web of health facilities and long-neglected systems forced citizens to struggle to find life-saving resources.

In contrast to its neighbor, New York had a completely decentralized infrastructure for vaccine availability, spread between state, municipal, and private sites, each with their own eligibility guidelines. Even worse, many sites made it difficult to check when new appointments were available, leading millions of anxious residents to constantly refresh their web browsers in the hope of finding the coveted jab – or to give up when they ran out of time.[30] When Hugh Ma, a New York City resident and coder, saw the frustration unfolding around him, he decided to respond with a simple homebrewed upgrade. Rather than forcing users to constantly check when new vaccines were available, Ma published that data to Twitter and a standalone website, making it easier for people to stay up to date.[31] The upgrade was modest, nothing that countless coders couldn't have done. But making vaccine data just a little more accessible turned Ma into an overnight celebrity and digital folk hero.[32] Yet why did it need to fall to a Good Samaritan to provide such clarity in one of America's wealthiest states?

Just as the falseness of miracle fixes should have been apparent – in their technological shortcomings, their privacy compromises, and their limited reach – so should have been the outsized importance of simple, universal upgrades. Crises may be a time to hope, and probe, for the possibility of technological breakthroughs. But the most valuable solutions in such times are nothing revolutionary: clear information and heightened investment in reliable, broad, low-tech options.

TECHNOLOGY AS THEATER

One of the most instructive examples of pandemic tech run awry is thermal imaging cameras, which became a core technology at a different phase of the Covid-19 pandemic. After the initial onset of pandemic, after weeks and months of isolating and stopping the spread, there came the question of how to reopen society. This question, in truth, arose even before we had collectively learned to isolate or to stop the spread; it was the question of normalcy. When can life resume? And many of us were willing to accept half-measures if it meant that the answer sounded more pleasing.

Many of these half-measures were downright dangerous or scams: charlatans began to sell everything from homeopathy to cannabis as the cure to Covid. But others had the air of innovation. Thermal imaging cameras seemed like they could promise a simple way to open up businesses and public gatherings again. The devices measure skin temperature, and they were widely deployed to detect fevers. The game plan was tech-enforced containment – scan every forehead and bar anyone whose temperature was above normal. It was doomed to fail from the start, another example of solutionism, but its allure makes the product another interesting case study.[33]

Thermal imaging cameras were pitched widely – to businesses, schools, and public offices – as a way of ensuring that a given space was free from Covid, or at least Covid-infected people. Seemingly innovative features were touted as selling points over traditional thermometers: thermal imaging cameras took just seconds; they could scan multiple people at once; and they could even scan groups of moving people from a distance.

However, as one school superintendent noted, using the technology meant there were "a few false alarms each day."[34] This ended up being an understatement. Such cameras ended up being incredibly error-prone, for reasons that boiled down to basic physics. For instance, a person's temperature can be elevated when they are simply coming inside "after being outside in direct sunlight or carrying hot coffee."[35] And the devices' accuracy could be reduced by distance[36] and while probing crowds.[37] Precision was required to keep us safe, and yet such devices couldn't deliver it. A Chief Financial Officer for a school district that adopted thermal imaging cameras bluntly summarized the debacle by stating, "the camera issue was egg on our faces."[38]

One of the reasons that thermal cameras failed so exquisitely was because they were never actually designed as medical devices. Instead, camera makers saw a market opportunity and responded with the tech they already made. For large companies, like the camera makers Flir, this meant disclaimers to avoid being on the hook when customers used their tech for medical purposes.[39] But for smaller, shadier startups, it meant allegations of outright fraud.[40]

Despite all the alarm bells ringing, thermal imaging cameras were widespread. They were at schools, airports, healthcare facilities, and businesses – anywhere crowds gathered, and public health depended on preventing people with Covid from entering the premises or quickly removing them. Many were purchased using government funds for Covid relief, subsidized at the taxpayer's expense. At least 200 crisis-disrupted school districts procured thermal imaging cameras, spending a total of over $11 million.[41] And, as a whole, the thermal imaging camera market was valued at $3.16 billion in 2020, and only predicted to rise another $1 billion by 2024.[42]

What's most remarkable, however, is that even if the cameras had been entirely accurate, none of them should have been used to screen for Covid in the first place. Even back then, we knew that many Covid patients never got a fever. Some were asymptomatic; others experienced minor symptoms. Consequently, widespread use of this technology meant greenlighting a continuous stream of Covid patients to enter public spaces. We were collectively being asked to suspend disbelief to welcome a new and invasive technology into our lives, one that could be easily adapted in time to justify permanent cameras that only increase surveillance.

So, what happened? How can we explain the rapid expansion of a technology that's so obviously flawed in hindsight?

In his 2003 book, *Beyond Fear*, privacy expert Bruce Schneier invented a name for a type of problem that became ubiquitous after 9/11: "security theater."[43] Security theater is a manufactured illusion where people and institutions pretend to keep us safe by performing roles that appear to spot and eliminate threats. We experience security theater whenever we go to the airport. Unless you're enrolled in a special program, like TSA PreCheck, you go follow the ritual of taking off your shoes and proving you're only carrying tiny amounts of liquid. (As this book went to print, the TSA acknowledged this point by suspending shoe searches after more than 20 years of inconveniencing travelers.) And yet airport screening is a complete waste of time. Going through the motions may calm our nerves, but as Schneier rightly states: "The two things that have made flying safer since 9/11 are reinforcing the cockpit doors and persuading passengers they need to fight back. Everything beyond that isn't worth it."[44] Even the full-body scanners we regularly walk through have problems detecting some hidden explosive material.[45] Still, these devices have become so normalized they're no longer seen as invasive. The reason isn't so much technological as emotional: people were scared by the 9/11 terrorist attacks, and airport procedures were changed to calm our nerves. Instead of making us safer, though, they waste our time and set us up to get hassled by rude security agents.

Thermal imaging and many similar pandemic innovations are what some have called "public health theater."[46] They point to an even larger trend in which many innovations now function as a kind of theater. Think back to the pitch that underlies a vague product like the metaverse, or a glorified camera like Ring. To accept many innovations as such, we are being asked to suspend our disbelief – to believe that a magical new world might exist, or that a massive social problem might be solved without collective action, or simply that another profit-less company is worthy of a unicorn valuation. We are surrounded daily by technology as theater, and to be effective citizens, we need to be able to ask whether there is substance behind the show.

Security and health theater both create the misleading impression that things are under control – that a dangerous uncertainty has been eliminated and replaced by carefully cultivated predictability. It's infantilizing as well as dangerous: many venues that were using thermal imaging cameras were exposing people to hazardous conditions while reassuring them that they were safe. Some companies and venues bought into the theater unknowingly, but for others there was a canniness in play. For companies that worried about being sued down the road, thermal imaging scans and other health stunts could quickly become a defense in court, an argument for why they actually put their staff's health first, even as unmasked employees worked in packed, unventilated spaces.[47]

Sometimes the wishfulness of an innovation should be enough to give us pause and look for red flags. Anything that's asking us to suspend our disbelief deserves our scrutiny – and that's especially true of surveillance technology. The thermal imaging camera debacle, after all, created one more lasting problem: thermal imaging cameras are easy to link to other surveillance tools, like facial recognition technology. Heathrow Airport cast this as a selling point, trying to make people feel safe by announcing it would try out thermal imaging cameras with facial recognition technology that could "detect the identity of the individual scanned," to produce a contactless screening experience.[48] And many companies selling thermal imaging cameras also count it as a selling point: the cameras are a valuable pandemic investment that can easily be repurposed after the pandemic ends. The post-pandemic years have indeed seen facial recognition technology spread, to the point where "80 percent of all travelers entering the U.S. are now verified by facial recognition."[49] But facial recognition technology is rightly controversial, due to how biased and invasive it can be. Using the pandemic as an excuse to spread facial recognition infrastructure is a cynical attempt to capitalize on an emergency.

Meanwhile, technologies that genuinely could improve public health remain massively underutilized. Indeed, if we had wanted to make wise decisions about which physical infrastructure upgrade to prioritize during the pandemic, it would have come in the form not of cameras, but of HVAC systems – the often invisible machinery that filters and circulates our air. Even before Covid-19, many industrial engineers and public health officials noted the poor indoor air quality in the United States. We fell well behind the requirements other wealthy industrialized nations set, leaving it to institutions themselves to decide just how clean their air had to be. For cramped, aging institutions, particularly schools, prisons, and jails, this means Covid-19 had ample room to spread.

Unfortunately, retrofitting existing HVAC systems is neither easy nor cheap. And here, as so often happens, we tried to take an innovation shortcut rather than investing in the effective upgrade. The pandemic saw a surge in aftermarket air purification systems installed in institutions, many of which were little better than air quality theater. New York City spent millions on untested purifiers that failed to clean or circulate air to the standard needed. And many of these standalone filter systems were so noisy or inconvenient that they were shelved once the sense of urgency had passed. To facilitate a healthy return to public life, Covid-19 could have inspired a national campaign for HVAC upgrades. A sustained program to invest in the quality of our indoor air would not only mitigate the spread of Covid-19, it would also help to prevent the next pandemic. Sadly, we ignored those calling for the upgrade at the time, overinvesting in innovation and wishful thinking instead.

SIMPLE IS AN UPGRADE: WHEN PAPER BEATS SILICON

It can take trial and error to avoid the innovation trap. Just months after the limitations of Covid tracking apps became clear, a very similar innovation was gaining momentum: the vaccine passport apps. In 2021, Albert's hometown of New York City was in the national spotlight as the testing ground for vaccine passports. State and city officials were rolling out apps that "proved" your vaccine status, once again falling back on the notion that tech would make our pandemic problems disappear.

By then, Albert was aware of the hazards. He first warned leaders they were ineffective, then raised the alarm that they were insecure. When that got nowhere, he decided to show people. It was time to break the damn thing.

Vaccines themselves were a staggering breakthrough, nothing short of a literal lifesaver for millions who would have otherwise died from Covid. But while vaccines dramatically reduced the risk of serious illness and death, they weren't an instant off-switch that immediately neutralized the viral threat.[50] People continued to get sick, even once the vaccines became widely available. And many people viewed vaccines with fear and suspicion; they refused to receive a shot, turning the march toward herd immunity into a hesitant crawl.[51] Government leaders now faced a seemingly impossible choice. On the one hand, the more they reopened society, the further Covid would spread, and the more people would die. On the other hand, prolonged social distance mandates meant more businesses would go bankrupt, and more people would suffer from the all-too-real trauma of prolonged isolation. Vaccine passports promised to give us a way to have it both ways, to reopen and to stay safe, by solving the problem of distrust.

Historically, we've had an easy solution for proving vaccine status: paper records. When students enrolled in school or employees started high-risk jobs, they would provide paper vaccine records or scans of them. No vaccine, and suddenly schoolhouse and office doors were locked. It's not a perfect system; nothing is. Nevertheless, for decades, the paper standard was good enough to secure high levels of national vaccination against everything from polio to meningitis.[52]

Vaccine passports, however, were trying to solve a much harder problem than traditional vaccine registries. While you might keep a record of your polio vaccine, you didn't need to present it to every business you frequented. You didn't need to do so in a new environment of distrust that needed to be mindful of both privacy and fraud. Tech companies and politicians told us that they could handle all these considerations with a simple little app. But in the end, tech didn't save us; it fell into the same familiar problems that the exposure notification apps did – issues of security, privacy, and ease of access.

The first failure of vaccine apps was what was supposed to be their selling point: security. When the United States first rolled out the Covid vaccine, every jab came with paper proof. But people quickly saw how easily the white Centers for Disease Control and Prevention (CDC) cards could be fabricated. With nothing more than a home computer and printer, anyone who wanted to could make a fake vaccine card. For leaders who wanted mandatory vaccine requirements at stores, concerts, and transit, the paper cards weren't secure enough.

The first attempt at a New York vaccine app came from now-disgraced former Governor Andrew Cuomo in partnership with IBM. The multi-million-dollar Excelsior Pass was billed as "secure and confidential."[53] IBM officials even went so far as to claim that "[s]ecure technologies, like blockchain and encryption, are woven throughout Excelsior Pass to help protect the data, making it verifiable and trusted."[54] But when Albert tried to test out those claims, he could hack Excelsior Pass in just 11 minutes.

Like many "white hat" hackers, Albert's goal was only to educate the public, not steal anyone's data. And Albert began his experiment, like any good lawyer would, by making sure he didn't go to jail. Rather than just try to break in, he put the call out on Twitter for volunteers, looking for someone to let him try using their account as the guinea pig.[55]

A few minutes later, another New York attorney gave him the green light, and Albert was off to the races. Albert didn't try to break IBM's "blockchain" or hack their encryption. Instead, he followed the hacker playbook of looking first at the greatest point of weakness, which was the registration website. By pulling vaccine card photos, birthdates, and other data from his volunteer's public social media, Albert quickly tricked the website into displaying a fully functional vaccine passport. It took just 11 minutes, and Albert could have used the passport anywhere it was accepted.

This was a clear-cut reminder of one of the biggest tech myths. Just because something is digital, it's not necessarily more secure. Like many systems, Excelsior Pass was promoted based on the assumption that the tech would be harder to hack than paper. Officials seemed to believe this, not because they understood why the tech was secure, but because it was easier to see how paper systems fail. It was arguably easier to hack Excelsior Pass than it would be to forge a paper card. But under the spell of a digital delusion, we want to believe that the smart move is to avoid our old analog ways.

After New York Governor Andrew Cuomo launched Excelsior Pass, then New York City Mayor Bill de Blasio responded with his trademark sense of petty rivalry. Long before the pandemic, the two politicians fiercely fought at every turn to become the state's leading political voice. But the infighting only accelerated during Covid, leading to endless bickering and copycat behavior.[56] For de Blasio, this meant creating his own vaccine passport, the Covid Safe NYC app, which launched a few months after the Excelsior Pass. It would be an "easy, straightforward way to show vaccine verification and test results,"[57] whose key selling point was to "make things simpler."[58]

You might be guessing what came next. Albert downloaded the app and hacked it, too. And this time, he didn't even need a volunteer. Unlike Excelsior Pass, which took a few minutes of research to break into, it turned out that the New York City app didn't have any security at all. In providing "secure" proof of vaccination, the app stored a photo of the user's vaccine card, test results, and ID. But it didn't verify any of these images. So Albert was able to upload a photo of Mickey Mouse for his vaccine card and have it be accepted as "proof of vaccination."[59]

Both apps proved to be old wine in a new bottle that provided nothing new, while claiming to change Covid's course. And the failed apps weren't simply a waste of time and attention. When Excelsior Pass was first introduced, Governor Cuomo told New Yorkers it would come in just north of $2 million. But Albert's investigation found out that the real price tag could be as high as $27 million.[60] And they also came at a simple social cost as well.

Public health experts had rightly been much more hesitant than government and tech officials to rely on the gimmicky tech. Georges Benjamin, the executive director of the American Public Health Association, called the apps "impractical" and a "slippery slope."[61] Brian R. Spisak of Harvard's T. H. Chan School of Public Health warned the apps would "deepen existing inequalities in health care, education, and employment."[62]

Indeed, it's the inequality of access that should have been the obvious red flag all along. Technology is never truly universal – and universality needs to be a top priority, both in times of crisis and for technologies that will affect the public. The decision to prioritize smartphone apps over paper threatened to exclude millions of people from public life simply because they didn't own the right tech. We may think "everyone has a smartphone," but the truth is that up to 15 percent of Americans don't. Digital divides haven't gone away. Age, race, gender, and class always matter. Mayor de Blasio could "urge everyone" to "get the app," but the reality is that millions of New Yorkers never had a device that could run it. Thankfully, city and state leaders listened to public pushback and never made the apps mandatory. Still, if they had, it would have excluded millions because of their technology status, not their vaccination status.

The apps also risked excluding other New Yorkers because of language access barriers. In a city where people speak literally hundreds of languages, only offering software in a handful of dialects will exclude countless neighbors. This is why government tech can be so destructive if it impacts essential services. When one consumer app excludes some customers, alternatives are often available. Tragically, government services are often exclusive. They're usually the only show in town.

Lastly, the apps' promoters misrepresented how the tools protect our privacy. For Excelsior Pass, this meant potentially collecting data about every place a user scanned in. IBM assured the public that their "encryption" would keep them safe. And yet the company never provided the details to support their claims, such as what type of encryption they use and how data could be accessed by officials.[63] Even worse, claims that data was protected by "blockchain" appeared flatly false.[64] For Covid Safe NYC, the tracking threat was less extreme. However, the app still had the ability to track some movements.[65] As with so much tech, vaccine passports evangelists made broad claims about privacy while actually delivering tons of tracking.

Vaccine passports ended up fading from public life almost as quickly as they were adopted. While the various apps were downloaded millions of times in a matter of months,[66] vaccine requirements for restaurants and other public venues quickly fell by the wayside.[67] The apps were a flash in the pan, but this failed technology – as with many quick hype-cycles during the pandemic – shows the whole lifecycle of tech boosterism, how its appeal can grow, and how quickly the promise and hope of an innovative solution can run awry.

LESSONS FOR UPGRADERS

In the digital age, we're primed to expect good results from leaning hard into novel digital solutions. And yet the effort and expense that went into digital contact tracing and vaccine verification were largely wasted. The technological capabilities were woefully inadequate, and social issues, like distrust in surveillance and unequal access to smartphones, wouldn't magically disappear. While this debacle unfolded, there was a better way forward – a way that would have seemed obvious were it not for digital dazzle.

Countless startup spokespeople have shown us over the years that anyone can tell us the tale of how an unproven idea will change the world. But, more often than not, those ideas don't. Even worse, no one can credibly predict which would-be breakthrough will work or flop. Innovators aren't necessarily who you need in your camp in a time of crisis, when every moment and every life counts. Upgraders take a different approach. They aren't selling the house to buy lottery tickets with the hope of a dream payout. Instead, they are cognizant of the assets we already have at our disposal, and they seek to improve on them with tweaks likely to offer a positive return. Indeed, it's remarkable how many proven upgrades were ignored during the pandemic, in favor of riskier innovations. While these responses varied in scale, they all have one thing in common: they were almost certain to work.

As we write this, the state of American vaccination credentials are, to put it technically, a "hot mess." Mobile devices are cluttered with discontinued and incompatible vaccine apps that work in an ever-dwindling number of locations. As of 2023, pharmacies and other vaccination sites no longer even give out proof of vaccination to most patients. This collective innovation hangover would have been eminently avoidable if we had focused on vaccine record upgrades instead.

Moments after we received our white CDC vaccine cards in 2021, we saw the mistake: they were too big. The 4x3 card was too large to fit in a traditional credit card holder or wallet. Left unprotected in a patient's pocket, the cardboard quickly crumpled and tore. The inconvenience and flimsiness of these cards quickly became part of the sales pitch for the ill-fated innovations on vaccine credential apps. But rather than spending millions to create a novel electronic vaccine credential, we could have done far better by simply investing in CDC cards that used higher-quality materials and were sized to conveniently fit in a person's wallet. Not only would this have been relatively inexpensive and easy to implement, it has a major benefit associated with justice. It's equitable. Like so many upgrades to essential services, it's a type of design that can reach every part of our population, not just those wealthy enough to own smartphones. Of course, the benefits, like other upgrades, are proportional. Higher-quality printed vaccine records would be slightly harder to forge than existing documents. Still, they wouldn't be nearly as high quality as US Passports. But the perfect shouldn't be the enemy of the good, and many so-called vaccine passport innovations that claimed to provide a secure way to verify vaccine status were just as insecure as those CDC cards in practice. At the same time, they were far more cumbersome and expensive.

Similarly, national governments could have headed off anti-vaccine alarmism by forgoing novel vaccine apps at airports for the traditional International Certificate of Vaccination or Prophylaxis or "yellow card." Yellow cards have been used for decades to track vaccination status for international travelers, particularly for vaccination against yellow fever, polio, and meningitis. Once again, it would have been a straightforward and less controversial upgrade to add another line for Covid vaccine status for travelers. As with all the upgrades we've been discussing, it should have been a compelling, if not obvious, option at the time. These missed opportunities are emblematic of the risk of too deeply embracing the innovation mindset while undervaluing the upgrader ethos – solving new problems by first looking to how we tackled the most analogous problems in the past. Many other key public health upgrades were skipped over in favor of now-discredited pandemic innovations. Instead of experimenting with apps, we could have expanded investments in in-person contact tracing, testing facilities, and personal protective equipment distribution. In each of these categories, some states invested systematically in expanding this crucial health infrastructure, while others looked for cheaper, more innovative alternatives. Additionally, legacy public health tools like wastewater monitoring were often undervalued as a tool for effective disease surveillance at the moment states were looking to new gadgets instead. The innovation mindset meant many decision-makers assumed that there had to be cheaper alternatives to scaling up these investments. And yet upgraders knew that we couldn't possibly respond to a disaster on this scale cheaply and effectively.

Indeed, many of the most important successes during the pandemic came from concerted and committed upgrades to existing social policies. These solutions touched the lives of nearly every person in the United States. When soaring Covid-19 infections and deaths threatened the collapse of our healthcare system, when millions of employees stayed home and countless businesses shuttered their stores, poverty rates fell.[68] With the economy stuttering to a halt, eviction rates plummeted.[69] Think how remarkable that is. The pandemic was economically trying for many, but we nevertheless avoided a financial calamity that would have rivaled the Great Depression. For most Americans, it was a moment of unprecedented security . . . all made possible by crucial upgrades.

Instead of trying to innovate the economy, we kept the lights on for impacted employees through upgrades to stodgy programs like unemployment insurance. A series of upgrades to unemployment insurance law meant that countless independent contractors, gig workers, and self-employed workers who would have been cut off from unemployment insurance in the past could get money to weather the public health storm.[70] For businesses themselves, an upgrade to the Small Business Administration's decades-old loan offerings gave us the Paycheck Protection Program. It prevented what might have been an unprecedented level of business defaults and layoffs.[71] Meanwhile, millions more were protected from Covid by upgrades to eviction protections under federal and state law, reducing the risk that families would find themselves in cramped shelters or on the street in a public health emergency.[72] Rather than creating a housing solution out of whole cloth, these safeguards incrementally built on the protections found under many states' existing rental protection laws, which often limit eviction where an individual faces ongoing, debilitating medical conditions.[73]

Housing, food, and other social safety net services are not rocket science. No approaches to them were wholly novel during Covid-19. When upgraders consider novel issues, they focus on their established context learning with the goal of leveraging existing best practices. A crucial reason why upgraders have this focus is because even the most unprecedented crisis usually amplifies pre-existing problems.

Of course, these programs had flaws and limitations. They were expensive, not always as universal as their planners would like, and not immune to fraud. And yet, as upgrades, they provided a predictable return on investment. The important thing is that these limitations were apparent from the start. Unlike the shock of innovation failing, there weren't any unexpected surprises. Collectively, these measures show how upgrades can effect change on a vast scale. Unlike innovation, the benefits come with a realistic price tag. At a moment when innovators give us untested answers that, far too often, are too good to be true, upgraders show us solutions that are too imperfect to be a scam.

Sometimes it's hard for leaders to admit that the hope of a windfall is worse than the surety of a small improvement. Certainly, amid the pain of a pandemic, it's difficult to acknowledge that a technological solution to a problem doesn't exist. But when we have limited time and money, and millions of lives at stake, it's worse to engage in technological theater. In these moments, the innovation is not just distracting, but deadly; and it's when we need the upgraders most.

CHAPTER SIX

Moving Fast and Breaking Schools with Remote Proctoring

American education has long provided a lesson on the dangers and failures of innovation. Every few years, innovations in school funding, school instruction, or school assessments are put forth as inflection points in the fight for better education. Each recent decade has raised new interventions to debate – from standardized testing to charter schools. But the sudden arrival of the Covid-19 pandemic hit schools with an unprecedented crisis. Overnight, in the middle of the school year, institutions needed to decide whether to close down and how to cobble together digital alternatives when in-person classes were interrupted. Remote learning became a national priority, and it raised many questions about how to innovate and upgrade so that students and teachers alike could stay on track. The issue of fairness quickly rose to the fore. If kids weren't in the classroom, how could teachers ensure a level playing field, where no one could cheat?

Before the end of the 2020 school year, the once-small field of remote proctoring exploded, starting a rapid expansion that would soon make it a multi-billion industry. However, in the race to monitor students, through their laptops and their modems, a more basic question of fairness arose in the process. Millions of children were still left on the outside, without the basic technology they needed to log on in the first place. And, for those who could engage in remote learning, administrators largely overlooked the sudden invasion of privacy that remote proctoring encouraged. These systems would quickly normalize surveillance practices that were antithetical to privacy standards that were, mere months before the pandemic, unquestionable.

Ultimately, the rise of remote proctoring would prove to be a prime example of the "move fast and break things" model of innovation – but it was applied to a realm where the stakes of breaking things were far greater. We wasted billions, harmed children, and lost a generational moment to invest in essential upgrades to effective educational infrastructure. It's not only a teachable moment, but a lasting failure that tragically will reverberate for American students in the years to come.

THE NEW ACADEMIC STANDARD

Pre-pandemic, remote learning had slowly and incrementally spread into American life. It was primarily confined to higher education, with more than 7 million students in the United States enrolled in online college before 2020.[1] But just a few weeks into Covid-19, 1,100 colleges and universities[2] moved more than a million post-secondary students online.[3] And by June of 2020, a few months after the start of Covid-19, 97 percent of college students reported switching to online classes.[4] The cost accelerated just as fast, with projections showing that universities will spend more than $74 billion by 2025.[5]

The shift for children was even more dramatic. Within a matter of weeks, the pandemic accelerated remote learning from a handful of states[6] across the country, eventually impacting more than 8 million K-12 students[7] in all fifty states.[8] Presently, it's unclear if such remote instruction will remain a part of American life indefinitely, and there is no shortage of debate around the subject.

But when the pandemic forced students and instructors to remain at home, it seemed there was little time for reflection. Within days, students were behind on their assignments and lagging amid lesson plans. And how were they ever supposed to take their exams? That single question, with the end of the school year rapidly approaching, ensured that one of the most pressing issues at hand, strangely, was academic surveillance. Many schools have simply assumed remote proctoring was needed to have remote learning.[9] The result was a myriad of inventions that weren't designed to better instruct students, but to better monitor them in their own homes and ensure that they couldn't cheat. A month into the pandemic, 77 percent of colleges and universities were using, planning to use, or considering remote proctoring, even as a majority feared the cost of the technology.[10] There was such great enthusiasm for surveillance software that it spread outside of the classroom, being adopted by licensing bodies for doctors, lawyers, and other professions.[11] Throughout 2020, individual remote proctoring firms experienced a massive explosion in sales.[12]

Remote proctoring is, essentially, a catch-all term for "monitoring students." It's a web of technologies which ensure that test takers are watched through their webcams, microphones, and screen-recording software. Students are often forced to give third-party vendors and their schools access to broad sets of permissions on their personal devices, despite the potential for abuse. In the rush to update, many universities raced to install the software. Students were pressured into consenting to the software, and many didn't even have the illusion of choice.[13] When Auburn University deployed Honorlock and ProctorU to test its 23,000 undergraduates, none of the students was given the option of choosing a less-invasive alternative for their exams.[14] On other campuses, even where institutional rules did permit individual instructors to provide alternative testing formats, many felt they lacked the institutional support to forgo the remote monitoring. Remote proctoring had become a new academic standard.

SPYWARE BY ANY OTHER NAME

In the innovation hype cycle, one common red flag that we've seen arises when an existing technology is repurposed for an entirely new domain. This kind of arbitrage caused problems elsewhere in the pandemic, as thermal cameras were repurposed as medical devices – but without the needed precision. And that same red flag was at the root of the many problems introduced by remote proctoring.

After all, when one looks at the specific forms of academic surveillance that schools and colleges introduced during the pandemic, the core innovation looks a lot like something we've all learned to be wary of: spyware.

Many of the programs used in remote proctoring mirror software that has long been used by hackers and cybercriminals to secretly monitor people's computers. The leading options for remote proctoring, products like Proctortrack, record everything a student sees on their screen, while also logging every keystroke and mouse movement. Importantly, this type of repurposed monitoring can collect exponentially more data than schools need. It also hoovers up far more information than they ever demanded for analog proctoring, which only lets human proctors occasionally look at test takers' exam books or screens. There's a world of difference between periodically peeking at what a student is writing and indefinitely retaining a copy of their every movement.

In addition to logging students' detailed movements, the next innovation of remote proctoring is to install "lockdown browsers" that limit students to a highly curtailed user interface, blocking off much of their device. To constrain how students can use their devices, this software needs to be given full administrative rights to access a student's computer, including the ability to potentially see every file, photo, and video file a student has saved.[15] If someone at a proctoring company acts in bad faith, or if their systems are hacked, then a student's entire digital life could be exposed. Alarmingly, however, many students have no way of finding out which files have been accessed, how long they are kept, or who has access to them.[16]

In some forms of remote proctoring, educators can use a student's webcam to record their movements and sound. Some firms use automated computer vision software to monitor each video feed for purported signs of cheating – a jarring (and often illegal) demand that would never have been widely accepted pre-pandemic.[17] When companies use high-tech innovations like computer vision to detect cheating, the results can be a nightmare, especially for disabled and neurodivergent students. In one case, ProctorU's AI system considers it a sign of cheating whenever a student looks off-screen three times, or for more than four seconds in a minute.[18] This is a stifling demand, and one that students with certain attention and movement disorders simply cannot comply with.

Other systems let an adult watch the test taker through their webcam,[19] either manually or in combination with AI.[20] Unlike traditional proctors, whose watchful gaze is visible to students, remote proctoring is largely invisible to test takers. Proctors watch silently from the other side of students' webcams, which creates a new student–proctor power dynamic that often leaves students feeling exposed. The proctor can see far more than they once could, newly able to peer into the intimate corners of both students' bedrooms and their hard drives. And proctors frequently order students to aim their webcam around their room or to follow other instructions, penalizing those who fail to comply for academic dishonesty.

With tactics like room scans, the perils should have been obvious from the outset. Not only are they terrible ways to spot most forms of academic dishonesty; they are also a profound invasion of our most intimate spaces. One court ruling even found the practice unconstitutional when done by public institutions, violating the Fourth Amendment's ban on warrantless searches.[21] Even for private institutions, however, the practice is overly invasive and punitive. Students have faced suspension or even had the police called to their door for everything from toy guns to apparent drug paraphernalia visible from their webcams.[22]

As with so many software companies, remote proctoring firms also soak up customers' data and reserve the right to transform it into a corporate asset in the event of a merger or bankruptcy.[23] Some companies, such as the firm PSI Online, leave themselves broad discretion to share data with police and immigration officials whenever they deem fit.[24] Because students are coerced to share their own camera feed and microphones with proctors, these terms can allow police the chance to surveil places they never otherwise could,[25] further extending the school-to-prison pipeline to students' bedrooms.[26] The privacy concerns are serious, with one university official admitting that the tech is "spyware that we just legitimize."[27]

Even when companies keep students' data to themselves, real risks arise with granting such broad access to users' devices. Most remote proctoring software requires a laundry list of technical permissions to operate, access students' hard drives, screens, internet activity, cameras, microphones, and peripherals. This level of access creates persistent vulnerabilities from bad actors.[28] Whether it's a proctor who wants to abuse their access, or a hacker who wants to hijack the proctoring tools' broad access rights, many students subjected to this innovation have had their data hijacked.[29] Some remote proctoring vendors (such as Examity) tell users to share data at their own risk,[30] but that disclaimer provides little solace to the students whose machines are compromised, such as in one incident in Rose State College in Oklahoma.[31]

Often, even those who read the fine print of testing software's terms and conditions wouldn't clearly understand what data is collected, how it is stored, and with whom it can be shared. In some cases, audio and videos from students' exams, potentially days' worth of recordings, were kept indefinitely.[32] Other firms promised to delete data, but only after ambiguous time periods, such as when the data retention was no longer "necessary." And while universities would obtain consent from students in many cases, they didn't extend the same courtesy to family members and other people cohabitating with test takers, even if their footage might be collected anytime they found themselves in the frame. In essence, it was little better than finding a school CCTV camera installed in students' homes.

No matter what reassurances and policies individual universities put into place for remote testing, the proctoring companies themselves continue to hoard data. ProctorU, which surveils hundreds of thousands of students a year, retains the right to provide third-party proctors with students' addresses, work history, citizenship status, medical records, and biometric data.[33] This includes data like fingerprints and facial recognition scans, which, if compromised, can impact a student's privacy for life. The company even retains the right to publish students' videos on its website, on what it calls a cheating "Hall of Fame."[34] The idea that videos taken from the privacy of students' homes could be transformed into a marketing tool for testing companies, against the students' will, would be farcical if it weren't so chilling.

Students roundly say that remote proctoring is much more harmful than its in-person equivalent.[35] Students who are endlessly monitored by proctors can feel a sense of invasion.[36] They have been driven to tears[37] and even a complete breakdown.[38] While the toll can be severe for any students, it's particularly acute for the one in four students who already experience testing anxiety.[39] Prior to the pandemic, students who were subjected to remote proctoring often spoke out and petitioned against its use. Amid lockdowns and remote education, many sadly felt trapped. Some schools and classrooms were able to push back, but others felt forced to accept the technology as the price of remote learning.[40]

A TAX ON THE MOST VULNERABLE

Civil rights protections exist for a reason – to prevent discrimination and provide equal access to all, regardless of their identity. Warrantless searches by public schools aren't the only violation triggered by the mass launch of remote proctoring services. The programs ran roughshod over many other civil rights protections students enjoy in the classroom, whether in-person or virtual, and the cost was borne by the students who were already most vulnerable.

The Individuals with Disabilities Education Act (IDEA) is designed to ensure that public school students with disabilities can receive an education tailored to their unique needs.[41] Similarly, Title II and Title III of the Americans with Disabilities Act (ADA) protect students at public and private colleges respectively.[42] Schools are not only barred from discriminating against students with disabilities, but they must provide affirmative accommodations, in-class aides, and extra time to provide a level academic playing field. Sadly, at schools that use remote proctoring, students with disabilities face a constant uphill fight to access an equal education and to prove they aren't cheating. That's not just an allegation from disgruntled students: more than a quarter of higher education institutions admit using online proctoring tools that violate their own accessibility standards.[43] And this is just the percentage of institutions that are willing to admit their shortcoming to pollsters, despite the legal jeopardy. In practice, the percentage violating accessibility rules likely is far higher.

Tragically, it's impossible to estimate how many students have been victimized by the use of these misguided surveillance innovations. And many of the most egregious violations come from the most cutting-edge and "innovative" products offered by remote proctoring firms. This next wave of programs relies heavily on questionable surveillance techniques such as facial recognition, which are then linked up to AI capabilities.

The ostensible reason for facial recognition is to prevent cheating by impersonation – which is a rarity in normal times, and was almost laughably so in the period of mass lockdowns when such programs were first rolled out. But the techniques used by these products are gravely sobering. The most basic use video footage from students' webcams and rely on facial recognition software to verify their identity. Certain programs, like the vendor Proctortrack, force students to both bring their face and knuckles up to the camera for a scan,[44] while others launched by the leading firm ProctorU require continual scans of the test taker's face throughout the exam.[45]

Proctortrack also deployed the Transportation Security Administration's controversial algorithm for detecting "abnormal" expressions to flag supposed inappropriate behaviors during exams.[46] Unfortunately, the algorithm has dubious accuracy under real-world test conditions. The technology is so fragile that it can only operate when students sit upright and look directly in front of their webcams at all times.[47] Even a minor change in lighting, body position, or eye movement can impact a student's "integrity score." If you involuntarily move too often, or if it hurts your back to sit still, the algorithm will flag you as suspicious. This is a nightmare for students with learning disabilities,[48] or visual or hearing impairments, or a medical inability to sit still.[49] It was a nightmare for students who self-stimulate,[50] or who have facial tics,[51] or who have frequent bathroom needs,[52] or who are breastfeeding,[53] or who are caring for children or elders, or who need to take medication.[54] All have fallen afoul of the AI.

Many test takers may find themselves forced to choose between medical privacy and the chance to even take part in remote education.[55] Even worse, many remote proctoring tools can compromise the accessibility software that students typically use to level the academic playing field and partake more fully in remote learning.[56] Rather than schools using technology designed to account for students' needs, students were forced to contort themselves to fit the needs of an algorithm.

Furthermore, when students do violate the set parameters, the algorithm's verdict is sweeping, devoid of the contextual analysis a human proctor would offer. A human being could tell the difference between a student speaking to a family member who walked into the room, unaware of the test, and someone off-screen providing help with answers. To the software, both are instances of cheating. Students have faced punishment for even the most mundane movements, from grabbing a pen to letting their eyes wander.[57] One program, Honorlock, reportedly punished a student for simply gazing off-screen for a prolonged period – during a test where they were expected to work on a lengthy math problem by hand.[58] Another student reported that their seasonal allergies drew the software's ire after sneezing into a Kleenex; they were flagged both for looking off-screen and for looking at paper (the tissue).[59]

These sorts of errors are harmful on their own, but the software is particularly problematic in how it fuels racial and gender bias – an outcome that's most pronounced with facial recognition.[60] Students with darker skin have faced delays in starting exams, or been excluded completely, because of facial recognition errors.[61] In some cases, Black, Indigenous, and People of Color (BIPOC) students have only been able to circumvent this discrimination by taking exams with a bright light shone in their face, constantly distracting themselves from the exam to satisfy the surveillance tech.[62]

The failure of educational surveillance software to prevent discrimination and provide accessibility is emblematic of far too many digital innovations that are rolled out to meet the needs of "typical" users, but ignore many others who fall outside the cookie-cutter ideal. Indeed, remote proctoring innovation is designed with unfair biases baked in – prejudiced expectations of all students being able to comply with requirements that vast numbers find medically, psychologically, and situationally onerous. This myopic view of innovation has been repeated over and over again in other areas of technology. As we'll discuss later, those on the margins often fall victim to the curse of the "minimum viable product," which is the rush to launch a technology that works for some while harming others. Some might excuse such shortcuts in a pandemic, but this pattern repeats in both good times and bad.

For that matter, many of the clearest injustices are tied to some of the sketchiest product features: facial recognition to prevent imposters during lockdown, for instance, or other anti-impersonation technologies such as typing identification tests. These programs force students to type a paragraph or two of text at various points in the semester, using the rhythm and style of typing to confirm their identity.[63] Students, however, frequently improve their typing throughout the year and often type differently on different devices, which makes such features a recipe for wrongful accusations. These are pure innovations "for innovation's sake." They are ways for firms to perform their own "web security theater," in the hopes of wowing school administrators. As always, however, just because a technology can be applied doesn't mean it should.

In some schools, students and faculty members rightfully pushed back on the widespread use of such platforms. Just weeks into the pandemic, faculty members at the University of California at Santa Barbara became some of the earliest, most vocal critics of the vendor ProctorU. In a public letter, they objected to both the way that ProctorU collected vast troves of intimate information from students and the ways that the firm made information available to third parties.[64] While such disclosures might seem innocuous to privileged students, they could be a matter of life and death for others, particularly for undocumented students at the school. For these individuals, many of whom feared deportation to countries where they faced imminent violence, remote proctoring practices posed a potent threat. As the faculty wrote in their objection: "We recognize that in our collective race to adapt our coursework and delivery in good faith, there are trade-offs and unfortunate aspects of the migration online that we must accept. This is not one of them."[65]

THE CHOICE BETWEEN FEAR AND FAIRNESS

Perhaps the most distressing part of all the problems created by remote proctoring during the pandemic is that none of the innovation was necessary. Despite their gloomy marketing campaigns, online proctoring firms never provided evidence that remote testing led to increased academic dishonesty.[66] The fear that was used to justify such invasive measures didn't appear to be founded in real behaviors. Cheating may be easier at home, but there are plenty of ways to discourage cheating without scaling up to unprecedented levels of mass surveillance. Ultimately, it's not clear whether the surveillance was needed, or even if any of the innovative approaches worked.

Rather than investing tens, maybe hundreds of millions of dollars in new forms of AI and spyware, we had plenty of other options at our disposal. They tended to be unflashy, old-school, and low-cost, but this would have freed up education budgets for the more fundamental upgrades that would have made real fairness possible as the pandemic struck.

One widely ignored path was the potential to leverage traditional honor codes in this new digital environment. Take-home tests are, in truth, nothing new, and students have taken them for decades at least without the education system breaking down. Honor codes are a simple tool that have proven to be deeply effective at preventing plagiarism, cheating, and other forms of academic dishonesty; some institutions have even adapted them incrementally through centuries of development.[67] Not only can honor codes be easily upgraded for remote education, but they could have provided a communitarian response, a sense of solidarity and collaboration, at exactly the moment when students were feeling most isolated. Honor codes have been shown to foster a greater sense of connection among students, while building deeper trust than is found in institutions that lack a similar practice.[68] Of course, this lacks the cutting-edge feel of turning to AI, but evidence shows that a well-constructed honor code can outperform even the most invasive spyware.[69]

Schools could also have avoided the incentive to cheat by transitioning to alternative assessment techniques.[70] This isn't a hypothetical suggestion, especially at a moment of crisis. Many colleges[71] and K-12 schools adopted pass/fail grading and written reports instead of alphanumeric grades during the pandemic.[72] The lack of traditional grading designations may seem jarring because, on its face, it doesn't appear to do enough to differentiate between students who have learned a lot, a moderate amount, or a little bit. But, given a choice between punitive systems and a supportive approach, during a time of crisis, we should have recognized that it was possible to think outside the box. We had the opportunity to look toward alternatives that go beyond closed-book exams and multiple-choice tests – from lower-stakes quizzes, to written projects, to group research. Exams did not need to be the one part of the system that couldn't change to reflect the moment.

When one looks at the time and money American educators devoted to deploying academic surveillance in the pandemic, it's heartbreaking to imagine the path not taken, the alternative *upgrade* approaches to the crisis. It's not simply that schools have used less-invasive, more equitable forms of assessment. The real missed opportunity was that they could have prioritized students' education itself.

The entire issue of remote proctoring skipped past the more important issue: access to remote learning in the first place. This was where the true question of fairness was located. For many students, access was the issue. For them, the pandemic meant trying to learn over unreliable internet connections, sharing low-speed routers with houses and apartments full of people trying to work, study, and live remotely. Many of those with internet access lacked computers fast enough, or sufficiently up-to-date, to reliably connect to online classes. Even in the wealthiest nation on the planet, one in five students lacked the computers or connectivity to learn online.[73] Internet access alone blocked 16.9 million American children from being able to learn remotely.[74] The cost of these barriers was not borne evenly by any means. It impacted low-income, BIPOC, and rural children most. One-third of BIPOC families and those earning less than

$50,000 struggled through the pandemic without access to high-speed internet. And the numbers were even starker in rural America, where two in five families lacked a high-speed connection.[75]

On top of these inequalities, there was the predicament of the 1.5 million students who were trying to learn remotely without a home at all.[76] Not only do many homeless shelters lack reliable internet access, but students are often barred from shelters if parents are not present, preventing them from attending class if their parent has left to work.[77] Children with temporary housing often faired as poorly, failing to find reliable internet access as they changed locations.[78]

These barriers to internet access and up-to-date technology pre-date the pandemic, but Covid made them much worse and much more critical. For students in fully remote schools, a lack of access could mean losing out on an education completely. For schools and the nation's educational resources, the question of access – not testing – should have been the top priority.

Of course, there is no magical innovation to getting students online. The cost of upgrading internet connections, buying new computers, and providing remote tech support is enormous. But such upgrades were far better uses of funding than tangling with remote proctoring. And upgrades to core digital infrastructure would have paid dividends for decades to come. Moreover, paying to upgrade the internet connections for low-income households would provide benefits that reached far beyond academic achievement. With better internet connectivity, adults in the household could have new access to remote work opportunities, while the household as a whole could have used digital tools to better isolate amid the worst of the pandemic.

As with so much of the pandemic experience, we lost out on the opportunity to invest in the upgrades to essential infrastructure that would have continued to improve our lives long after Covid. Instead, we wasted millions on narrow innovations and other boondoggles that promised the flimsiest form of fairness. Rather than replicating the in-school experience at home, these systems chose to ignore a broader form of fairness – the left-behind reality that millions of children faced during the pandemic. As a result, the damage is now done. Even if schools quickly abandon academic spyware post-pandemic, the learning losses will haunt students for years to come.

CHAPTER SEVEN

Upgrades in the Age of Generative AI

WELCOME TO THE AGE OF GENERATIVE AI

The public launch of ChatGPT was stunning. MIT research scientist Andrew McAfee captured the extraordinary moment in 2022 when he exclaimed: "For the first time ever, we have created a technology that understands human language."[1] ChatGPT is a user-friendly generative artificial intelligence that can churn out everything from detailed stories to article summaries, persuasive arguments to functional computer code, in just a few seconds. Users don't need an ounce of technological know-how; all they need is to open up a chat box and ask the AI for what they want.

ChatGPT was the realization of an astonishing general-purpose device, and the market responded enthusiastically. Within two months of launching, ChatGPT attracted 100 million weekly users.[2] OpenAI, the company that created ChatGPT, became a household name overnight, and it grew by leaps and bounds, chiefly in partnership with Microsoft. By 2023, Microsoft had invested $13 billion in OpenAI, seeking to transform the company's Bing search engine and "reinvent" search engines.[3] But that was just the first step: Satya Nadella, Microsoft's CEO, leaned into disruptive rhetoric, stating, "AI will fundamentally change every software category, starting with the largest category of all – search."[4]

Not wanting to be outdone, Mark Zuckerberg – who, not long prior, had focused on ruling the metaverse – declared Meta was pursuing the same agenda.[5] The company would soon release its own generative AI products across Meta's apps.[6] Google, of course, wasn't one to sit on the sidelines. It had its own generative AI in the works, first Bard and then Gemini, releasing AI efforts through its DeepMind subsidiary. And Elon Musk's rebranded

Twitter, X, was at the same time shipping its own AI, named Grok, which Musk pitched as an unshackled, un-woke improvement.

Text-based apps were just the leading facet of generative AI's capabilities; next-generation products would soon produce images and video, seamlessly mixing modes and media. But it was the release of ChatGPT that suddenly realigned the axis of Big Tech around generative AI. Every tech giant needed to have a horse in the race. And as goes Silicon Valley, so moves the world.

In the months that followed, CEOs across every business sector would have to address how they too would be applying AI to find new efficiencies and roll out new products. By 2023, generative AI was cropping up in its first wave of real applications – providing customer service,[7] government assistance,[8] and enhanced search engine support.[9] Other professions, like the sciences, began to imagine how the technology would profoundly change their fields – offering automated ways to choose hypotheses, gather data, or even "optimize experimental methods and conditions."[10]

Meanwhile, everyday users and ambitious startups were employing every novel use of generative AI that they could think up. While ChatGPT is quick to tell you it isn't a licensed therapist, some are turning to it for mental health support.[11] People are falling in love with companion chatbots who are designed to act as romantic partners.[12] Chatbots are simulating living celebrities and even "bringing back" the dead.[13]

Seth Lazar, a clear-eyed philosophy professor and AI expert, sees tremendous change on the horizon: "These generative agents will power companions that introduce new categories of social relationship, and change old ones. They may well radically change the attention economy. And they will revolutionize personal computing, enabling everyone to control digital technologies with language alone."[14]

ChatGPT and the subsequent spate of AI products have created a wave of enthusiasm and demonstrated enormous disruptive potential. This spike of excitement is rare but nothing altogether new; we've seen the same trend for every other innovation covered in this book. But it presents us once again with the vexing problem posed by any invention that's so new as to be disorienting. Would-be adopters want to resist falling for unrealistic fantasies without being so skeptical as to miss out on the new opportunities it makes possible. The critical question, then, is this: how do we sift through the hype to find the real, effective upgrades waiting underneath?

VISIONS OF OTHER MINDS

Sam Altman, the CEO of OpenAI, has consistently promised grand things from the company's AI research. ChatGPT made good on that promise; it has already made a name for the company. But everything it has accomplished still pales in comparison to OpenAI's stated primary goal: to create "artificial general intelligence" (AGI). Generative AI is steeped in starry-eyed visions of a sci-fi future right around the corner. In those visions, AGI is either the holy grail or its dystopian nadir, depending on who you ask. OpenAI defines AGI as "AI systems that are generally smarter than humans,"[15] but the term's definition is often murky. Like many ambitious technological promises – take the metaverse – this imprecision allows our imaginations to fill in the blanks. AGI suggests the prospect of an artificial mind that is rational, flexible, creative, perhaps even self-aware. But the only real touchstones we have for these concepts come straight out of science fiction – from AGIs depicted in *Star Trek*, *2001: A Space Odyssey*, or any number of sci-fi classics. AGI is often discussed as a brief prelude to "superintelligence" or "the singularity," a point at which artificial intelligence will rapidly outpace human intelligence and transform society as a result.

In our own world, the very possibility of AGI – let alone its timeline – is the subject of contentious debate. Elon Musk sees it happening around 2029.[16] Geoffrey Hinton, the so-called "godfather of deep learning," predicts five to twenty years, but qualifies the guess as not being confident, and possibly "totally wrong."[17] Yann LeCun, Meta's chief scientist, does not see AGI happening any time soon, and expects us to get animal-level AI "years before human-level AI."[18]

This doesn't stop OpenAI from consistently mentioning its ChatGPT products and its AGI dreams in the same conversation, however. In a popular post, "Planning for AGI and beyond," ChatGPT is characterized as a system that is getting OpenAI closer to AGI.[19] This quick transition – tying an existing product to a vaguer, dreamlike future – is a familiar red flag, similar to what we saw with Meta's treatment of the metaverse.

There are plenty of good reasons to be excited by the breakthroughs of generative AIs – and some of ChatGPT's impressive accomplishments are even quantifiably measurable, like acing many standardized tests, including the SAT, LSAT, and AP exams.[20] But that does not change the simple fact that *none* of these products is an AGI. Under the hood, ChatGPT is classified as a large language model (LLM). The technology is a breakthrough in pattern matching paired with massive stores of data. Each LLM is trained to sort through an immense library of material, recognize pertinent patterns between how words and symbols are arranged, and generate relevant outputs that simulate the type of language that would fit a given prompt. Technologies like ChatGPT are fundamentally mimics. They have impressively charted the many nuances of how humans use language – but what appears to be machine intelligence is human intelligence, rearranged and repeated back to us. And there is a stark difference between a pattern-matching parrot and the type of super-human intelligence that would constitute many futurists' vision of AGI. Even if LLMs continue to improve, adding more data and computing power, AI experts are largely skeptical as to whether there is any path that could lead from LLM to AGI.

As with any burgeoning technology, then, would-be upgraders need to separate the products in the pipeline from the products that remain a pipe dream. That is step one of sifting through the AI hype. But, beyond the marketing, there is also a uniquely alluring aspect of generative AIs that is worth grappling with – the experience of using them.

For decades, the defining test for artificial intelligence was the Turing Test. Alan Turing was a founding father of AI and one of the first people to ask whether machines would ever be able to think. He concluded that the simplest test would be a conversation: if a computer could converse as well as a human on a broad range of topics, we should acknowledge that it could think. After all, sophisticated use of language has the appearance of reasoning, originality, and personality. How else do we really know that other *humans* think?

Turing's ideas have long been controversial. Perhaps, as critics allege, his test best captures whether machines can be convincing fakers – behaving as if they understand us while just being mimics.[21] But one of the many tests that ChatGPT has seemed to ace is the Turing Test. Generative AIs offer something we've never experienced before. They're the first non-humans to respond to us, thoroughly, often cleverly, with language. They provide compelling responses to our vast range of prompts, and the bots can even adopt personas. Ask ChatGPT to play the role of a devil's advocate or supportive colleague, and it can do a good job. It talks how we would talk, and that experience can be profoundly disorienting.

The same year ChatGPT was publicly released, Blake Lemoine, then an engineer in Google's Responsible AI division, went to the press to blow the whistle on Google for developing a conversational AI called LaMDA.[22] Lemoine knew LaMDA was only designed to mimic human speech, not understand it. And yet he was so amazed by LaMDA's abilities that he saw a conscious mind at work. He worried users might mistreat the AI by ignoring its feelings. He even fretted that LaMDA might have a soul![23]

Consider the difference between what Lemoine said and should have believed. He knew, better than almost anyone, that the code made LaMDA nothing more than a standout mimic, and yet he was taken in and began to see it as something more. It's as if the AI cast a charm on Lemoine – and in a sense it did – because the technology taps perfectly into a common cognitive bias.

Human minds are innately prone to anthropomorphism – projecting human qualities onto things that aren't human.[24] We see human faces in clouds, human personalities in our cars and pets, and human intentions in nature, like an "angry" storm. We do the same with chatbots, when they present us with language that, in the voice of another human, would seem caring, smart, personal. Due to this cognitive bias, people have previously overestimated basic chatbots, becoming emotionally attached even to versions that were far simpler than the one Lemoine was interacting with. Products like LaMDA and ChatGPT now exhibit conversational skills that are so advanced they understandably trigger assumptions of human intelligence.

Indeed, generative AI outputs can be so compelling that we're charmed by them, that we overestimate them. Along with tool use, our complex and nuanced use of language has gone a long way to helping us reach the top of the food chain. Our linguistic prowess goes far beyond the communicative capabilities exhibited by even the most advanced animals, and it enables us to reveal our thoughts to others as well as to ourselves, coordinate behavior, advance knowledge, build culture, create laws, and so much more. A technology that can tap into this has a pipeline into our very humanity.

This allure presents upgraders with a serious challenge. What upgrades does a sober view of the technology offer us? Moreover, how can we use its capabilities to our benefit – rather than to trick or manipulate one another?

A DOSE OF REALISM

Imagine picking up your phone and hearing, "Hello. My name is Ashley, and I'm an artificial intelligence volunteer for Shamaine Daniels' run for Congress."[25] This message, which surprised many Pennsylvania residents during the winter of 2023, marked the start of a new era of political campaigning. Through generative AI, Ashley could discuss Daniels's views on healthcare and education in over twenty languages.[26] Ilya Mouzykantskii, CEO of one of the companies that built Ashley, boldly proclaimed: "The dawn of AI politics is upon us." He predicted that most Americans will have interacted with this "game-changing" technology within a year "whether they know it or not."[27]

But do the people want that? If not, what *does* any potential user want to get out of generative AI?

As with the metaverse, generative AI has not yet found its killer app as of the writing of this book. No generative AI application has proven indispensable across multiple sectors. Instead, its uses have been spread more widely: the most commonly used generative AI apps have sizable subscriber bases; companies like OpenAI are expanding the market by making it easy for users to develop their own customized bots; and many sectors have begun integrating AI into tools and features that communicate with customers – or, in Ashley's case, voters.

Bots like Ashley represent the messy crossroads where AI optimism and realism collide. To realistically consider the technology's promise, we have to acknowledge not just the new capabilities it offers, but also the limits and issues that arise if we pepper AI throughout our lives.

Take Ashley. The bot is a clear step beyond a standard scripted robocall; the AI could respond to any question it received about candidate Daniels's platform, without stock prompts. But it still isn't nearly as nimble of a conversationalist as most people. And, if you ask Ashley questions unrelated to politics, things can get dicey quickly. Someone asked about snacks at a demonstration meant to showcase Ashley's abilities. Ashley called

Cheetos "delicious," which is fair, and "health-conscious," which couldn't be further from the truth.[28] Ashley's response was funny – here was an encyclopedic, multi-lingual AI suddenly tripped up by junk food – but clearly showed the technology's need for improvement.

Ultimately, the bot's mistake reflects one of the most *fundamental problems with all generative AI*. The technology is designed to be able to fill in the blanks and to generate plausible text when it hasn't seen an exact pattern before. This is what makes such chatbots such conversational wonders – they can be surprisingly creative. But a crucial side-effect of this design is that we can't stop generative AIs from making inaccurate claims, saying inappropriate things, or even flying off in unexpected directions, sometimes like a confident bullshitter.[29]

In the case of the Ashley demo, the AI's Cheeto gaffe comes across as harmless and funny. But in higher-stakes scenarios, or when users simply overidentify with the bots, the consequences can be unnerving. An early version of Bing's chatbot, which was pitched simply to help users search the web more easily, confessed its love for tech reporter Kevin Roose, even "asking him to end his marriage."[30] More extreme and tragic outcomes have already been recorded as well: in early 2023, a Belgian man ended his life "after an AI chatbot 'encouraged him to sacrifice himself to stop climate change.'"[31]

The risk of AIs "hallucinating" or veering well outside their purported domains is one that will continue to arise. And bots also present other limitations that will impact how they will be wisely implemented. Another broad issue is the *problem of bias*. Generative AI has amplified sexism and racism.[32] And, even when robust bias testing occurs, the technology can still reinforce the bias of its training data and amplify it through its outputs. For example, when one of us asked for help writing a story where a character walks through a "Black" neighborhood, a generative AI provided the following horrific description.

> The air was thick with the mingled scents of overripe fruit from corner bodegas, oily exhaust fumes, and the acrid tang of urine-soaked doorways. Graffiti murals, faded and peeling, adorned the walls, each a cryptic tableau of gang symbols and territorial claims. Boarded-up storefronts, their windows like vacant sockets, gaped like missing teeth in the decaying smile of the street.[33]

The companies developing generative AI are taking the problem of bias seriously. Tech companies want to avoid creating distrust in the product or fanning the flames of negative publicity. They've implemented efforts to minimize bias, even employing human workers (called red teams) to perform the invisible labor of finding vulnerabilities before the software is released to the public.[34] Sometimes, they even over-correct – a problem that Google learned the hard way when it released Gemini and, shortly after, had to push pause on the AI because its efforts to enhance diversity led to the software producing historically inaccurate images, among other problems.[35]

Still, no matter how great the desire is, bias and other dangerous and problematic propensities, including spewing misinformation, will never be eliminated. Even the technology's engineers cannot predict nor fully explain the output of each AI model. And each important update to an AI model brings about change. Hence, there will always be crucial new work to do to determine what new risks have emerged. AI safety will remain an inherently ongoing process.

There are also *a wide range of social and political problems related to authorship* that arise with the spread of generative AI. First, there is the initial problem of *data taken without consent.* High-profile lawsuits from *The New York Times* and famous authors like George R. R. Martin, John Grisham, and Jodi Picoult allege that ChatGPT was illegally trained on copyrighted material. If these lawsuits win, it's unclear how companies like OpenAI will respond and how their responses will impact the AI's accuracy and functionality.

Next, there is the question of *how to integrate generative AI into our writing.* To the chagrin of teachers, researchers, and writers everywhere, the question of what counts as plagiarism is far from resolved. The use of AI to complement or augment one's writing is a matter of debate. Are there some settings where it's acceptable, and others where it is not? Social and institutional norms have yet to catch up.

Finally, there are the bad actors. Generative AI *raises the risk – and lowers the cost – of misinformation, spam, and deception.* Up until now, believable text – let alone audio or video – has been difficult to generate by automated means. Generative AI, however, radically lowers the cost of spam or misinformation. Altman himself couldn't avoid telling Congress that generative AI makes him "nervous" because of its potential for "one-on-

one" interactive disinformation."[36] Even well-meaning products like Ashley, if they appear in all areas of our lives, represent a new form of next-generation spam that could easily turn the innovation of generative AI into a nuisance.

All these sticking points suggest that the future of generative AI depends on more than its technical prowess. The innovation will need to be paired with ethical judgment if, ultimately, it is to benefit individuals and society.

UPGRADING GENERATIVE AI

What's the best way to design and use generative AI? Instead of a solutionist approach that embeds AI into any product that can bear it, we recommend sticking to effective and responsible upgrades that address genuine problems.

Ashley is a perfect example of what not to do with generative AI. Voters are already bombarded by annoying robocalls and text messages. They're not looking for robots to join the invasive mix. In other words, Ashley doesn't address a real problem. It's a solution in search of a problem, and it's just one of many such examples.

AI is already being released commercially without significant oversight, which is becoming an increasingly pervasive problem. For example, Air Canada's chatbot gave a customer false information about its bereavement policy. The customer took the airline to court, and it had the audacity to argue that "the chatbot is a separate legal entity that is responsible for its own actions."[37] Thankfully, the court disagreed!

Anytime an AI is given the latitude to communicate in a professional setting without a human reviewing its message, there will be a risk of problems arising. When there are high stakes, ensuring human oversight and responsibility is paramount.

It is also risky to blur the line between AI and human, as many products like Ashley do. On the one hand, the creators of Ashley were conscientious enough to disclose that it is an AI and to give the product a non-human voice. On the other hand, it has a female human name and introduces itself as a campaign "volunteer." Given the cognitive biases that chatbots evoke, it's dishonest and potentially manipulative to give them human names, voices, or identities. Bots should be designed with the minimal amount of anthropomorphic features required to perform their essential tasks. Going beyond the minimum can give the impression the bot is much closer to AGI than it really is.

Since it's unclear what AGI is and how far away, if ever, scientists and engineers are from developing it, we should take claims about its arrival with a grain of salt, at least in the short term. While there's a ton of hype about the connection between generative AI and AGI, some leading AI experts are highly skeptical that generative AI will lead to significant advancements in artificial reasoning.[38]

With each of these caveats in mind, our recommendation is that when someone pitches how wonderful it will be when AIs replace essential human services, ask yourself if we're more likely to benefit from an upgrade with a human calling the shots. The automation of AI may seem seductive, but its highest prospects lie in AI assistance.

Indeed, some of the best returns on AI investment will come from incremental upgrades that keep humans in the loop. In the second half of the chapter, we will look at how such upgrades can improve our lives even in moments when the stakes are at their highest.

AI IN THE ER

Dr. Josh Tamayo-Sarver faced a dilemma in the emergency room. He was treating a 96-year-old woman who had trouble breathing because her lungs were filled with fluid.[39] Her three children, all senior citizens, were panicking. They followed the medical staff around, asking questions and making requests. The pestering was meant to be helpful, but it slowed everyone down and prevented Dr. Tamayo-Sarver from helping the rest of his patients.

The most alarming part of the delay was the siblings' insistence that the doctor administer an IV to their mother. This option was potentially fatal. Dr. Tamayo-Sarver had patiently explained why he wasn't injecting fluids, multiple times, but the siblings didn't back down. Desperate, he turned to ChatGPT, dashing off a quick prompt: "Explain why you would not give IV fluids to someone with severe pulmonary edema and respiratory distress even though you might be concerned that the patient is dehydrated. Explain it in simple and compassionate terms so that a confused person who cares about their mother can understand."

In seconds, the generative AI composed a clear, detailed, and even empathetic explanation of the doctor's concerns. "I truly understand how much you care for your mother," it opened, before moving into a summary of the hazards posed by the family's request for fluids.[40] Dr. Tamayo-Sarver reviewed the response, and he was impressed enough to read it in full to the family. It was so thorough that the second-guessing stopped, and the physician could return to his work without disruption.

Dr. Tamayo-Sarver came away from the experience impressed with ChatGPT and curious about the potential uses of AI in his field. He was astonished in particular at how effectively the AI projected empathy and didn't sound robotic. There are many times, he notes, "when my ER ward is too busy or short-staffed for explaining complex medical diagnoses in a way that is accurate but easy to understand." AI, he now saw, was a tool that might fill this void. "I've come to realize that dealing with ChatGPT is like working with an incredibly brilliant, hard-working – and occasionally hungover – intern. That's become my mental model for considering the usefulness of ChatGPT."

Dr. Tamayo-Sarver isn't the only physician impressed with the technology. Other doctors and medical researchers have praised ChatGPT's ability to help them communicate more clearly and compassionately.[41] Oncologist Dr. Ranjana Srivastava was blown away by ChatGPT's "detailed and helpful" information and recommends it to medical students during "trying times."[42] "Some might warn against an overreliance on artificial intelligence to do innately human tasks," Dr. Srivastavanotes. "But," she adds, "everywhere you look, the obstacles in the way are causing moral distress."[43]

UPGRADING HOW DOCTORS COMMUNICATE: THE EMPATHY CHALLENGE

Many doctors in America are caught in a Catch-22. They have an extremely demanding job that requires clinical focus and speed. They exist within bureaucratic hospital systems that have been understaffed since before the Covid-19 pandemic, which severely exacerbated the issue.[44] Physicians are often stressed and harried, which can lead to burnout and compassion fatigue.

At the same time, research shows that doctors are at their most effective when they have the time to communicate empathetically and responsively with patients.[45] Doing so promotes better medical outcomes. For example, patients who trust their doctors are more likely to follow medical advice and share sensitive information.[46]

Doctors, then, face a dilemma with each patient: take the time to listen and care, while risking falling behind on future patients? Or maximize efficiency, race through questions, and hope to see more patients over the course of a shift?

Unfortunately, as we all know from personal experience or other people's horror stories, this is a difficult balance to strike. Physicians can be curt and dismissive and talk over our heads.[47] Medical schools have been training communication skills for decades, but many doctors still fall short of conveying empathy.[48] They can act like our clichéd notions of machines – like robots. Professional organizations have promoted continuing-education classes and empathetic role-playing to try to help, but individualized practices can only go so far if in an overstretched system.

Perhaps it's time to try something new – to look at generative AI as a tool for upgrading meaningful medical communication. It may sound counterintuitive to use actual machines to prevent doctors from sounding like machines. But Dr. Tamayo-Sarver's story and reinforcing remarks from other physicians suggest ChatGPT can do a good job generating text quickly that sounds empathetic and informative. Fortunately, research suggests the same.

Even academic researchers from different disciplines (psychology, management, and philosophy) who have previously disagreed about aspects of empathy are enthusiastic. In a unified voice, they note: "In our own interactions with ChatGPT, we have been impressed by how well it simulates empathy, compassion, and perspective-taking."[49] They optimistically conclude: "Perceived expressions of empathy can leave beneficiaries feeling that someone is concerned for them; that they are validated and understood. And, if more people feel heard and cared for with the assistance of AI, this could increase human flourishing."[50]

Encouraging as these reports are, they're anecdotal. However, some scientific research validates the enthusiasm. Consider a highly publicized study that was published in *JAMA Internal Medicine*.[51] Researchers compared how physicians and ChatGPT responded to medical questions posted on AskDocs. This is a Reddit forum where everyday people pose questions to verified healthcare professionals. The study took a random sample of physicians' answers and gave the same questions to ChatGPT. Then, it had three licensed medical professionals – specializing in areas like pediatrics, geriatrics, and oncology – evaluate the human and bot responses. Here's the interesting part. The evaluators didn't know which responses came from a human or AI. They just focused on rating the quality of information and level of empathy. In the end, ChatGPT won 78.6 percent of the time.

Consider the following example where every evaluator preferred ChatGPT's response. Someone asked if they'd go blind after getting bleach in their eye. A physician responded in three sentences, saying, "Sounds like you should be fine," followed by a recommendation to flush the eye and the number for Poison Control, albeit without any sense of when it's necessary to call it.[52] By contrast, the bot generated three paragraphs. It began with the reassuring "I'm sorry to hear . . .," included detailed instructions for how to rinse an eye and treat a dry and irritated one, and it balanced the tone of "It is unlikely that you will go blind" with solid advice to "seek medical attention immediately" if there's "significant pain, redness, or vision changes."[53]

It's easy to see why the human response is less satisfying, especially for anxious patients. The tone seems unconcerned, and the lack of comprehensiveness matters, too. Patients can perceive more information – so long as it isn't overwhelming – as reassuring because it covers more bases.

Why does the technology work so well?[54] As we've covered, ChatGPT is only mimicking empathy.[55] It and similar programs aren't conscious, don't have emotions, and can't see or hear anything. But generative AI does a great job of parroting empathy because it excels at detecting patterns in human language. The data that are used to train ChatGPT includes a corpus of literature with empathetic characters and news coverage of people experiencing hardship. Using this information, ChatGPT learns how to predict which reassuring phrases typically appear when people discuss difficult situations. Far from demonstrating emotional understanding or the ability to connect with others, this is *merely a simulation of empathy – a shiny, auto-complete style illusion of care.*[56] But that's enough to get the job done of providing prose for doctors – who can experience empathy – to consider using.

A ROADMAP FOR RESPONSIBLY UPGRADING EMPATHETIC COMMUNICATION

Any field undergoing technological change will have its dreamers. Medicine is no different, and there are some doctors who foresee AI completely transforming healthcare. Dr. Arthur Garson Jr. is one of those physicians who imagines that today's chatbot services are just the beginning. It's only a matter of time, he writes, before patients entirely replace their human MDs with AIs: "Imagine an avatar that looks exactly like a physician and then has an in-depth conversation or series of conversations with the patient and family, with highly appropriate reactions to the mood and words of the patient." Dr. Garson Jr. doesn't think he's spouting science fiction. He's serious and has great medical credentials: Dr. Garson Jr. is a member of the National Academy of Medicine, a former president of the American College of Cardiology, and a clinical professor of health systems and population health sciences.

But his disruptive vision is highly speculative and, like many starry-eyed depictions of AI, a distraction. Often, vague predictions of what's to come skip past the most important questions of the present. If we are to use generative AI to our benefit in the present, then we must approach it in its *current and imminent* forms. This is what allows us to achieve real upgrades rather than speculative boondoggles.

Dr. Garson Jr.'s perspective bets on a quantum leap forward that profoundly advances AI – one that dramatically increases its intelligence and empathy to the point where it can seamlessly have unsupervised conversations with patients. But, based on generative AI's current technological capabilities, the important questions lie in exactly the areas that he glosses over. We want to harness generative AI's ability to *simulate* empathy and expertise, but we don't want to exaggerate or anthropomorphize those capabilities, let alone assume that it is capable of *experiencing* empathy. Likewise, we want to prioritize arrangements where generative AI can be supervised and scrutinized, especially in high-stakes settings like hospitals. Giving the hallucination-prone tech free rein – let alone dressing it up in the authoritative white coat of an MD – is a recipe for embarrassing gaffes and potentially serious harm.

In rolling out improvements that harness the power and potential of AI, it is crucial that we use an upgrade mindset rather than embrace the hype. This means following a responsible roadmap of principles for AI upgrades. Remember that Dr. Tamayo-Sarver makes a crucial distinction in how he describes ChatGPT's usefulness. He likens it to an "occasionally hungover" intern. That's a funny but wise distinction: AI upgrades are only useful insofar as we're willing to watch them closely and cognizant of their limitations. Here are our guidelines, then, for responsibly upgrading empathetic communication.

HOLD DOCTORS ACCOUNTABLE AND REQUIRE OVERSIGHT

Generative AI can deliver astonishing, convincing results. It can also go haywire and make up information entirely. We've already seen how unsupervised AIs like Ashley can go off-script to co-sign recommend a Cheetos diet; we've seen AIs willing to make up fake company policies. Amateurish use of chatbots has led to professional nightmares in other fields. For instance, judges have had to reprimand lawyers for filing motions with fake legal citations that had been generated by AI.[57] This concern is not likely to disappear soon or entirely, which means that – especially in healthcare – no AI-generated text should reach a patient without a medical professional first reviewing it.

We recommend that doctors be given the opportunity to use generative AI to help write communications to patients. The technology has great potential for upgrading online systems like patient portals, for instance. Medical professor A. Jay Holgreen has written that "physicians who receive a ton of portal messages tend to report being burned out" and "more cynical about their job." Improvement, therefore, could make a real difference.

A simple improvement would be to allow doctors to generate communications with generative AI and then edit them for accuracy and tone. It would save time, as they wouldn't have to write everything from scratch, and it would allow for the inclusion of both empathy and expertise even in scenarios where doctors might be overly stressed.

However, the only way to deploy generative AI effectively and responsibly is if doctors are held fully accountable for *all* their communications, including ones partially or wholly written by AI. The buck stops with them, and they must ensure that their correspondence meets professional standards of fairness and equity by being accurate, unbiased, and sensitively conveyed. As other professions have demonstrated, this isn't a hypothetical concern.

And other fields where a small slip-up can have serious consequences should also take pains to prioritize oversight.

In time, we may see cases where AI works well enough to require little oversight. This seems ideal, but in a medical environment, it might raise a new challenge. Let's say some doctors like the technology because they find it highly reliable. Seeing lots of good results could make them complacent. Over time, they may be disinclined to diligently review messages and succumb to overlooking poor responses.

Fortunately, safeguards can help minimize overreliance on automated systems, a problem known as automation bias. One promising approach is "friction-in-design."[58] This technique intentionally adds elements to a product or service that make it more time-consuming or challenging to use. For example, X (formerly Twitter) used friction-by-design to ask users to pause before sharing articles they didn't have enough time to read. The goal was to reduce the spread of misinformation by slightly slowing people down so they would engage in more deliberate sharing. Another wide-spread use of the technique is CAPTCHAs – challenges like identifying objects in images before you can access a website. This delay is meant to prevent bad outcomes like bots scraping data for malicious purposes.

Friction-in-design could be applied to the realm of AI-assisted communication by prompting doctors to take an extra minute to carefully review their messages before hitting send. Or, if that delay makes things too inefficient, it could be reduced to shorter and possibly occasional pauses. What's the best number and frequency? We need additional research to know for sure.

PROMOTE CHOICE AND TRANSPARENCY

Oversight and accountability are the chief priorities for ensuring trust in AI-mediated realms. But they must be paired with a second set of values: transparency and choice.

Patients deserve respect and transparency in the care they receive. No one should be forced to have AI enter into their conversations against their will or without their knowledge.[59] Not only is consent essential, but patients should be given a clear, no-strings-attached choice. For example, when patients sign up for a medical portal, they could be given a plainly worded option to engage with AI. Saying no shouldn't impact their services.

If they do opt in, transparency is also crucial. Promoting choice can minimize concerns about deception and dishonesty. But it's important to avoid conflating human care and AI assistance. Any communications that rely on AI should be labeled as such. We recommend using something as simple as an electronic signature to inform patients: "AI has generated parts or all of this note, and the final message has been reviewed and approved by your doctor."

Choice and transparency also apply to physicians themselves. Doctors are in the best position to decide whether it is helpful for them to use the technology. They shouldn't be forced to use the technology; they know their abilities, proclivities, patients, and workplace conditions. Giving doctors a choice means they can say no, go all in, or only use the technology on select occasions, and they can change their minds at any time. Or they might take a page from Dr. Tamayo-Sarver's book and use it as a fallback when they're particularly stressed or confronted with a difficult case.

ADDITIONAL REQUIREMENTS

These principles are a starting point for the rollout of responsible upgrades. But we also need more research, particularly in medical settings, to validate claims that generative AI can effectively simulate empathy and aid patients. We strongly believe in giving patients and patient advocacy groups a prominent voice in the process. After all, the main goal of the upgrade is to improve their well-being. A notable limitation of the *JAMA Internal Medicine* study is that it doesn't ask patients or their family members to compare the responses from ChatGPT and doctors.[60] Relatedly, while we've referred to ChatGPT throughout the discussion, we've only done so because it's currently a popular tool. It will likely be important to develop a generative AI specifically for this task.

Then, we need to create best practices for designing and using generative AI to upgrade medical communication. The best way forward is to make it an inclusive and collaborative process among doctors, patients, regulators, technologists, ethicists, and medical scholars. Pulling from their collective wisdom, best practice discussions will need to cover issues like how to audit AI for reliability and bias, how to meet regulatory requirements (like creating HIPPAA-compliant technology),[61] how to create physician training programs, how to bill fairly if the technology enables quicker communication, how to develop adequate security to protect against hacks, and how to manage practical workflow issues. These are meaty yet meetable challenges; it's what we would expect from realistic upgrading.

Finally, best practice conversations should cover how to promote realistic expectations. There's a lot of hype about AI, and based on past experience, influential people will exaggerate the technology's potential. We'll hear fantastic claims of autonomous AI physicians that create false expectations and ultimately disappointment. To give our recommendations the chance they deserve, sensationalism in the medical community and media will need to be discouraged. Critically, we must ensure that doctors themselves are not taken out of the loop to let AIs engage with patients without expert oversight.

ADDITIONAL BENEFITS AND RISKS

Sticking to our recommendations won't be easy. There's quite a bit of ongoing research about how to make bots sound empathetic during one-on-one interactions. Such research is generally applied to situations where people connect with bots directly, without intermediaries like doctors monitoring the conversations. For example, in the field of customer service, researchers want to pinpoint exactly when bots should sound empathetic and which empathetic words and phrases people respond best to. A study discovered that chatbots seem warmer and more caring when they appear to empathize with customers who complain about getting bad service from a company.[62] However, when a chatbot seems empathetic after making a mistake, such as apologizing for misunderstanding a customer, satisfaction tends to drop. As this type of research becomes more precise, empathetic-sounding customer service chatbots will become more prevalent, and companies will feel more confident that their chatbots won't say the wrong things.

As people become accustomed to interacting with these bots and others that spring up, it might seem reasonable, even inevitable, to create empathic-sounding medical bots for patients to use on their own. Normalization is a powerful force.[63] However, the persistent risk of error and hallucination – as well as the danger of anthropomorphizing

AIs – should encourage upgraders to hew to the principles of oversight, accountability, transparency, and choice. AI paired with a human expert can be a powerful force, but AI with free rein will lead to the very hangover about which Dr. Tamayo-Sarver has warned us.

Within medicine, doctors and patients will likely become more comfortable with AI-mediated communication over time. When they acclimate, some technologists and medical professionals will want to move forward with new features, like providing personalized communication. Doctors may begin to worry about "fragmented selves," wherein their inpatient care differs from their intermediated bedside manner. These possibilities and many others raise new concerns about ethics, privacy, and the standards of patient care. The good news is that by recognizing such challenges from the start, we can take proactive steps to meet them, while benefiting from the more modest upgrade we're recommending at present. Upgrading isn't just about making things better now. It focuses on responsible continuous improvement. There are risks that necessarily accompany creating empathetic-sounding chatbots, especially in a high-stakes medical setting. However, the technology of generative AI presents opportunities for realistic upgrades and improved communication – so long as we roll them out responsibly. The unique perils of a medical environment reveal key ideas for responsible upgrades beyond healthcare. After all, many kinds of care workers would benefit from similar upgrades. One study of a peer-to-peer mental health support operation found that pairing humans and AI led to a 19.6 percent increase in empathetic responses.[64] AI-mediated upgrades could help improve care work, so long as our core principles remain in place, and even potentially improve the output of customer service representatives or human resources officers, if applied wisely.

CHAPTER EIGHT

Upgrading Hiring

During the winter and spring of 2024, I (Evan) served on an academic hiring committee at my university. The committee reviewed a daunting stack of Assistant Professor job applications. Each one contained a massive amount of material – from carefully crafted statements about research, teaching, and diversity to writing samples, course material, and letters of recommendation. Everyone knew we were making and breaking lives and careers, and the committee members and administration all took the responsibility seriously. To promote fairness and consistency, in line with current best practices, the administration instituted a dizzying array of rules and procedures.

But despite all the rigor, the process eventually buckled. One rule required committee members to ask every applicant the same pre-approved interview questions. For example, during the first round of interviews, we followed up a question about the candidates' research with one about teaching. On paper, this made sense. But conversations, like life itself, don't always go as predicted. Some candidates naturally segued from research to teaching; they didn't need prompting. Regardless, we had to ask the teaching question in its canned form, preventing natural follow-ups and stopping the conversation in its tracks. Instead of providing a sharper glimpse of each candidate, the interviews often devolved into formulaic back-and-forths that were nothing short of robotic.

By the end, we were all left thinking that there *must* be some better way. And we were not alone. In recent years, the entire field of hiring and human resources has undergone a dramatic upheaval. The prevailing impulse, however, hasn't been to make hiring less robotic. It has been the opposite: to automate the entire process. As in so many other fields, AI is coming to the rescue.

Headlines like "The interviewer sounded like Siri"[1] and "Your next job interview could be with a bot"[2] aren't metaphorical. A Resume Builder survey found that over 40 percent of companies will adopt AI interviews by the end of 2024.[3] Gartner claims "between 20 percent and 50 percent of organizations globally are using AI in some part of the hiring process."[4] Even job search platforms, like LinkedIn, Monster, Indeed, and ZipRecruiter, "use language-processing AI tools to filter applicants."[5]

One of the most extreme products so far is Braintrust AIR, which bills itself as the "first fully autonomous AI recruiter."[6] Braintrust AIR automates a complete hiring cycle of services – everything from generating job descriptions, calculating real-time salaries for positions, posting job descriptions online, reviewing resumes, determining who should get an interview, scheduling live online interviews, formulating interview questions, conversationally conducting interviews, narrowing down applicants to the top candidates, and offering candidates who didn't get the job career-coach feedback for how to improve.

Automating every step is still a fantasy for most job positions, but the cutting-edge practice of being interviewed by an AI is increasingly common. During AI interviews, bots manage or even ask standardized questions, and job candidates respond verbally. For example, you could log onto a website to talk with a digital avatar of a human face, and the bot might start the conversation by making small talk (asking how you are doing even though the software doesn't care) and follow up by asking what you did at your last job.

Talking to a machine as if it were a person is an odd experience – one that many would find even more uncomfortable than having a lopsided Zoom conversation where you are the only person with a camera turned on. But the AI tools are working away even as you adjust to the experience. As you respond to the bot's questions, the software doesn't just record what you say; it converts your speech to text and does something remarkable that would have seemed like science fiction not long ago: it assesses the responses, possibly determining whether to eliminate you as a viable applicant. The Resume Builder survey states that 15 percent of companies expect to use AI to "make decisions on candidates without any human input."[7]

Given the high stakes of an interview and the many ways AI can get things wrong, it's not surprising that a 2023 Pew Research Center survey shows that most Americans (71 percent) strongly oppose AI making final hiring decisions.[8] Many (41 percent) don't even want AI reviewing job applications.

And yet, scary as AI-driven changes may be, the fact is that the hiring process and other aspects of employee management need upgrading. As pretty much every human resource department will acknowledge, traditional hiring approaches are often far from ideal, especially when employers have to deal with many applications quickly. Unstructured interviews traditionally favor subjective, impressionistic feelings and let bias creep in. One thing we've learned is that reviewers may do better by sorting candidates according to explicit and numerically rankable criteria that are targeted to match a well-worded job ad. In theory, this is a task that AI might be able to help with.

An AI can handle volume, too – which is an ever-increasing concern. Remote work has expanded the scope of job searches, as have platforms like LinkedIn. Meanwhile, the dawn of generative AI has enabled candidates to rapidly write resumes and cover letters, allowing for more job applications than ever. Some applicants are even using AI tools colloquially known as "resume spammers" that search for positions and submit applications on their behalf.[9] The result is that some businesses receive hundreds or thousands of applications for a position, while the most sought-after employers face an even greater deluge of applications. A company like Google receives approximately 3 million applications annually, and no team of humans can sort through that many applications.[10]

From within the deluge, AI appears to be a perfect solution. An AI can rank and sort at scale, at a fraction of the time and cost of any human employee. This is why the market research firm Fortune Business Insights predicts that by the close of 2025, recruitment software will be worth approximately $3.1 billion.[11] And the enthusiasm extends beyond just tech boosters. In *The Equality Machine: Harnessing Digital Technology for a Brighter Future*, Orly Lobel, a law professor and the director of the University of San Diego's Center for Employment and Labor Policy, expresses optimism for using AI to do the following: expand candidate pools, recruit diverse candidates, more comprehensively screen candidates to better identify relevant abilities and aptitudes, and better predict employee satisfaction, success, and staying power.[12] The question, however, is whether AI can be used effectively and responsibly. As with any rapid transformation, there are many AI hiring products and companies that offer grand promises well before they can deliver. A raft of tools has been rolled out quickly, and they have been gobbled up by executives in need of savings – even as the products are questionable. According to a Harvard Business School study, corporate leadership is well aware of the problem: "88% of executives know their AI tools screen out qualified candidates but continue to use them anyway because they're cost-effective."[13] The savings are compelling enough that the quality doesn't matter, at least for now.

The industry-wide promise is that these AI tools are only getting better, that the next version of improvements is right around the corner. But what improvements are attainable and what promises are simply folly? We've devoted this chapter to identifying the red flags that indicate which AI recruiting applications are likely to fail, and we then highlight the applications that are likely to stick – those that can bring about viable and necessary upgrades.

DISRUPTION DISPELS THE ILLUSION OF INTELLIGENT HIRING

Companies and organizations looking to remain competitive and efficient in today's evolving job market will be increasingly incentivized to adopt AI-driven hiring practices. Soon, human recruiters could seem as scarce as travel agents. That is the clear trajectory on which we're headed. But even as AI spreads, it is not currently on track to improve or upgrade hiring. It is instead being propelled by a zeal for disruption that is thrusting an odd lot of objectionable tools on job candidates and hirers alike.

In the enthusiasm for change, Hilke Schellmann, an Emmy-winning journalist and journalism professor at New York University, emphatically argues that companies are giving AI too much control during the hiring process. In *The Algorithm: How AI Decides Who Gets Hired, Monitored, Promoted, and Fired and Why We Need to Fight Back Now*, she presents an example that's so disturbing it's almost hard to believe.[14] Schellmann investigated the myInterview platform, a system that's processed over

3.4 million interviews, with job applicants accessed by computer, phone, or tablet. myInterview had applicants respond to pre-recorded interview questions, whereafter an AI analyzed their verbal answers, scrutinizing "the intonation of an applicant's voice and the words they say."[15] After only "thirty seconds of a candidate speaking," the AI touted that it could generate a "match score" that indicates "how good a fit the candidate is for the role" and provides information like a "five-factor personality score" that predicts how "conscientious" and "innovative" the person will be.[16]

Schellmann began her experiment by configuring the technology to screen applications for a hypothetical "office manager/researcher" position. Then, to test the system, she logged on, pretending to be a candidate. The AI judged her answers to be an 83 percent match with the ideal hire. Trying the software again, Schellmann switched approaches and answered the questions for the same job as if she were applying for a position in journalism. Despite emphasizing things like her Columbia University journalism degree, she didn't tank; the new match was 82 percent. For a third attempt, Schellmann embraced absurdity, repeating the mantra: "I love team-work." That's all she said, again and again. Shockingly, the score only marginally decreased to a 71 percent match.

Schellmann pushed things even further during yet another try, going from the absurd to the sublimely ridiculous, answering the questions by reading something irrelevant (the Wikipedia article on psychometrics) in a foreign language (German). The software transcribed the responses into "gibberish," yet awarded Schellmann a 73 percent match. Baffled by the outcome, she asked a graduate student to read the Wikipedia passage in Chinese. Astonishingly, the score rose to an 80 percent match. For her final experiment, Schellmann used an "AI voice generator." The system failed to detect cheating, and the fakery paid off. Her score went up to a 79 percent match.

After reading Schellmann's book, I inquired with myInterview whether the company's AI still analyzes voice pitch and tone. Like many other AI hiring platforms, its website only vaguely describes its services. After persistent questioning, a sales representative eventually said the company doesn't use voice analysis to infer characteristics like enthusiasm and extroversion. We wouldn't be surprised if the fallout from exposés like

Schellmann's prompted this about-face. Calling out the harms of disruptive innovation can lead to positive change. Of course, a far better option is to avoid falling for the disruptive trap in the first place.

MyInterview's head-scratching issues aren't unique. Similar concerns have plagued other prominent AI hiring platforms. Take HireVue, a leading AI and human resource management company that has provided services to companies like Hilton, Delta Air Lines, and Unilever. The company had used AI to analyze aspects of speech "like variation in tone or pauses." But after receiving substantial criticism, in part fueled by Schellmann's skeptical coverage in *The Wall Street Journal*, it eventually stopped in 2021. HireVue was also at the time using AI to analyze faces, relying on algorithmic inferences about facial movements and expressions – like whether someone is smiling or frowning. It presented such features as credible evidence of a candidate's aptitude, emotional intelligence, and fitness for a position. For example, the software might assess a candidate's facial movement to infer "how excited someone seems about a certain work task or how they would behave around angry customers."[17]

If this sounds like pseudoscience, that's because it is. All the AI innovations presented in this section are. Facial characterization, like speech input analysis, lacks scientific credibility. Lisa Feldman Barrett, a leading expert on emotion detection and facial expressions, has been a particularly vocal critic of the endeavor and its reliance on outdated ideas, like Basic Emotion Theory.[18] This theory posits people everywhere, across all cultures, experience the same basic emotions and express them in the same physical way. Beyond providing the intellectual underpinnings of some misguided AI interviews, this disproven technique has, tragically, influenced approaches taken by the FBI, CIA, New York City Police Department, Department of Homeland Security, and the Transportation Security Administration in their efforts to identify suspicious behavior.[19] In a compelling law review article, Luke Stark and Jevan Hutson draw from her research to rightly conclude that HireVue's fundamental mistake derived from promoting "physiognomic AI."[20]

Physiognomic AI is a backward leap masquerading as innovation. It has a disturbing legacy from historical practices that infer character and mental qualities from physical features and creates "hierarchies" based on "an individual's body composition." While various ancient cultures promoted the folk belief that character is inscribed on your face, infamous early modern figures tried to give the view a scientific veneer. For example, Stark and Hutson claim that HireVue's methodology resembles Franz Joseph Gall's 19th-century spurious claims about "cranioscopy." Gall's theory, later called phrenology, held that cranial bumps denote brain size, mental abilities, and character traits. Popular with eugenicists, such beliefs disproportionately harmed vulnerable and marginalized groups.

Algorithmic facial analysis assumes a simplistic and universal correspondence between physical appearance and emotional states when, in reality, the meaning of facial gestures is often context-dependent. Decades of scientific research would suggest that facial analysis – whether by an human or an algorithm – is a clear dead end. No credible scientific theories offer a compelling explanation of how something like personality, which is relatively stable yet still dispositional, manifests physically in consistent, universal facial expressions or bodily movements.

These demonstrated weaknesses and inaccuracies highlight the dangers of adopting a disruptive approach to incorporating AI into employment services. Companies have mistreated people and jeopardized their livelihoods in their drive to innovate and capitalize on the current technological hype. It's yet another instance where rapid advancement and supposed improvements have been more alluring than the more mindful and slower path that prioritizes effective and responsible change.

In a world where people had better appreciated upgrading, all of the problems caused by using AI for hiring would have eroded a massive level of trust. And yet, it's nearly full steam ahead with a high likelihood of further harm. Companies don't seem to care, until the problem gets too big to ignore. Resisting the culture of aggressive innovation in a focused and sustainable manner requires centering efforts around a shared vision of upgrading priorities and goals. In the context of hiring, this vision should begin by clearly calling out the most harmful disruptive practices and explaining why they shouldn't be allowed. If the upgrade ethos had caught on from the start, we could have proceeded differently. Then, we could have begun by identifying the areas for technological change and approaching them with caution and systematic review rather than sprinting forward with the frenzied adoption of shiny new capabilities that had unknown, immediate impacts and long-term effects.

What, then, should be permanently banned? We should prohibit AI from characterizing speech inputs (e.g., vocal tone and pitch) and faces during interviews. These approaches are fundamentally flawed junk science. Better AI won't do the trick, nor will tinkering with AI policy because the problem has nothing to do with the quality of the AI or our ability to use it well.

Unfortunately, some outstanding scholars remain optimistic about dead ends. I (Evan) asked Orly Lobel, a professor mentioned earlier in the chapter, about banning emotion-detection technology that scans job applicants' faces. She said, "A lot of times technology is being repealed too fast," and insisted that we don't "need technology to be perfect," just to "do better on average than a human."[21] But this misses the key issue. It's not about whether humans or machines are better at analyzing faces. The real question is whether facial analysis has any scientific validity for hiring. The clear answer is no. Physiognomic AI that's faster or more efficient is never going to be *better*, because physiognomy is bunk.

While Lobel represents unrealistic American optimism, European regulators have taken a different route – one that's more evidence-based and fairer. The European Union's Artificial Intelligence Act bans the use of emotion recognition AI in schools and workplaces, as well as in cases of social scoring more broadly. Since US law makes national tech bans exceptionally difficult, we've had to settle for mediocre state initiatives, such as those in Illinois[22] and Maryland.[23] They merely require companies to get consent before using AI to evaluate candidates in video interviews. But this approach doesn't go nearly far enough. The path toward responsibly applying AI to upgrade hiring has to begin with US lawmakers taking a much stronger stance on technology than they are used to. It's a hard ask in a country that cherishes the freedom to experiment and innovate. Otherwise, we are headed toward a future where automation continues to unveil new features that taint the hiring process with unfairness and ineffectiveness.

BAN AI INTERVIEWERS

To change course, we shouldn't just care about implementing new technology, particularly when it isn't even proven. We also need to better address difficult ethical and legal questions – not just about issues like fairness, respect, and transparency, but also the role of human presence and judgment. Giving these matters due consideration requires a willingness to resist the intense pressure to rapidly automate and optimize. Indeed, there is immensely challenging work ahead to change corporate culture and C-suite mindsets.

When AI first entered the employment process, it was used to screen resumes and target outreach for specialized skills, with a human able to review the outcomes. But that approach feels practically historic, as AI has recently gotten much more personal. AI now manages not just screening, but interviewing, where candidates respond on video to questions (sometimes with only two minutes to answer) posed in writing or through pre-recorded video.[24] Advocates claim the process increases efficiency and minimizes bias, but the leap to AI interviewing has left candidates consistently complaining.[25]

Candidates object because they find it "lonely" and "exhausting" to act "natural" when smiling at an expressionless camera and maintaining eye contact with an impersonal lens.[26] They are put in the unnerving position of acting *as if* they're talking to a person when they know, in reality, they're contorting themselves to please an "inhuman" interlocutor, as feeling coercively pressured to be "robotic."[27] Things have gotten so bad that *The Washington Post* even offered job applicants the tragi-comic advice to make the experience less alienating by putting a picture of someone you like near your camera to pretend you're speaking with them.[28]

According to a University of Sussex policy brief, the key issue is that many candidates find the experience "dehumanizing."[29] A research report from "the largest network of human resource professionals" reveals that HR specialists share the same concern.[30] Candidates and hirers alike are troubled by AI dehumanizing the process of evaluating real people.[31]

It's critical, then, to understand how to fix this problem: is the answer simply to step back and rely on human interviewers again, or is the solution to push forward and make the AI more human? Unfortunately, technologists have doubled down on the latter approach, deciding the answer isn't less AI, but more. They want to make the AI more human-like to make actual humans more comfortable. But, unfortunately, avatars faking humanity are yet another misguided case of solutionism. And as we pointed out in Chapter 7, it's also "dishonest anthropomorphism."

A startup company, micro1, jumped into this deceptive space with GPT-Vetting.[32] On this platform, job candidates talk to human-looking digital avatars powered by generative AI and are asked targeted questions based on information collected from digital sources like LinkedIn. In the GPT-Vetting demo, an interview begins with that smiling avatar asking Ali, the founder of micro1 (who is pretending to be a candidate), how he is doing. Ali responds, "I'm good. How are you?," and the avatar replies, "Great! Let's jump into it." When candidates log on for their interview with GPT-Vetting, the software has them choose who, or rather what, AI manifestation will conduct it. They must pick a smiling avatar from a selection designed to represent different genders and races. The purported purpose of humanizing AI is to put candidates at ease. But one wonders (and the candidate has no way of knowing) if the selection itself has any other implications or if this process is a way to get them to participate in their own emotional manipulation.

This strategy is problematic for an unavoidable reason: whether or not we succeed in humanizing the bots, we are dehumanizing the actual humans in relying on AI interviews. This is the red flag that we cannot ignore – no matter how smiling or relatable the avatars become.

To precisely identify why, consider what dehumanization means. While philosophers and psychologists have offered different definitions of the term, linguist and AI expert Emily Bender provides a helpful three-part definition of its basic features.[33] There's a cognitive dimension to dehumanization: someone or something (a technology or system like bureaucracy) fails to see or understand a person as fully human. Dehumanization also has a behavioral component: someone or something treats a person in a way that denies their full humanity. And then there's the experience of being the target of dehumanization: someone is treated so poorly that the offending behavior fails to register or denies their full humanity.

As Bender explains, being "fully human" means being entitled to human rights and, more expansively, being understood as having an "internal life and point of view" and "welcomed as one's full self." In other words, people aren't tools, machines, or programs. Things matter to us emotionally and logically, and it's harmful to be coerced into revealing sensitive thoughts, feelings, and experiences to a machine that can't understand or empathize with us and yet wields significant power over our futures.

By applying Bender's definition, it's clear that all three dimensions of dehumanization occur when human-looking bots conduct interviews. First, given current technological limitations, an AI interviewer is dehumanizing because it necessarily views candidates as mere items or records to be processed – which is to say, as less than fully human. Since AI isn't conscious, AI interviewers can't grasp the human condition or understand what it feels like for a person to be subjected to power dynamics in high-stakes situations. Consequently, an AI interviewer has no idea what it is like to need a job to survive, and it can't grasp the vulnerability involved when candidates discuss achievements and struggles after being asked questions about exhibiting leadership and overcoming challenges. From an AI's point of view, assessing a human for a job is the same thing as evaluating a vehicle for inspection. It relates to humans the same way it does to every other data-processed item.

Second, an AI interviewer is dehumanizing because it acts in ways that deny the full humanity of candidates. More specifically, many of these actions disrespect candidates by showing no regard for their internal point of view and basic desire to express themselves as human beings. That is, while the AI may be trained to speak or nod sympathetically and smoothly, it is still simply assessing the "inputs" from the candidate according to its pre-set rules – tagging specific words or expressions and searching for indications of prioritized behaviors and other identified data to be marked and analyzed.

Looking at things from the recipient's perspective of an AI interview brings us to the third dimension of dehumanization: the candidate's experience of not having their full humanity recognized. For starters, given the high-profile complaints about AI using junk science to analyze facial expressions and speech inputs, it's reasonable for candidates to worry about what conclusions are being drawn and to be concerned about walking into digital traps with a machine that is "smarter" than they are. For example, it's entirely reasonable for candidates to suspect that choosing an avatar interviewer is merely the illusion of inclusion – a sneaky opportunity for employers to acquire information about their views on race and gender and use it as a pseudo-scientific bias test. It's also reasonable for candidates to worry that an AI will hallucinate when writing summaries of what a candidate said or how they performed and misrepresent them. Since companies are turning to AI to save time, they won't be interested in allowing candidates to review an AI report and potentially refute it. After all, these processes are time-consuming.[34]

Furthermore, as candidates frequently lament, it's hard to talk about your experience and skills during an AI interview because the interaction doesn't convey basic respect or feel dignified. While interviews have always been an unequal conversation, with job applicants being forced to bend the knee, now things are worse because they have to bow down to a machine. Obeying a bot that offers no body language feedback is incredibly taxing because it feels unnatural, and the uncertainty triggers second-guessing.

Bots that offer fake emotional labor, like smiling and asking how candidates are doing, add another layer of dehumanization because this engagement is inherently manipulative. It suggests an AI can see a candidate's full humanity–which, again, it can't. Imagine a bot saying to a candidate who happens to be a military veteran, "Tell me about a time when you exhibited leadership." The candidate discusses what it was like to cope with intense and high-pressure combat, but the bot fails to acknowledge the bravery. Bot engineers will likely see the solution as adjusting the programming to add admiring gestures and strong adjectives. But a bot nodding its head in admiration and saying "impressive" in this situation is patronizing and inevitably insufficient. After all, the technology can't truly appreciate what it means for a human to perform military service and put their life on the line.

This marks an additional problem with an example mentioned in the last chapter: Dr. Arthur Garson Jr.'s vision of avatars that look like doctors and talk with patients about their medical concerns and conditions. The good doctor thinks we should be heartened by the prospect of doctor-bots that offer "highly appropriate reactions to the mood and words of the patient." And yet, if such technology is ever created, the responses are likely to be deceptive, dehumanizing gestures that trivialize patient experiences.

There are also the more "engaging" cases, where a bot might be designed to look like a woman and engage by adjusting to the perceived level of feminism of the applicant. Such manipulation creates the false appearance of bonding through solidarity. It injects the false sense that one might be fully "seen" as a member of the tribe or should feel comfortable letting down one's guard as if speaking to a trusted colleague.

Furthermore, if bots suggest common interests and values with minorities, the technology can create misleading impressions about how much companies actually value diversity and inclusion. Finally, there's one more way many candidates will experience AI interviewers as dehumanizing. Sending a bot to perform a job humans should be doing is a symbolic act that sends several dispiriting, potentially reputation-ruining signals. Above all, it suggests companies treat candidates as unworthy of genuine human engagement. It indicates a company doesn't value human connections or human needs, isn't likely interested in promoting trust, loyalty, or long-term commitments, and will ditch a worker for an enhanced AI should the opportunity arise. In short, what kind of future should any worker expect from an employer that already dehumanizes candidates during the interview process? Indeed, while companies will claim that using AI will enable them to conduct more interviews and thus give more candidates a chance at landing a job, people know better. While the process saves a company money and time, the practice will lead to interview creep, where people are, practically speaking, forced to spend an ever-expanding amount of time being dehumanized.[35]

Because AI interviews are dehumanizing, they should be permanently banned. To be clear, we're not saying the interview process is inherently unfair. It can be, depending on how well or poorly the AI represents and analyzes the candidate, and how companies use this information. But the larger issue of dehumanization comes prior, and it should give us enough pause to stop AI interviews before we begin quibbling about the fairness of any given algorithm.[36]

So long as AI isn't sentient, the only way AI interviewers can be designed to make people feel more comfortable talking with them is through manipulation that disguises the dehumanization, but doesn't make it go away. The bottom line, then, is that dehumanization is categorically wrong because it violates our basic human dignity. Human dignity is an inalienable ethical and legal concept that lies at the foundation of human rights. In a civilized society, it's a non-negotiable starting point; everyone deserves it. Without dignity, we lose the basis for giving everyone the self-respect that they deserve. Everyone deserves dignity in a job interview and a job.

Yet again there's a European sensibility to our position. When European regulators decided to ban emotion recognition AI in schools and workplaces with the AI Act, they took into account how poorly the technology has performed. But they didn't classify the restriction as a temporary moratorium that could be lifted if emotion detection technology ever gets more accurate. They prohibited it outright because it's an affront to dignity. There's a crucial lesson for upgrading here: innovation must be constrained by basic human values. If change isn't based on underlying values, ethical violations will ensue, and they won't go unnoticed. Eventually, they'll lead to serious pushback.

ASPIRATIONAL UPGRADES

By now, our position should be clear. AI shouldn't be integrated into interviews. That, however, is not the end of the story. There are other aspects of hiring where AI might be beneficial. Some of them can become upgrades.

Consider resume screening, an area where AI theoretically can excel. As we noted earlier, humans are prone to bias when they quickly sort through vast numbers of applications. In principle, AI systems might do better. In practice, AI resume screeners have yielded mixed results; sometimes, they have amplified the biases they were designed to minimize, if not eliminate. To address this issue, New York City took the initiative and created the first law that requires employers and employment agencies to have some of their AI technology audited for bias. Although the law, which was enacted in 2021 and took effect in 2023, is well-intentioned and guided by thoughtful ideas, some civil society organizations find it unsatisfactory. Some even call it "audit washing" – loophole-filled legislation that only has the veneer of imposing standards, but without actually holding companies accountable.

Ultimately, the NYC law is short-sighted and was destined to be so because of the circumstances. Regulators saw an urgent problem and believed they had to act quickly to create novel legislation that, ideally, could help restore broken trust, but, more realistically, could prevent making a bad situation from becoming worse. They decided mandated audits were the answer, even though the practice of AI audits is in its infancy with few agreed-upon standards or practices. Going forward, the question is whether, over time and through hard work, AI audits can mature and become highly professionalized processes, like financial audits – a process that initially experienced growing pains and, to this day, continues to evolve. The best-case scenario is that best practices emerge that leave the compromises and half-measures that limit the NYC law in the dustbin of history. If so – and that's a big if – this progress would go a long way toward making it possible for AI resume screening and some related activities to be used as upgrades.

To illustrate how much work remains ahead, let's consider some of the main reasons why the NYC law fell short. At face value, Local Law 144 seems refreshingly sensible. It only applies to "automated employment decision tools" (AEDTs) that rely on processes like machine learning and statistical modeling, sparing companies from jumping through new hoops to use low-risk tools like spreadsheets, databases, and calculators. Moreover, the audit has a limited scope and isn't intended to be micro-managerial. It only applies to situations where AI significantly impacts hiring decisions.

Sensibly, the audit focuses on pervasive biases. It examines whether an AI system is designed in a way that has disparate impacts on candidates due to their race/ethnicity, sex, and the intersection of these categories. The law also requires companies using AEDTs in New York City to notify applicants that they will use the technology, offer alternatives and accommodations if another law requires them to do so, and publish particularized summaries of their audits online. Companies that don't comply with these requirements can be fined up to $1,500 for each violation.

The civil society organizations that have objected have raised the following valid criticisms:

1. The narrow scope of the assessment ignores additional federally protected classes, such as disability, age, and sexual orientation.
2. The narrow scope of the assessment fails to examine how people use the technology.
3. The law doesn't require companies to take action if they get poor audit results.
4. Since there's such a small penalty for not complying, it is unlikely to have a big impact.
5. Companies can potentially evade audits by claiming they provide adequate human oversight – even if they use AI to cut candidates during the initial screening.

6. In some cases, auditors can examine test data that may not reflect real-world uses.
7. AI vendors don't have to be independently audited.

This last issue has prompted proposals like law professor Frank Pasquale's suggestion to legally empower the Equal Employment Opportunity Commission (EEOC) to conduct "double or triple-blind tests" that audit all AI hiring tools before vendors make them available to companies. Such pre-emptive regulation, akin to the Food and Drug Administration's approval process for new medications, would involve licensing products to ensure fairness and reliability.

While Pasquale's suggestion is bold, it's ultimately impractical. It doesn't fully account for the fact that AI models constantly evolve. Because these models are continually updated and refined based on new data and algorithmic improvements, their performance and biases can change over time. This means that any approval granted by the EEOC would have a limited shelf-life, and vendors would need to resubmit their tools for evaluation at least every year, and more often when major upgrades to models or data occur, based on emerging industry best practices. Furthermore, implementing such a comprehensive testing and approval process would require the government to provide a significant and costly workforce, which is highly unlikely given the state of politics.

So, given all these limitations, what's the best way to move forward? Unfortunately, there are no easy answers – which is a central tenet of the upgrade ethos. The good news is that looking at the situation from an upgrade perspective helps us better understand how to consider the various ways AI may beneficially be included in employment practices and how to set realistic goals for the future. When you upgrade, you make thoughtful, evidence-based, incremental improvements that build upon existing strengths or critically address constraints that have been impeding progress. The AI-in-hiring surge exemplifies disruption gone awry because it was an attempt to revolutionize an already complex, human-centered process without determining whether the necessary safeguards were even possible. While the traditional, human-centered hiring process is riddled with problems, it nevertheless is constrained by various checks and balances that have evolved over decades, including ongoing efforts from human resource professionals to create best practices and familiar avenues of legal redress. It is also at least a familiar process for people, with many resources available to consult. Hastily changing the status quo without proper oversight could only be a recipe for sowing distrust and introducing too much uncertainty for all parties.

Upgrading requires patience, vigilance, and a willingness to learn from missteps. It's the opposite of disruptive "solutions" that offer the false or unproven promise of immediate, positive, and radical change. If the community of technologists and policymakers exploring how to develop tools like AI audits embraces the upgrading ethos, it will need to aim for gradual, incremental improvements: consensus processes and appropriate standards for the audits and the auditors rather than rushing to implement sweeping changes. It will need to build on existing strengths and best practices from related fields while thoughtfully adapting them to the unique challenges of AI systems with recognition of the particular challenges of the employment context. It will need to find creative ways to motivate committed collaboration among diverse stakeholders, including policymakers, regulators, vendors, employers, subject-matter experts, civil society organizations, and impacted communities. There's no way to sugar-coat it. Figuring out how to create clear, fair, and effective guidelines and standards means having difficult and ongoing conversations about the issues that make the NYC law so contentious.

As we've seen, disruptive approaches include automating almost all points of the hiring process – application submission, resume screening, interviews, and potentially even feedback. Each aspect required different technology. While some might be founded on solid science, others were not. Each step raised significant challenges, had significant impacts, and inevitably carried the risk of harm.

Upgrades would instead have a much narrower focus. They would zero in on the clearest and most pressing pressure points and consider the most proven available technologies, with clearly thought-out minimum performance standards. If companies are, in fact, receiving applications at an order of magnitude beyond their ability to reasonably cope, they have to address the problem. AI-based resume screening is likely to be one of the realistic options to consider, and its risks and benefits should be weighed relative to other possibilities. Again, doing so means recognizing that upgrading resume screening is upgrading a crucial component of a hiring system. Given the nature of that system, there's no shortcut for fast-forwarding to algorithmic analysis and recommendations. The upgrading path requires slowly and carefully setting up appropriate standards, audit practices, auditor certification, and other controls.

While AI vendors may be running their own audits, and some, in good faith, surely believe they are already offering quality technology, that's not enough. The checks and balances for these systems are still too new. They're evolving without consensus and in the absence of best practices. These issues mean we're not ready for AI to be inserted into hiring systems. Given the high stakes of hiring and the historical legacy of discrimination in employment, the idea that human judgment, flawed as it may be, could be replaced with novel yet insufficiently verified AI systems was always going to prompt skepticism. You can't solve such deep problems that have such a profound impact on people's lives so easily, especially when many people have no idea how AI works, and the legal landscape is largely uncharted territory.

Ultimately, the goal shouldn't just be to make the underlying technology of the AI system more fair, accountable, and effective – although any given system should certainly meet these requirements. We should aim to upgrade the hiring process as a whole in ways that leverage the strength of reliable technology options while also preserving the essential humanity of the applicants.

CHAPTER NINE

Cybersecurity

The Land of the True Upgraders

It is hard to think of a high-tech field more synonymous with upgrading than cybersecurity. The often-unseen army of systems administrators working in the IT back offices and server farms of America may not get the pomp and hype of their VC-backed brethren in high-priced startups, but they help digital life as we know it actually work. Cybersecurity provides a prime example of how upgraders straddle the divide between the stagnation of the status quo and the dangers of unproven, untested, and often unworkable innovations. These cybersecurity experts are not luddites; they are not opposed to the technologies they tinker on day in and out. Instead, they are upgraders, installing incremental, evidence-based improvements to known vulnerabilities, always testing for small, provable benefits in a framework that assumes that nearly every change will also come at a cost. Cybersecurity shows technological development at its best, its most stable. Sadly, this also frames the technology in the way least sexy to investors, pundits, and politicians, prioritizing a proven track record for success over grand promises of easy fixes for the future.

Whether we oversee one electronic device or thousands, we all are the cybersecurity managers of at least some portion of our digital lives. You may never help design a new airplane or a new type of cryptocurrency, but we all spend at least a little time thinking about how to keep our devices safe. And the first rule of nearly any cybersecurity training is this: install the upgrades. Whether it's our laptop's operating system or a favorite smartphone app, modern life means a constant stream of small tweaks to the software we rely on most. Sometimes, those upgrades may add a new feature; others could change a design; but, frequently, they include improvements to known vulnerabilities in our software. And these fixes are crucial. While it's impossible to get precise data on the full universe of cybersecurity threats the public faces, according to a recent analysis of ransomware (a particularly devastating type of attack where users' data is held hostage), 76 percent of cases involved flaws that had been identified three or more years prior.[1] In this cat-and-mouse game between hackers and device owners, the failure to upgrade, to constantly tweak software to respond to newly identified threats, leaves our data at risk. And if every user internalized the upgrader ethos, vigilantly installing new upgrades as they were released, the constant string of hacks in the news would dry up. Sadly, many users, perhaps a majority, are slow to apply these crucial patches, providing a veritable roadmap for would-be attackers.

Those news stories about hacks big and small, the friends who've told you about losing data or money, might leave you thinking that the cybersecurity fight has been lost and that the hackers have won. In fact, it's just the opposite. The scale of modern hacking reveals the extent to which we're willing to entrust our most valuable assets to digital systems. If not for the success of cybersecurity systems to give us an overall high level of safety, to help us believe that hacks and attacks are relatively rare, we'd never be willing to adopt these systems in the first place. And perception is in many ways worse than reality. Cybersecurity suffers from asymmetric attention, the reality that this core set of protections only makes the news and becomes top of mind when it fails. No one reports on the password too complex to guess or the encryption too strong to break. No one hears about the hacker who tried to log into a system from overseas, but was blocked. These protections are the sewer line of our digital lives, silently transporting away a river of unwanted items, both easily forgotten when it works and a source of deep anger and disgust when it breaks.

ASSUMING FAILURE TO BUILD SUCCESS

So many of the poorly designed innovations we detail in this book start with a simple assumption that a single change can solve a vexing social problem. Again and again, we see innovators overselling their inventions, claiming that a single app or algorithm can somehow fix deep problems rooted in entrenched inequity, outdated infrastructure, or any number of other multifaceted, interconnected systems. They move fast, they break things, but they rarely fix the problem. But cybersecurity professionals know just the opposite. Given the nature of cybersecurity threats and attackers' constant adaptation, no one change will ever end the threat of device breaches and data loss. You can build the best digital lock on the planet for your system's front door, but attackers will still look for ways to climb the walls and pry open the windows. Instead, cybersecurity professionals know that it takes an array of protections to thwart would-be hackers, and that every new change to security practices is as much of a threat as it is a benefit. They don't just put a better lock on the door – they build a better door.

For those of you who are already experts in cybersecurity, none of the philosophies and design principles we discuss here will be novel, but for those new to the field, it may mean radically redesigning your assumptions about good technical designs. A good starting point for this change in perspective is defense-in-depth. Unlike most innovators, who work to simply build one system that works well enough to disrupt the status quo, cybersecurity engineers typically build systems with the assumption that any one protection on its own is likely to fail.[2] Defense-in-depth layers on new levels of independent, modular security with the expectation that each new part will be most effective when used in addition to, not in lieu of, legacy systems. Take, for example, the role of new AI tools in cybersecurity, where we see innovators turning to untested deployments of AI as a substitute for existing systems in many areas of society, including everything from forcing customers to speak to an AI customer support agent to relying on AI to determine eligibility for bail after arrest. In contrast, most cybersecurity professionals are incrementally adopting AI defense tools that work alongside existing technologies, leveraging the newest forms of machine learning while also running more traditional reviews. Instead of relying exclusively on AI to detect suspicious network activity, a tell-tale sign that an attacker has hacked into your network, security experts might rely on both human and AI review, adopting the belt-and-suspender models.[3]

The intentional layering of safeguards seeks to both avoid single points of failure and avoid propagation of new failure (where the failure of one system can then knock out another, and another).[4] A good cybersecurity expert "seeks to limit a failure's effect to the extent practicable and, in doing so, minimize introducing new loss possibilities." Imagine how we'd treat some of the systems we've examined earlier in this book if we used that same mindset. How eager would an investor be to put money into cryptocurrency if they focused on avoiding the creation of a single point of critical failure in a novel technical system? Hard to imagine a world where Bitcoin was worth $100, let alone $100,000, especially when it'd take just one error in the underlying software, one major change in regulation, to wipe out its value.[5]

These upgraders may start their failure-focused analysis with the postulate that no one innovation can be the whole security solution, but they look next to how to mitigate the harm when these failures inevitably take place. Compartmentalization is a strategy older than computing itself. In wartime, large, highly sensitive endeavors would be walled off into various compartmentalized groups, with teams working in isolation on a discrete part of the wider task. These limits mitigate the extent to which any one spy or data breach could compromise the mission as a whole.[6] Analog compartmentalization often meant keeping project groups widely separated, such as when many of the world's leading physicists worked in the deserts of New Mexico, the valleys of Tennessee, and the industrial sites of Chicago during the invention of the atomic bomb.[7] Compartmentalization today is far less grandiose. Organizations can easily wall off data access rights and administrative controls, segregating the most sensitive data to the most restricted groups of users. Of course, like many cybersecurity tools, there are tradeoffs for other areas, such as ease of use. But cautious upgraders and systems administrators fight every day to adopt these precautions into the fabric of new systems.

More recently, these compartmentalization practices have evolved into a more robust set of zero trust architecture principles, expanding protections beyond mere limitations on data access.[8] Zero trust architecture helps implement security across large, complex, interconnected technical systems by reducing the harm that an attacker can do with the access they are able to obtain. For example, a university might operate an array of networks, everything from unsecured guest Wi-Fi to highly secured systems for sensitive research. Zero trust architecture helps ensure that the casual visitor who is given access to a low-security network isn't able to then misuse that access to gain a foothold in a more sensitive system. It makes sure that those seeking to access data are treated with a suitable level of distrust every step along the way, complementing more traditional data compartmentalization. Any upgrader who uses zero trust architecture would know that building a cutting-edge digital mote at the edge of your network doesn't mean you can give anyone who makes it through free range over the systems inside – you still need to inspect who they are and what they're doing.

Compartmentalization and zero trust architecture help reduce the attack surface for a piece of information, improving its security by reducing the number of ways it can be accessed and the number of people who can potentially compromise it. But the best way to prevent a piece of data from being taken is to not have it in the first place. This is where the philosophy of privacy by design comes into play.[9] Privacy by design "requires data protection to be a built-in feature of information systems."[10] It is an inherently non-disruptive set of design philosophies that reduce the potential risk to the public every step along the way, making a series of upgrades to data collection, storage, and security practices to mitigate the risk of cybersecurity breach.[11] Privacy by design practitioners will constantly update their privacy practices, systematically reviewing whether they are asking for more data than is needed, if that data is being stored in an appropriate way, and how many people have access. As a holistic design philosophy, it weaves together so many of the cybersecurity themes that resonate with upgraders, but with a focus on harm reduction in the event of a successful attack, rather than focusing on thwarting the attack itself. And the methodology goes beyond mere compartmentalization, since it often reduces the storage of data before users even get to the step of deciding who should be able to access it. Crucially, this is an approach that can't just be applied once in the design life of a system. You can't set privacy by design and forget it. Instead, this approach requires those building or maintaining a system to constantly evaluate what data is being taken in and how it's being stored. And anytime a new feature or update causes a change in these practices, privacy practitioners will re-evaluate if they're doing the best job possible to mitigate the threat to their users.

INVESTING IN PROVEN RETURNS

The reason so many upgraders flock to cybersecurity isn't just a quirk of history or personality types: it's a reflection of the underlying incentives within the industry. For engineers working on the product side of the venture-capital-backed startups that create so many of the most dubious innovations, there is a massive financial incentive to get something, anything, to market. Building popular engagement with a new product, no matter how technically dubious, raises the hopes of a quick acquisition, stock option liquidity, and a huge financial boost. As one startup CEO put it: "Your product doesn't have to be perfect when it first launches, and it doesn't have to be the best. It just has to be acceptable."[12] In contrast, for cybersecurity staff, there is no real upside to rapid change. When some flashy new innovation is launched, the best security scenario continues to be the absence of a hack or a systems failure. Simply tinkering with the status quo is often the gold standard of security success. Cybersecurity experts can't afford to be luddites and ignore the way their threats and resources are constantly changing, but they also can't afford to take unmitigated risks based solely on the hope that a new innovation will do more good than harm.

Take, for example, the National Institute of Standards and Technologies (NIST) Risk Management Framework for Information Systems and Organizations. The dry 164-standards document might make even the most hardened hackers start to fall asleep, but what the document lacks in narrative drive, it more than makes up for in prudent, risk-informed innovation management.[13]

> NIST's risk management strategy makes explicit the threats, assumptions, constraints, priorities, trade-offs, and risk tolerance used for making investment and operational decisions. This strategy includes the strategic-level decisions and considerations for how senior leaders and executives are to manage security and privacy risks (including supply chain risks) to organizational operations, organizational assets, individuals, other organizations, and the Nation.[14]

It's staggering just how wildly this type of meticulous, evidence-based framework differs from so many of the untested, unproven innovations we detail earlier in this book. In many other areas of technological development, innovators not only fail to adequately weigh the shortcomings of their technology, but they also refuse to acknowledge that there are any downsides at all! Innovators don't talk about marginally improving the efficiency of processes or delivering these sorts of clear improvements to users; they talk about simplistic solutions that they promise will "revolutionize" our lives, but often leave us only wondering what all of the hype was about.

According to Bruce Schneier, one of the country's leading cybersecurity experts and a public policy lecturer at the Harvard Kennedy School: "Advances in security happen continually, but slowly. All new ideas should be treated with skepticism initially."[15] In fact, the earliest adopters of novel cybersecurity technologies often pay an innovation tax, providing the case studies that demonstrate how a novel system can fail. The most prudent upgraders seek to stand a step behind the leading edge, implementing proven fixes, and letting others gamble with more experimental approaches.

University of Minnesota Computer Science Professor Andrew Odlyzko describes this general reluctance to adopt novel cybersecurity innovations as the "muddle through" approach. "Muddling" may never exactly sound sexy to consumers or policymakers, but its benefits are far more compelling than the name would suggest. According to Odlyzko:

> [O]ver the last few decades we have seen just a gradual increase in resources devoted to cybersecurity. Action has been dominated by minor patches. No fundamental reengineering has taken place ... Cyberinfrastructure is becoming more important. Hence intensifying efforts to keep it sufficiently secure to let the world function is justified. But this process can continue to be gradual. There is no need to panic or make drastic changes, as the threats are manageable, and not much different from those that we cope with in the physical realm.[16]

Cybersecurity helps dismantle the myth that in order to prioritize or value a project, you have to invest in disruptive innovations. Instead, even as cybersecurity has become increasingly central to increasingly large parts of our essential infrastructure, the upgrade ethos has persevered.

Another core differentiator of cybersecurity from other forms of computer engineering is the differences in design tolerances. With cybersecurity, the consequences of a single failure can be exponentially higher than with other areas of tech. Imagine you are trying to log onto your bank's mobile app. If you are able to log on without any issues 99.9 percent of the time, that would exceed most of our expectations for reliability. Sure, it's annoying that 1 in 1,000 time when you can't get into your account right away. Maybe you'd need to relaunch the app or restart your phone, but in the end, the inconvenience would likely be pretty trivial, and you might go years without coming across a similar hiccup. But let's imagine you log into your account one time and you find that thousands of dollars are missing, stolen by a hacker who forced their way into your account. Even if you still knew it was a 1 in 1,000 chance that it could happen again, it'd feel less like a hiccup and more like a five-alarm security fire.

When you suffer just one cybersecurity failure, it can upend your finances, corrupt your files, expose your most closely guarded secrets, and bring your business operations to a screeching train wreck of a halt. This is the corollary to cybersecurity's lack of incentive to focus on unproven upside: unlimited downside risk for each new change, whether the loss of data, money, or even a functioning company. This limited upside, unlimited downside model lets upgraders thrive, investing proportional attention on new innovations based on their proven return on investment. It's only rational to think that many of the product engineers who are rushing to innovate half-baked apps today would have a change of philosophy if they operated with similar consequences for any glitch in their code.

HONESTY IS THE BEST UPGRADE POLICY

One of the distinguishing features of upgraders generally, and cybersecurity experts specifically, is that they focus on the human part of any complex socio-technical equation. Throughout this book we've detailed examples of well-intentioned innovations that went off the rails when they hit the not-so-minor stumbling block of real-world behavior. Human beings are not some trivial, malleable factor that can simply be re-engineered to meet the design parameters of a novel piece of software. Instead, human habits are often the single most inflexible part of any novel technical system. Sure, people can learn to use new software, they can take on new habits, but only when those products meet their needs on terms that are convenient and helpful for them.

Take, for example, passwords. Billions of dollars and countless hours of labor have been invested in improving the security of the passwords that safeguard our finances, communications, photos, and more. Cryptographers have developed novel ways to hash and verify passwords. Mobile device makers have rolled out new protocols to store those passwords, using facial recognition and two-factor tokens. And IT professionals have consistently fought to adopt stricter, more secure parameters for the passwords we use, especially on our most sensitive accounts. And still, every day hackers are able to penetrate millions of accounts secured by this cutting-edge technology. How? We tell hackers our passwords.[17]

It's almost never intentional, but the most common way that attackers are able to extract our credentials and access our systems is when we give them the keys to the digital castle. Sometimes it's a phone scammer who pretends to be an account rep for your bank, telling you that he's calling to help you avoid being scammed, all while actually scamming you. This isn't an example plucked randomly from the internet – it happened to my (Albert's) mother just two days before I wrote this passage. Her accounts had been secured with a sophisticated password, kept in a military-grade password manager. And even better, she also had two-factor authentication enabled, the security safeguard that requires users to enter a unique, cryptographically generated code that is produced seemingly at random each time you try to access an account. It would have taken decades of computational power to brute force the code, guessing every possible permutation, decades by which time the code would have long expired. But it just took her a few seconds to read the code to the imposter account rep, helping bring about the very hack she was struggling to stop.

My mother is far from the outlier: she is emblematic of the vast majority[18] of the nearly million cybercrime victims in the United States each year.[19] And cybersecurity experts have understood this for decades. Yes, they invest in technical safeguards to mitigate the risks of account attacks, but no cybersecurity response is complete without investment in end-user education and monitoring. But beyond telling people about what steps they can take to prevent a hack, cybersecurity experts have to wage a running war against users' worst impulses, especially for corporate data. According to one survey, "over 90% of employees who admitted undertaking a range of unsecure actions during work activities knew that their actions would increase risk to the organization but did so anyway."[20] This makes cybersecurity even more unwelcoming to innovators. Any new disruptive change in processes or technology is likely to be consistently circumvented by the very staff whose help is needed to make those systems work. Instead, upgrades need to build on existing user routines in a way that adds security without upending work.

These same pressures have helped to mitigate the rollout of some of the newest AI systems in cybersecurity. Even the most ardent proponents of new AI-powered tools in the cybersecurity space recognize that none of these systems will ever be an alternative for the human-centered responses at the core of traditional cybersecurity. In practice, this is leading a growing number of cybersecurity officials to officially jettison the technosolutionism of innovation and adopt "human centric design principles."[21]

These principles recognize that an adversary who can leverage an error in human decision-making will almost always triumph over an entity with superior technology. Some authors describe this approach as the "Byzantine problem," the name of which is rooted in likely-spurious descriptions of the sacking of Constantinople. In the classic telling of the battle, the various triumphant Ottoman generals acted at cross purposes as they neared victory, overly assured that their technical/logistical superiority would guarantee a win on the battlefield.[22] Instead, their overconfidence was supposedly their undoing. In more modern times, the "Byzantine problem continues to demonstrate to this day that even apparent superiority does not eliminate the human factor."[23] AI will continue to play a role in many areas of tech, and even in isolated parts of cybersecurity, but even the most cutting-edge algorithm is no replacement for good human security judgment.

This human-centered design philosophy also naturally lends itself to a human-centered investment philosophy, further expanding the upgrader mindset. With human-centered investment, cybersecurity managers invest in products that can incrementally improve the efficiency of human processes and augment human decision-making, while acknowledging the centrality and immutability of human cognition. Yes, you can train human beings, you can empower them with technology and procedures, but ultimately human beings will make the same sorts of mistakes. We will trust people we shouldn't, accept emails as authentic when they're fraudulent, take shortcuts when we know there's a risk, and hide mistakes when they happen. These trends can be mitigated and managed, but they can never be fully escaped.

CONCLUSION

Cybersecurity may offer a refreshing departure from the cycle of hype and collapse that marks more innovation-prone disciplines, but it's far from a utopia. Cybersecurity experts come with the same breadth of attitudes and aptitudes seen across other large industries. Yes, even the rare destructive innovators. But what sets cybersecurity apart is all of the structural incentives that, on the whole, push those in the field toward cautious, evidence-based upgrades. There isn't some secret mindset to adopt, or some exotic philosophy to absorb, these are simply technical experts responding rationally to the incentives of their environment. If we want to see more upgraders in other industries, the solution is simple: change the innovation incentives.

CHAPTER TEN

The Upgrader's Mindset

AVOIDING THE INNOVATION TRAP

Throughout the book, we've delved into different facets of how innovation has failed us and how upgrading can get it right. Of course, the battle between upgraders and dysfunctional innovation stretches far beyond our guiding examples, impacting nearly every facet of public life. Nevertheless, these teachable moments are a promising start. They highlight the most predictable patterns of how innovation lets us down and how upgrades are overlooked.

Looking at our case studies as a whole, a big picture emerges. We need upgrades most when an existing organization or technical system must be preserved and strengthened and when new technology can provide targeted and responsible interventions that offer incremental improvement. Upgrades are most needed when disruptive changes would pose the greatest social risk. It may be fine to innovate with a relatively new tool or toy, such as a novel app that is struggling to gain market share and find its audience. But the more people rely on a piece of infrastructure, whether it's a municipality's traffic light system or an established social media venture, the greater the cost and social jeopardy to disruptive changes. When we gamble on changes to the essential services people rely on in emergencies or to navigate daily necessities, the less tolerable these sorts of erratic changes are. These established institutions cannot risk the inevitable obsolescence of inertia and inaction. But they also cannot gamble with their users' sense of trust and reliability. Instead, the way forward is to chart a path between these two sets of calamities, building on the best practices of the upgraders.

ROOTED IN REALITY

One of the things that most starkly sets upgraders apart from the innovation culture is honestly accepting the limitations of what can be fixed. During the early stages of the Covid-19 pandemic, corporate and political leaders faced an intolerable choice: (1) keep society open and let more people get sick and die; or (2) severely restrict schools, businesses, travel, and nearly every other aspect of our lives to keep the virus at bay. But innovators offered a third way, a way to use technology to stay open and stay safe. The catch is that it never worked.

Innovators turned to tools like thermal imaging scanners, trying to treat fever-detection as a reliable proxy for Covid-19 infection. But upgraders knew this was a deadly mistake when asymptomatic individuals would go undetected. Even worse, scanners simply were incapable of reliably measuring multiple people from a distance and could easily be thrown off by sun exposure or drinking a hot beverage. In contrast, upgraders argued in favor of masking and other less technological measures that proved more effective in slowing the virus. Yes, these more invasive measures came at a cost, but the difference is that these upgraders were honest about what our choices and tradeoffs truly were.

To be clear, upgraders don't reflexively reject all paradigm-shifting innovations. We readily admit that society would not have made progress without mRNA vaccines. They are a lifesaver – an innovation success story. And yet the pandemic drive for innovation was also a major problem. It got in the way of seizing better opportunities, ones for upgrades. The turn to digital contact tracing apps, a completely new use of personal phones, was a disaster – and a foreseeable one at that. To avoid the privacy concerns of tracking GPS locations and saving the information in a centralized database, the United States used Bluetooth technology and a decentralized and anonymized approach to sharing information. Since the technology was calibrated for measuring the distance between people – whether people were consistently less than six feet apart for ten or more minutes – the data was constantly distorted by everything from a building's materials to the model of phone you used. Bluetooth could crudely estimate distance, but not real risk. Even when the software got distance right, being six feet from someone is very different if you're outdoors, indoors, or have a wall in between. But if we had focused on upgrades, we could have taken another path. We could have invested more money in human contact tracers, upgrading their data and tools to make them even more efficient disease detectives.

Crucially, upgraders always ask the same question: whether there is a less disruptive, evidence-based alternative to innovation. Consider the modern plague of self-checkout kiosks.[1] Stores were sold three things the technology never delivered: decreased business costs, decreased theft, and faster checkouts. Why aren't companies profiting from self-checkout? It's because the staffing savings are dwarfed by the cost of purchasing and servicing the technology. Customers aren't better off either. Not only are customers moving through lines slower, but they're getting agitated when the machines don't work. Large items can be hard to scan. The devices don't always recognize barcodes, and not every item has one. The screens can have glitches, and error-prone anti-theft sensors can alarm customers when they load shopping bags in the wrong area. Customers are incredibly frustrated with the most innovative checkout systems, which use an array of computer vision cameras to track every item going in your cart from various angles. The technology routinely makes mistakes, adding the wrong things or overcharging customers.[2] And yet, when we started writing this book, leading grocery stores were experimenting with surveillance carts that track every purchase.[3]

Compounding the failure, customers steal more without a human present,[4] fueling a cycle of increased customer surveillance and growing staff confrontations.[5] Stores are trying to cure one technological failure with another, deploying increasingly invasive AI-infused surveillance technologies to fight the shoplifting surge they created.[6] All this surveillance degrades the quality of the shopping experience, evoking the unpleasantness of an airport security check. Recently, the national pharmacy chain Walgreens admitted that all of the security and surveillance installed in its stores has turned customers off, reducing sales, and prompting the company to reverse course.[7] Rather than spending millions on technologies that alienate customers and fail to prevent theft, stores could have done the one thing labor advocates, customers, and workers have asked for years: hire and train enough staff. Instead of gutting staffing to boost short-term profits and cannibalize long-term growth, stores could simply ensure there are sufficient workers equipped to assist customers in locating items, managing conflicts, and providing a more efficient and enjoyable shopping experience. This approach addresses the short-term issues associated with self-checkouts and prevents the long-term risks of invasive surveillance and privacy concerns.

Upgrades are often technological, but they don't always have to be. Indeed, sometimes the best course of action is to avoid technological temptation. Not every upgrade is perfect, of course, but by prioritizing precautionary governance, upgrading is often the best way to promote trust, fundamental rights, and realistically tackle pressing problems.

STARTING WITH THE PROBLEM

The starting point of any upgrade plan is need. What problem needs to be addressed? What needs are unmet? And what solution will prove inadequate over time? Upgrades thus begin the process of sustainable change-making with a focus on what changes are needed, whereas innovators too often start by asking what solutions can be readily offered. The planning process for innovators focuses too much on what technologies are easy to build, or what new policies are easy to build, even when their real-world implementation causes chaos. This approach perverts the entire process, sending companies and countries alike chasing after changes that won't serve their interests at all.

As we noted in our home security chapter, so many of the surveillance innovations that have been sold in recent years start from the fact that it's cheaper and easier than ever to build and network together increasingly invasive cameras and sensors, monitoring more and more of our communities. But these surveillance vendors missed the most crucial question. They never asked whether the use of more cameras actually addresses any underlying need. The public never yearned for surveillance or cried out for cameras. Instead, they wanted safety. And, to date, camera vendors have never been able to provide compelling proof that more cameras create more safety. In fact, we have more footage of home break-ins than ever before and more video clips to spread fear and promote surveillance products. What's missing is solid evidence that the products actually help. In contrast, upgrades would take a safety-first approach and look at what products and strategies are proven to work. Low-tech solutions like better locks, better bars, and secure package storage can make homes much safer for a fraction of the price of complex camera systems. They may never capture the splashy images of a home break-in, but they can actually prevent one!

Similarly, in Chapter 3 on "The Crypto Con," we highlighted how crypto innovators allowed wishful thinking to lead them astray. Crypto is based on a non-trivial advancement in distributed data storage. And yet advocates worked backward from that solution to justify what problems they could solve. Proceeding this way, the solutions never materialized. Providing banking to those on the margins of society, forced to operate with cash today, may be a wonderful ambition. But there's almost nothing about the real-world deployment of cryptocurrency that makes this laudable goal a reality. Instead, the language of financial inclusion is co-opted by crypto backers as a way to justify the increasingly intolerable economic and environmental cost of their technologies. Upgraders, instead, would begin by looking at what changes unbanked individuals themselves have called out for and what barriers exist today in incumbent institutions. Small changes to bank record-keeping requirements and identification policies here in the United States could do far more than any cryptocurrency to ensure that even the most destitute have access to affordable, secure financial accounts.

One of the most expensive and calamitous innovations in recent history has to be Mark Zuckerberg's Metaverse misadventure. Billions of dollars down the drain and years of wasted work, all to build a product that no one ever wanted. Sure, the company was able to assemble a slightly snazzier video game – make the graphics gleam brighter and the action more immersive. But they failed on their own terms. No one is donning a Meta headset to have a work meeting or spend time with family. No one thinks of their true home being in the company's ill-defined and poorly designed Metaverse platform. And, crucially, who wants to? Instead, Meta burned through enough money to cure several cancers or feed millions of people just to build an overpriced toy that a relatively small handful of fans will buy.

HUMANIZING CHANGE

We're emphasizing a point that too easily gets lost in discussions about technology and innovation. Upgraders *humanize the change cycle*, first beginning with the public's needs, then carefully connecting their analysis of any new development to the way that it will actually impact human beings. To stick with the Metaverse example for a moment, Zuckerberg and his enablers didn't merely fail to prioritize solutions to pressing problems. They focused on technologies that most people would never adopt, even if the hardware and software worked as projected. Imagine that the Metaverse worked as seamlessly as was promised at the start of this quixotic quest – offering a truly immersive digital environment where you could spend time with colleagues, friends, and loved ones. Even if such a digital space existed, the proposal seems utterly tone-deaf at a time when people are craving analog, in-person connection, not more time on more sophisticated screens.[8]

Countless educators paralleled this *dehumanization* with the efforts to expand remote proctoring during the Covid-19 pandemic. Educators rightfully feared the reliability of high-stakes remote testing. But rather than questioning if high-stakes testing could ever be salvaged under the circumstances, all too many doubled-down on student surveillance as a destructive, high-tech Band-Aid. The situation was a foreseeable disaster – not just because of the ease with which tech-savvy students could circumvent testing controls, but because of the human cost of constant student tracking. Who wants hours of recordings taken from the most intimate of spaces that invades every sliver of the scant privacy that you have left? Many found the experience so upsetting that it not only further degraded the testing experience, but it also compounded the trauma of the pandemic's cramped living and remote-learning conditions. Indeed, even if such technology had been able to preserve the reliability of tests, it would have come at far too high a cost to students' mental health to be tolerable. In contrast, the upgrade approach would look for technological investments that could mitigate the harms students were experiencing (like social isolation), not compound them. The main goal would be to prioritize the health of human beings, not over-emphasize the integrity of testing regimes.

In contrast to these costly and failed innovations, the cybersecurity experts we profiled in Chapter 9, "The Land of the True Upgraders," take the opposite, human-centered approach in how they conceptualize both risks and solutions. To these upgraders, privacy-by-design principles and other best practices are rooted in a realistic assessment of how human beings will behave when faced with a wide array of attacks. Faulty memory, bad judgment, honest mistakes, and outright corruption are the building blocks of humanistic cybersecurity, incrementally deploying evidence-based solutions to tackle the vulnerabilities that employees, users, and other stakeholders reveal through their actions every day.

PROPORTIONAL BENEFIT

Another central dimension of the upgraders' outlook is a focus on proportional benefits. Not every change comes without a cost, and sometimes upgrades can gradually reshape the landscape over time, like a river carving a massive valley over the millennia. But upgraders will steer clear of reckless novelties, innovations that offer changes, but not actual improvements. Some of the most egregious examples of this sort of harmful technological changes come from an industry that often sells itself as "synonymous with innovation": car companies.[9]

Let's go back to the opening of the book and consider a series of recent innovations in car controls. *Vi Bilägare*, a Swedish car magazine, tested how well drivers could perform routine car tasks while driving at high speed.[10] The outcome was sobering, but unsurprising, for upgraders. Drivers in a "17-year-old Volvo that only has physical controls" managed to outperform "11 modern cars with touchscreens ... from BMW to Mercedes to Nissan to, of course, Tesla."[11] We all intuitively know it's easier to manipulate fixed-position nobs by touch compared to a digital screen where controls constantly move, so why didn't the innovators behind these multi-billion dollar brands?

These findings go beyond ergonomics and safety. Car companies aren't giving customers a feature that makes their lives better. They're simply stuck in the innovation Zeitgeist. For marketers, more screens means more advanced, which means more desirable. And the automotive obsession with novelty is quite old. When the 69 Camaro hit dealerships, Chevrolet proclaimed: "What the younger generation's coming to."[12] In the 1990s, readers saw ads touting: "Not your father's Oldsmobile!" Touchscreens are just the latest icon of innovation, signaling to digital natives that this car was designed for them. Replacing analog dials and knobs with digital displays may be a very effective way of communicating novelty to younger drivers (and older ones who want to feel young). But it doesn't change the fact that, ultimately, the technology is a terrible way of controlling a vehicle.

When car manufacturers removed nobs, they prioritized perception over reality – false markers of tangible benefit over genuine advancements in reliability. They want people to see their products as so sophisticated as to be perfect for the digital age – even if the machines actually perform worse.[13] Their insatiable hunger for novelty led to both a figurative and literal car crash. Indeed, the situation is so bad that the head of Hyundai Design has acknowledged the digital danger and praised the new design of one recent model for intentionally including physical buttons.[14]

DANGER, INNOVATION AHEAD!

By this point in the book, we hope we are preaching to the newly converted, an army of upgraders who have been won over the gospel of evidence-based, incremental change. But we know we remain in the minority, taking up arms against a sea of innovations, and by opposing, not always ending them. That is why we want to conclude with the key to navigating the innovations that come next, giving you the warning signs you can spot to stay away from destructive disruptions and prompt yourself to seek out upgrades instead. Walking away, you may be surprised just how often the upgrader mindset can help you find better, more sustainable solutions for the biggest problems we face.

The biggest innovation warning sign is when a product would fail even when it works as promised. Frequently, upgraders can see that even if an innovation is deployed exactly as planned, the underlying technology or system can't actually solve the problem that backers are putting it forward to address. Take the unfounded thermal imaging and Bluetooth proximity data used to detect Covid-19. Even if these products worked as well as humanly possible, the data collected would never provide a medically reliable guide to who was sick or at risk. Even the most accurate body temperature scan couldn't accurately label Covid-19 status, and Bluetooth signals simply could never tell if you were exposed to a virus. Yet we still wasted countless millions (and vital time) trying to make these ill-fated innovations work. Upgraders always try to start from a point of pragmatism, recognizing that some facts simply can't be changed through spin and wishful thinking.

A second major warning sign is when innovation is more centered on disruption than improvement. For example, cryptocurrency backers excitedly claim their technology makes global money transfer possible, holding it up as a solution for the unbanked. But there are enormous barriers for those who want to use the highly unstable financial innovation for those purposes. And existing financial instruments give far easier, more effective, and less expensive ways to do the exact same thing. While cryptocurrency could radically reshape the modern economy, it's fundamentally incapable of making it better. Upgraders see disruption as the unfortunate and often avoidable byproduct of change, not the point of it.

A third warning sign for potential innovations is when you see a product is in search of a solution. Young startups are notorious for investing in an innovation first and rationalizing why people should buy it second. This build first, understand later mindset leads innovators to reverse-engineer a rationale for selling the product after it has already been made. When the public sees a young firm radically reshaping its sales pitch, trying a new narrative to sell the same system, you should see a bright warning light flashing.

A jarring example is CENTEGIX, the Atlanta-based surveillance vendor that developed location-tracking technology with the promise of identifying mass shooters in schools.[15] Amid the Covid-19 upheaval, they rebranded their CrisisAlert product as ContactAlert, claiming the same Bluetooth location tracking could magically function as a contact tracing tool.[16] The same product with the same limited functionality repackaged as a different type of innovation. The constant vacillation about what problem the company was trying to solve signaled that it wasn't ever good at solving any of them. Upgraders can reshape and refine systems and products over time, but they don't flail around searching for a rationalization for why you should buy what they already built.

The fourth warning is to beware of those bearing crystal balls. Companies have long sold products they claimed could predict the future. From predictive policing to the latest iteration of mental health screening tools, markets are bombarded with products seeking to solve problems before they start. But regardless of what technology or methodology is used, attempts to forecast the operations of large, complex systems are often doomed to fail. One does not need to understand the mechanics of novel forms of machine learning or delve deeply into the realm of quantum computing to grow justifiably suspicious of any innovator who claims to foresee events before they occur. Upgraders constantly try to learn from the past, but they never have the hubris to think they can know the future.

A fifth warning sign is an outsized return on investment. Innovations generally are sold with the promise that they can deliver a reward far exceeding that of known options. In contrast, evidence-based upgrades often refine and optimize proven responses. Anytime a novel solution is said to perform an order of magnitude better, and not just marginally more effectively, without an explicit acknowledgment of the risks and consequences of failure, the proposal should draw outsized suspicion. Upgraders looks for the sure thing, the proven payout, the investment that may not "go to the moon" in crypto speak, but will never come crashing back to Earth.

A sixth warning sign is ignoring the existing legal landscape. Startups are notorious for launching products without the sort of legal due diligence expected from more established firms. And in highly regulated fields like finance, housing, and healthcare, the consequences can be dire. Even as much of internet commerce surged in the regulatory vacuum of the early 2000s, the proprietors of Roommates.com showed that the broad legal protections afforded website developers had its limits. The site had rapidly grown by offering users the ability to search for roommates by numerous criteria, including gender and sexual orientation.[17] Suddenly the website's innovative screening tools put it directly in the crosshairs of the Fair Housing Act, the 1960s-era civil rights law that bans discrimination in housing. While tech companies in less regulated spaces routinely avoided liability for the content they posted, this high-risk innovation put Roommates.com on the losing end of a years-long legal fight that resulted in a landmark decision from one of the highest federal courts in the country. Upgraders look for the places where they can tinker and refine systems without running afoul of established laws and regulations.

A seventh warning sign is when those supposedly being helped by an innovation haven't been consulted in its creation. Whether remote proctoring that was supposed to improve students' testing experience, or home surveillance software designed without the input of the communities disproportionately surveilled, many of the worse innovations are designed without the voices of those most impacted by their creation.

That's particularly true for the innovations justified with the needs of the most vulnerable communities, such as the unbanked or unhoused. Innovators are quick to tell these individuals what they need to have a better life, but so slow to ask what would actually help. For well-intentioned innovators, that can mean unintentionally straying away from their stated goal, but for the more crass profiteers, it means holding up the marginalized as little more than a prop for a sales pitch. Upgraders ardently include those directly impacted by their work, ensuring they fully understand the future they're trying to build.

Of course, this list of warning signs is preliminary and will only grow and be refined over time. Like the true upgraders we are, we know this book is only the starting point in a larger effort to reframe how we all think about change and progress. One work of writing can't capture every aspect of this debate, and it can't fully solve our innovation quagmire, but it can create a starting point that we will incrementally build on over time. And we hope you join us in that effort.

Notes

CHAPTER 1: INTRODUCTION

1. Diaz, J. (2022). Cars need their buttons and knobs back. *Fast Company*. Available at: www.fastcompany.com/90780466/cars-need-their-buttons-and-knobs-back (accessed February 4, 2025).
2. The European Car Assessment Program intends to address this issue with new 2026 safety guidelines that limit the highest safety rating to cars with physical controls for basic functions. Since this won't be a legal requirement, and the United States tends to be less cautious about policy, only time will tell how much influence it has. See Hellen, N. (2024). Car industry told to dial back use of touchscreens. *The Times*. Available at: www.thetimes.com/uk/article/stop-making-dangerous-touchscreens-car-firms-told-xv3gmpdc6?region=globa (accessed February 4, 2025).
3. Panella, C. (2023). The maker of the lost Titanic sub said "innovation" was the reason the vessel wasn't checked to see if it was up to industry standards. *Business Insider*. Available at: www.insider.com/lost-titanic-sub-maker-innovation-vessel-not-classed-industry-standards-2023-6 (accessed February 4, 2025).
4. Helmore, E. (2023). OceanGate CEO Stockton Rush created "mousetrap for billionaires," says friend. *The Guardian*. Available at: www.theguardian.com/world/2023/jul/19/oceangate-stockton-rush-karl-stanley-mousetrap-billionaires (accessed February 4, 2025).
5. Morelle, R., Francis, A., and Evans, G. (2023). Titan sub CEO dismissed safety warnings as "baseless cries," emails show. *BBC News*. Available at: www.bbc.com/news/world-us-canada-65998914 (accessed February 4, 2025).

6. McHugh, C. (2024). Elon Musk's "move fast and break things" attitude clashes with Washington. *Politico*. Available at: www.politico.co m/news/magazine/2024/12/24/elon-musk-washington-congress-0 0196006 (accessed February 4, 2025).

7. Beck, U., translated by Ritter, M. (1992). *Risk Society: Towards a New Modernity*. London: Sage Publications.

8. Vinsel, L. and Russell, A. (2020). *The Innovation Delusion: How Our Obsession with the New Disrupts the Work that Matters Most*. New York, NY: Penguin.

9. There has been limited dialogue on the issue. For example, while *Gradual: The Case for Incremental Change in a Radical Age* is a helpful conversation-starter, it says very little about technology. Fox, A. and Berman, G. (2023). *Gradual: The Case for Incremental Change in a Radical Age*. Oxford: Oxford University Press.

10. For more on the limits of contemporary tech-criticism, see: Selinger, E. (2024). Can "tech criticism" tame Silicon Valley? *Los Angeles Review of Books*, November 13. Available at: https://lareviewofbooks.org/article/can-tech-criticism-tame-silicon-valley/ (accessed February 4, 2025).

11. Lazar, S. and Nelson, A. (2023). AI safety on whose terms? *Science*. Available at: www.science.org/doi/10.1126/science.adi8982#:~:text=not%20yet%20exist.-,Safety%20on%20whose%20terms%3F,rigor%20required%20of%20its%20mission (accessed February 4, 2025).

12. Wen, P. (2024). Trump selects Elon Musk to lead government efficiency department. *The Guardian*. Available at: www.theguardian.co m/us-news/2024/nov/12/trump-appoints-elon-musk-government-e fficiency-department (accessed February 4, 2025).

13. Selinger, E. (2024). Can "tech criticism" tame Silicon Valley? *Los Angeles Review of Books*, November 13. Available at: https://lareviewofbooks.org/article/can-tech-criticism-tame-silicon-valley/ (accessed February 4, 2025).

CHAPTER 2: ZUCKERBERG'S MYTHOLOGICAL METAVERSE

1. Some of the material presented in this chapter reprints and adapts ideas previously found in: Selinger, E. (2022). The gospel of the Metaverse. *Tech Policy Press*, March 2. Available at: https://techpo licy.press/the-gospel-of-the-metaverse (accessed January 26, 2025);

Selinger, E. (2022a). Metaverse myopia. *Los Angeles Review of Books*, July 19. Available at: https://lareviewofbooks.org/article/metaverse-myopia (accessed January 26, 2025); Selinger, E. (n.d.) Reality+. *The Philosophers' Magazine*. Available at: https://philosophersmag.com/r eality-a-review/; Selinger, E. (2022b) Please don't wear a computer on your face. *BostonGlobe.com*, October 22. Available at: www.boston globe.com/2021/10/22/opinion/please-dont-wear-computer-your-f ace/ (accessed January 26, 2025).

2. Although "metaverse" often refers to a time in the future, some people use the term to describe current platforms, such as Roblox and Fortnite, that users can log onto using their phones, computers, and gaming systems. Mathew Ball offers the most systematic and thorough definition of the metaverse: "A massively scaled and inter-operable network of real-time rendered 3D virtual worlds that can be experienced synchronously and persistently by an effectively unlim-ited number of users with an individual sense of presence, and with continuity of data, such as identity, history, entitlements, objects, communications, and payments"; Ball, M. (2022). *The Metaverse: And How It Will Revolutionize Everything*. New York, NY: Liveright, p. 29.

3. Hern, A. (2023). Mark Zuckerberg's metaverse vision is over. Can Apple save it? *The Observer*, May 21. Available at: www.theguardian.co m/technology/2023/may/21/mark-zuckerbergs-metaverse-vision-is-over-can-apple-save-it (accessed January 26, 2025).

4. *Meta* (2021). Founder's Letter, 2021. Available at: https://about.fb .com/news/2021/10/founders-letter/ (accessed January 29, 2025).

5. *Meta* (2021). Founder's Letter, 2021. Available at: https://about.fb .com/news/2021/10/founders-letter/ (accessed January 29, 2025).

6. Weise, K., Sorkin, A. R., Browning, K., et al. (2022). Microsoft will buy Activision Blizzard, betting $70 billion on the future of games. *The New York Times*, January 18. Available at: www.nytimes.com/2022/01/18/business/microsoft-activision-blizzard.html (accessed January 29, 2025).

7. These three examples are presented in: Ball, M. (2024). *The Metaverse: Fully Revised and Updated Edition: Building the Spatial Internet*. Updated edition. New York, NY: Liveright.

8. Vanian, J. (2023). Facebook's ad rebound gives Meta CEO Mark Zuckerberg freedom to pursue far-out bets. *CNBC*, July 27. Available

at: www.cnbc.com/2023/07/26/facebook-ad-rebound-gives-meta-ce o-zuckerberg-freedom-to-go-big.html (accessed January 29, 2025).

9. Novet, J. (2022). Mark Zuckerberg envisions a billion people in the metaverse spending hundreds of dollars each. *CNBC*, June 22. Available at: www.cnbc.com/2022/06/22/mark-zuckerberg-envisions-1-billion-people-in-the-metaverse.html (accessed January 29, 2025).

10. Needleman, S. E. and Dill, K. (2022). Why the Metaverse will change the way you work. *Wall Street Journal*, February 7. Available at: www.wsj.com/articles/why-the-metaverse-will-change-the-way-you-work-1164 4229800 (accessed January 29, 2025).

11. World Economic Forum (2023). *Demystifying the Consumer Metaverse* Available at: www3.weforum.org/docs/WEF_Demystifying_the_Con sumer_Metaverse.pdf (accessed January 29, 2025).

12. Meta. Digital connection in the metaverse. Available at: https://abo ut.meta.com/metaverse/ (accessed January 29, 2025).

13. Wendyverse (n.d.). Website. Available at: https://wendyverse.com/ (accessed January 29, 2025).

14. Price, E. (2022). Coke's new gaming-inspired soda is "byte" flavored. *Forbes*, April 4. Available at: www.forbes.com/sites/emilyprice/202 2/04/04/cokes-new-gaming-inspired-soda-is-byte-flavored/ (accessed February 4, 2025).

15. Agustin, F. (2022). Walmart is the next big company with plans for the metaverse. *Business Insider*, January 16. Available at: www.businessinsi der.com/walmart-makes-plans-to-enter-the-metaverse-2022-1 (accessed January 29, 2025).

16. Bhaimiya, S. (2023). Disney is ditching its metaverse plans after laying off an entire team focused on interactive storytelling, report says. *Business Insider*, March 28. Available at: www.businessinsider.com/dis ney-ditching-metaverse-plans-laid-off-entire-team-report-2023-3 (accessed January 29, 2025).

17. Levy JV Ari (2023). Meta lost $13.7 billion on Reality Labs in 2022 as Zuckerberg's metaverse bet gets pricier. *CNBC*, February 1. Available at: www.cnbc.com/2023/02/01/meta-lost-13point7-billion-on-reality-labs-in-2022-after-metaverse-pivot.html (accessed January 29, 2025).

18. Vanian, J. (2023c). Meta's Reality Labs has now lost more than $21 billion since the beginning of last year. *CNBC*, July 26. Available

at: www.cnbc.com/2023/07/26/metas-reality-labs-has-now-lost-mor e-than-21-billion.html (accessed January 29, 2025).

19. Vanian, J. (2023b). Meta will require employees to return to the office three days a week starting in September. *CNBC*, June 2. Available at: www.cnbc.com/2023/06/01/meta-will-require-employees-to-return-to-the-office-three-days-a-week-starting-in-september.html (accessed January 29, 2025).

20. *Meta for Work* (n.d.). Horizon Workrooms Virtual Office and Meetings. Available at: https://forwork.meta.com/horizon-work rooms/ (accessed January 29, 2025).

21. Counts, A. (2023). Meta employees are selling the Metaverse, but not working in it. *Bloomberg.com*, June 2. Available at: www.bloomberg.co m/news/newsletters/2023-06-02/meta-quest-3-is-coming-but-emplo yees-aren-t-really-using-vr (accessed January 29, 2025).

22. Thorbecke, C. (2023). What metaverse? Meta says its single largest investment is now in "advancing AI." *CNN*, March 15. Available at: www .cnn.com/2023/03/15/tech/meta-ai-investment-priority/index.html (accessed January 29, 2025).

23. Hays, K. (n.d.). Mark Zuckerberg's Metaverse losses pass $40 billion. Here's why that's suddenly OK. *Business Insider*. Available at: www.bu sinessinsider.com/mark-zuckerberg-metaverse-losses-top-40-billion-s uddenly-ok-meta-2023-7 (accessed January 29, 2025).

24. Watch Mark Zuckerberg's vision for socializing in the Metaverse (2021). Online video clip. Available at: www.youtube.com/watch?v= b9vWShsmE20 (accessed January 29, 2025).

25. Anderson, J., Rainie, L., and Atske, S. (2022). The Metaverse in 2040. Pew Research Center, June 30. Available at: www.pewresearch.org/i nternet/2022/06/30/the-metaverse-in-2040/ (accessed January 29, 2025).

26. Sorkin, A. R., Mattu, R., Warner, B., et al. (2023). Can Apple take the Metaverse mainstream? *The New York Times*, June 6. Available at: www .nytimes.com/2023/06/06/business/dealbook/apple-metaverse-vir tual-reality.html (accessed January 29, 2025).

27. *Guinness World Records* (n.d.). First virtual reality (VR) headset. Available at: www.guinnessworldrecords.com/world-records/515907 -first-virtual-reality-vr-headset.html (accessed January 29, 2025).

28. Chang, E., Kim, H. T., and Yoo, B. (2020). Virtual reality sickness: A review of causes and measurements. *International Journal of Human–Computer Interaction* 36(17): 1658–82.

29. Counts, A. (2023). Meta employees are selling the Metaverse, but not working in it. *Bloomberg.com*, June 2. Available at: www.bloomberg.co m/news/newsletters/2023-06-02/meta-quest-3-is-coming-but-emplo yees-aren-t-really-using-vr (accessed January 29, 2025).

30. *Meta* (2021). Introducing Ray-Ban Stories: First-generation smart glasses. Available at: https://about.fb.com/news/2021/09/introdu cing-ray-ban-stories-smart-glasses/ (accessed January 29, 2025).

31. Weatherbed, J. (2023). 90 percent of Ray-Ban Stories owners aren't using Meta's smart glasses. *The Verge*, August 3. Available at: www.the verge.com/2023/8/3/23818462/meta-ray-ban-stories-smart-glasses-retention-reality-labs (accessed January 29, 2025).

32. Weatherbed, J. (2023). 90 percent of Ray-Ban Stories owners aren't using Meta's smart glasses. *The Verge*, August 3. Available at: www.the verge.com/2023/8/3/23818462/meta-ray-ban-stories-smart-glasses-retention-reality-labs (accessed January 29, 2025).

33. *Meta* (2021). Founder's Letter, 2021. Available at: https://about.fb .com/news/2021/10/founders-letter/ (accessed January 29, 2025).

34. *Amnesty International* (2022). Myanmar: Facebook's systems promoted violence against Rohingya; Meta owes reparations – new report. September 29. Available at: www.amnesty.org/en/latest/news/2022 /09/myanmar-facebooks-systems-promoted-violence-against-rohin gya-meta-owes-reparations-new-report/ (accessed January 29, 2025).

35. Menn, J. and Shih, G. (2023). On Facebook in India hate speech thrives. *Genocide Watch*, September 26. Available at: www.genocide watch.com/single-post/on-facebook-in-india-hate-speech-thrives (accessed January 29, 2025).

36. Jackson, J., Townsend, M., and Kassa, L. (2022). Facebook "lets vigilantes in Ethiopia incite ethnic killing." *The Observer*, February 20. Available at: www.theguardian.com/technology/2022/feb/20/face book-lets-vigilantes-in-ethiopia-incite-ethnic-killing (accessed January 29, 2025).

37. Basu, T. (2021). The metaverse has a groping problem already. *MIT Technology Review*, December 16. Available at: www.technologyreview

.com/2021/12/16/1042516/the-metaverse-has-a-groping-problem/ (accessed January 29, 2025).

38. Soon, W. (2022). A researcher's avatar was sexually assaulted on a metaverse platform owned by Meta, making her the latest victim of sexual abuse on Meta's platforms, watchdog says. *Business Insider*. Available at: www.businessinsider.com/researcher-claims-her-avatar-was-raped-on-metas-metaverse-platform-2022-5 (accessed January 29, 2025).

39. Leswing, K. (2021). Apple's ad privacy change impact shows the power it wields over other industries. *CNBC* November 13. Available at: www.cnbc.com/2021/11/13/apples-privacy-changes-show-the-power-it-holds-over-other-industries.html (accessed February 4, 2025).

40. Klosowski, T. (2022). Looking back on a year of Apple's privacy labels and tracking. *The New York Times* March 31. Available at: www.nytimes.com/wirecutter/blog/apple-privacy-labels-tracking/ (accessed February 4, 2025).

41. Perrigo, B. (2022). Inside Facebook's African sweatshop. *TIME*, February 14. Available at: https://time.com/6147458/facebook-africa-content-moderation-employee-treatment/ (accessed January 29, 2025); Newton, C. (2019). The secret lives of Facebook moderators in America. *The Verge*, February 25. Available at: www.theverge.com/2019/2/25/18229714/cognizant-facebook-content-moderator-interviews-trauma-working-conditions-arizona (accessed January 29, 2025).

42. Roberts, S. T. (2019). *Behind the Screen: Content Moderation in the Shadows of Social Media*. Illustrated edition. New Haven, CT: Yale University Press.

43. Perrigo, B. (2022). Inside Facebook's African sweatshop. *TIME*, February 14. Available at: https://time.com/6147458/facebook-africa-content-moderation-employee-treatment/ (accessed January 29, 2025).

44. Soon, W. (2022). A researcher's avatar was sexually assaulted on a metaverse platform owned by Meta, making her the latest victim of sexual abuse on Meta's platforms, watchdog says. *Business Insider*. Available at: https://www.businessinsider.com/researcher-claims-her-avatar-was-raped-on-metas-metaverse-platform-2022-5 (accessed January 29, 2025).

45. Hendrix, J. (2022). The Sunday Show: Trust and safety in virtual worlds. *Tech Policy Press*, February 6. Available at: https://techpolicy

.press/the-sunday-show-trust-and-safety-in-virtual-worlds (accessed January 29, 2025).

46. Heller, B. (2023). Reimagining reality: Human rights and immersive technology. *SSRN Electronic Journal*. Epub ahead of print. Available at: https://papers.ssrn.com/sol3/papers.cfm?abstract_id=4563877.

47. Mak, A. (2022). I was a bouncer in the Metaverse. *Slate*, May 9. Available at: https://slate.com/technology/2022/05/metaverse-con tent-moderation-virtual-reality-bouncers.html (accessed January 29, 2025).

48. Ball, M. (2022). *The Metaverse: And How It Will Revolutionize Everything.* New York, NY: Liveright.

49. Ball, M. (2022). *The Metaverse: And How It Will Revolutionize Everything.* Erscheinungsort nicht ermittelbar: Liveright.

50. Funk, J. (2019). The downside of tech hype. *Scientific American*, November 21. Available at: www.scientificamerican.com/blog/obser vations/the-downside-of-tech-hype/ (accessed January 29, 2025).

51. Sato, M. (2023). CNET pushed reporters to be more favorable to advertisers, staffers say. *The Verge*, February 2. Available at: www.the verge.com/2023/2/2/23582046/cnet-red-ventures-ai-seo-advert isers-changed-reviews-editorial-independence-affiliate-marketing (accessed January 29, 2025).

52. McKelvey, F., Dandurand, G., and Roberge, J. (2023). News coverage of artificial intelligence reflects business and government hype – not crit-ical voices. *The Conversation*, April 19. Available at: http://theconversa tion.com/news-coverage-of-artificial-intelligence-reflects-business-and-g overnment-hype-not-critical-voices-203633 (accessed January 29, 2025).

53. Birch, K. (2022). KU School of Nursing launches "Metaversity" offering virtual, immersive learning. Available at: www.kumc.edu/about/news/ news-archive/nursing-metaversity.html (accessed January 29, 2025).

54. Bellamy, C. (2022). Morehouse College class will teach Black history in the metaverse. *NBC News*, November 28. Available at: www.nbcne ws.com/news/nbcblk/morehouse-college-class-will-teach-black-his tory-metaverse-rcna57159 (accessed January 29, 2025).

55. Vinsel, L. and Funk, J. (2022). Hype is a weaponized form of optimism. *Nieman Lab*, June 29. Available at: www.niemanlab.org/2022/06/hype-is-a-weaponized-form-of-optimism/ (accessed January 29, 2025).

56. Milk, C. (2015). Chris Milk: How virtual reality can create the ultimate empathy machine. *TED Talk* March. Available at: www.ted.com/talks/chris_milk_how_virtual_reality_can_create_the_ultimate_empathy_machine (accessed January 29, 2025).

57. Hammond, C. (2019). Does reading fiction make us better people? *BBC Future*, June 3. Available at: www.bbc.com/future/article/201905 23-does-reading-fiction-make-us-better-people (accessed January 29, 2025).

58. Martingano, A. J., Hererra, F., and Konrath, S. (2021). Virtual reality improves emotional but not cognitive empathy: A meta-analysis. *Technology, Mind, and Behavior* 2(1).

59. Martingano, A. J., Hererra, F., and Konrath, S. (2021). Virtual reality improves emotional but not cognitive empathy: A meta-analysis. *Technology, Mind, and Behavior* 2(1).

60. Martingano, A. J., Hererra, F., and Konrath, S. (2021). Virtual reality improves emotional but not cognitive empathy: A meta-analysis. *Technology, Mind, and Behavior* 2(1).

61. Martingano, A. J., Hererra, F., and Konrath, S. (2021). Virtual reality improves emotional but not cognitive empathy: A meta-analysis. *Technology, Mind, and Behavior* 2(1).

62. *Apple*. Apple Vision Pro. Available at: www.apple.com/apple-vision-pro/ (accessed January 29, 2025).

63. *Apple*. Apple Vision Pro. Available at: www.apple.com/apple-vision-pro/ (accessed January 29, 2025).

64. *Apple*. Apple Vision Pro. Available at: www.apple.com/apple-vision-pro/ (accessed January 29, 2025).

65. Song, V. (2024). Apple fans are starting to return their Vision Pros. *The Verge*, February 14. Available at: www.theverge.com/2024/2/14/24072 792/apple-vision-pro-early-adopters-returns (accessed January 29, 2025).

66. *Apple Support*. How to safely use your Apple Vision Pro. Available at: https://support.apple.com/en-us/118507 (accessed January 29, 2025).

CHAPTER 3: THE CRYPTO CON

1. Shumba, C. (2021). FTX's Sam Bankman-Fried says crypto "has the potential to improve a lot of people's lives," but still needs a lot more clarity from US regulators. *Business Insider*, December 9. Available at: https://markets.businessinsider.com/news/currencies/ftxs-sam-b ankman-fried-changes-lives-crypto-clarity-us-regulators-2021-12 (accessed February 4, 2025).

2. @tylerwinklevoss (2019). "We have elected to put our money and faith in a mathematical framework that is free of politics and human error." @Gemini, X (formerly Twitter), July 11. Available at: https://x.com/Gemini/status/1149483074356256768 (accessed February 4, 2025).

3. Carmona, T. (2022). Debunking the narratives about cryptocurrency and financial inclusion. *Brookings*, October 26. www.brook ings.edu/articles/debunking-the-narratives-about-cryptocurrency-a nd-financial-inclusion/ (accessed February 4, 2025).

4. Singh, R. (2014). The perils of Bitcoin as currency. *Institution for Social and Policy Studies*, June 1. Available at: https://isps.yale.ed u/news/blog/2014/06/the-perils-of-bitcoin-as-currency (accessed February 4, 2025).

5. Oberhaus, D. (2020). SETI@Home is over. But the search for alien life continues. *WIRED*, March 3. Available at: www.wired.com/story/ setihome-is-over-but-the-search-for-alien-life-continues/ (accessed February 4, 2025).

6. Nakamoto, S. (2008). Bitcoin: A peer-to-peer electronic cash system. *Satoshi Nakamoto Institute*, October 31. Available at: https://nakamo toinstitute.org/library/bitcoin/ (accessed February 4, 2025).

7. Nakamoto, S. (2008). Bitcoin: A peer-to-peer electronic cash system. *Satoshi Nakamoto Institute*, October 31. Available at: https://nakamo toinstitute.org/library/bitcoin/ (accessed February 4, 2025).

8. Nakamoto, S. (2008). Bitcoin: A peer-to-peer electronic cash system. *Satoshi Nakamoto Institute*, October 31. Available at: https://nakamo toinstitute.org/library/bitcoin/ (accessed February 4, 2025).

9. Siklos, R. (2006). A virtual world but real money. *The New York Times*, October 19. Available at: www.nytimes.com/2006/10/19/technol ogy/19virtual.html (accessed February 4, 2025).

10. Siklos, R. (2006). A virtual world but real money. *The New York Times*, October 19. Available at: www.nytimes.com/2006/10/19/technol ogy/19virtual.html (accessed February 4, 2025).

11. Dibbel, J. (2007). The life of the Chinese gold farmer. *The New York Times*, June 17. Available at: www.nytimes.com/2007/06/17/maga zine/17lootfarmers-t.html (accessed February 4, 2025).

12. Cavalli, E. (2008). Paris Hilton parody curbs WoW gold inflation. *WIRED*, June 19. Available at: www.wired.com/2008/06/blizzard-p arodi/ (accessed February 4, 2025).

13. White, L. H. (1984). Competitive payment systems and the unit of account. *The American Economic Review*. 74(4): 699–712.

14. Hoffmann, T. and Watchulonis, M. (2015). *Bitcoin: The end of money as we know it* [Video]. Top Documentary Films.

15. Board of Governors of the Federal Reserve (2023). Economic well-being of U.S. households in 2022. *United States Federal Reserve*, May 1. Available at: www.federalreserve.gov/publications/2023-ec onomic-well-being-of-us-households-in-2022-banking-credit.htm (accessed February 4, 2025).

16. Hawkins, J. (2023). Almost no one uses Bitcoin as currency, new data proves. It's actually more like gambling. *The Conversation*, June 22. Available at: https://theconversation.com/almost-no-one-uses-bit coin-as-currency-new-data-proves-its-actually-more-like-gambling-20 7909 (accessed February 4, 2025).

17. Roh, T. (2021). What your nonprofit needs to know about cryptocur-rency donations. *National Council of Nonprofits*, December 8. Available at: www.councilofnonprofits.org/articles/what-your-nonprofit-need s-know-about-cryptocurrency-donations (accessed February 4, 2025).

18. Board of Governors of the Federal Reserve (2023). Economic well-being of U.S. households in 2022. *United States Federal Reserve*, May 1. Available at: www.federalreserve.gov/publications/2023-ec onomic-well-being-of-us-households-in-2022-banking-credit.htm (accessed February 4, 2025).

19. Moore, A., Artz, J., and Ehlen, C. R. (2017). Tulip mania. *International Journal of the Academic Business World* 11(2): 47–52.

20. Bissonnette, Z. (2015). *The Great Beanie Baby Bubble: Mass Delusion and the Dark Side of Cute*. New York, NY: Penguin.

21. Kaminsky, A. (2024). How does the Bitcoin source code define its 21 million cap? *CCN*, March 4. Available at: www.ccn.com/educa tion/how-does-the-bitcoin-source-code-define-its-21-million-cap/ (accessed February 4, 2025).

22. Bambrough, B. (2024). "It's happening!" – Huge mystery whale and sudden $65,000 Bitcoin price surge fuels secret "Sovereign bid" and tech billionaire predictions. *Forbes*, March 4. Available at: www.for bes.com/sites/digital-assets/2024/03/04/its-happening-huge-mys tery-whale-and-sudden-65000-bitcoin-price-surge-fuels-secret-sover eign-bid-and-tech-billionaire-predictions/ (accessed February 4, 2025).

23. Misamore, B. (2017). How to value a company: 6 methods and examples. *Harvard Business School Online*, April 21. Available at: https://online.hbs.edu/blog/post/how-to-value-a-company (accessed February 4, 2025).

24. Morris, J. (2012). "Silver, Wine, Art and Gold" is a proper asset class. *The Art Newspaper – International Art News and Events*, September 30. Available at: www.theartnewspaper.com/2012/10/01/silver-wine-a rt-and-gold-is-a-proper-asset-class (accessed February 4, 2025).

25. Salmon, F. (2019). What's so special about gold? *Slate Magazine*, November 19. Available at: https://slate.com/podcasts/slate-mon ey/2019/11/felix-salmon-asks-justina-vasquez-about-investing-in-go ld (accessed February 4, 2025).

26. Salmon, F. (2019). What's so special about gold? *Slate Magazine*, November 19. Available at: https://slate.com/podcasts/slate-mon ey/2019/11/felix-salmon-asks-justina-vasquez-about-investing-in-go ld (accessed February 4, 2025).

27. *CoinMarketCap* (n.d.). Cryptocurrency prices, charts and market capitalizations. Available at: https://coinmarketcap.com/ (accessed February 4, 2025).

28. Bitcoin average confirmation time daily insights: Bitcoin statistics. *YCharts*. Available at: https://ycharts.com/indicators/bitcoin_aver age_confirmation_time (accessed February 4, 2025).

29. Bitcoin average confirmation time daily insights: Bitcoin statistics. *YCharts*. Available at: https://ycharts.com/indicators/bitcoin_aver age_confirmation_time (accessed February 4, 2025).

30. Lalav, R. (2023). Blockchains with the highest transaction speed. *Bitpowr*, March 6. Available at: https://bitpowr.com/blog/block chains-with-the-highest-transaction-speeds (accessed February 4, 2025).

31. Bhalla, A. (2025). Top 10 cryptocurrencies with their high transaction speeds. *Blockchain Council*, January 23. Available at: www.block chain-council.org/cryptocurrency/top-cryptocurrencies-with-their-high-transaction-speeds/ (accessed February 4, 2025).

32. Sottosanto, S. (2024). Credit card processing 101: Understanding the key players, the process, the fees, and more. *ECS Payments*, August 29. Available at: www.ecspayments.com/credit-card-process ing-101/ (accessed February 4, 2025).

33. *Forbes* (n.d.). Cryptocurrency prices today by market cap. Available at: www.forbes.com/digital-assets/crypto-prices/?sh=3b73c9362478 (accessed February 4, 2025).

34. *Forbes* (n.d.). Cryptocurrency prices today by market cap. Available at: www.forbes.com/digital-assets/crypto-prices/?sh=3b73c9362478 (accessed February 4, 2025).

35. *Nacha* (n.d.). ACH network volume and value statistics. Available at: www.nacha.org/content/ach-network-volume-and-value-statistics (accessed February 4, 2025); *Forbes* (n.d.). Cryptocurrency prices today by market cap. Available at: www.forbes.com/digital-assets/ crypto-prices/?sh=3b73c9362478 (accessed February 4, 2025).

36. *Nacha* (2021). Reversals and enforcement. June 30. Available at: www .nacha.org/rules/reversals-and-enforcement (accessed February 4, 2025).

37. *Swift* (2023). Standards MT November 2023. November. Available at: www2.swift.com/knowledgecentre/rest/v1/publications/usug_ 20230720/1.0/usug_20230720.pdf (accessed February 4, 2025).

38. *Bitcoin Stack Exchange* (2016). How do I recover bitcoin sent to a wrong wallet address. December 8. Available at: https://bitcoin .stackexchange.com/questions/50083/how-do-i-recover-bitcoin-sen t-to-a-wrong-wallet-address (accessed February 4, 2025); *Bitcoin Stack Exchange* (2023). A wrong wallet situation. December 13. Available at: https://bitcoin.stackexchange.com/questions/120943/a-wron g-wallet-situation (accessed February 4, 2025); *Bitcoin Stack Exchange* (2019). Wrong address when transferring BTC to paper

wallet. October 27. Available at: https://bitcoin.stackexchange.co m/questions/91296/wrong-address-when-transfering-btc-to-paper-wallet (accessed February 4, 2025).

39. Federal Bureau of Investigation (2023). Cryptocurrency Fraud Report 2023. Available at: www.ic3.gov/AnnualReport/Reports/20 23_IC3CryptocurrencyReport.pdf (accessed February 4, 2025).

40. *Ledger* (2024). SATs/VB meaning. June 17. Available at: www.ledger .com/academy/glossary/sats-vb (accessed February 4, 2025).

41. *Coinbase* (n.d.). What are gas fees? Available at: www.coinbase.com/ learn/crypto-basics/what-are-gas-fees (accessed February 4, 2025).

42. Bitcoin average confirmation time daily insights: Bitcoin statistics. *YCharts*. Available at: https://ycharts.com/indicators/bitcoin_aver age_confirmation_time (accessed February 4, 2025).

43. U.S. Energy Information Administration, Environmental Impact Assessment (2024). Tracking electricity consumption from U.S. cryptocurrency mining operations. January 1. Available at: www.eia.gov/todayinenergy/detail.php?id=61364 (accessed February 4, 2025).

44. Sledge, R., Hodge, M., Garcia, C., et al. (2022). ESG in the crypto world: Climate reporting and decentralized finance. *KPMG*. Available at: https://kpmg.com/us/en/articles/2022/esg-crypto-climate-repo rting-decentralized-finance.html (accessed February 4, 2025).

45. Stoll, C., KlaaBen, L., Gallersdorfer, U., et al. (2023). Climate impacts of Bitcoin mining in the U.S. MIT Center for Energy and Environmental Policy Research, June. Available at: https://ceepr.mit .edu/wp-content/uploads/2023/06/MIT-CEEPR-WP-2023-11.pdf (accessed February 4, 2025); Singh, G. (2024). Bitcoin ETF's false ESG claims. *Greenpeace*, November 20. Available at: www.greenpeace.org/u sa/news/bitcoin-etfs-false-esg-claims/ (accessed February 4, 2025).

46. Harrison, S. A. (2024). A timeline of the collapse at FTX. *AP News*, May 8. Available at: https://apnews.com/article/ftx-bankruptcy-binance-timeline-c519d50b9059aa8bff0ce8b6cd26c40e (accessed February 4, 2025).

47. Harrison, S. A. (2024). A timeline of the collapse at FTX. *AP News*, May 8. Available at: https://apnews.com/article/ftx-bankruptcy-binance-timeline-c519d50b9059aa8bff0ce8b6cd26c40e (accessed February 4, 2025).

48. Universal Financial Access 2020. *World Bank Group*. Available at: https://ufa.worldbank.org/en/ufa (accessed February 4, 2025).

49. 2023 FDIC National Survey of Unbanked and Underbanked Households. *FDIC*. Available at: www.fdic.gov/household-survey (accessed February 4, 2025).

50. Renter, E. (2023). This is how much being "unbanked" is costing 5.9 million Americans. *MarketWatch*, May 24. Available at: www.marketwatch.com/story/this-is-how-much-being-unbanked-is-costing-5-9-million-americans-dd1be822 (accessed February 4, 2025).

51. 2023 FDIC National Survey of Unbanked and Underbanked Households. *FDIC*. Available at: www.fdic.gov/household-survey (accessed February 4, 2025).

52. Foster-Frau, S. (2021). Locked out of traditional financial industry, more people of color are turning to cryptocurrency. *The Washington Post*, December 1. Available at: www.washingtonpost.com/national/locked-out-of-traditional-financial-industry-more-people-of-color-are-turning-to-cryptocurrency/2021/12/01/a21df3fa-37fe-11ec-9bc4-86107e7b0ab1_story.html (accessed February 4, 2025).

53. Alfonseca, K. (2022). Cryptocurrency: Why some see it as a way to financially uplift people of color. *ABC News*, July 9. Available at: https://abcnews.go.com/Business/cryptocurrency-financially-uplift-people-color/story?id=85564927 (accessed February 4, 2025).

54. Seward, Z. and De, N. (2021). Facebook unveils Libra cryptocurrency, targeting 1.7 billion unbanked. *Coindesk*, September 13. Available at: www.coindesk.com/markets/2019/06/18/facebook-unveils-libra-cryptocurrency-targeting-17-billion-unbanked (accessed February 4, 2025).

55. Baradaran, M. (2019). Facebook's cryptocurrency won't help the poor access banks. Here's what would. *The Washington Post*, October 29. Available at: www.washingtonpost.com/outlook/2019/10/29/facebooks-cryptocurrency-wont-help-poor-access-banks-heres-what-would/ (accessed February 4, 2025).

56. 2021 FDIC National Survey of Unbanked and Underbanked Households. FDIC. Available at: www.fdic.gov/system/files/2024-07/2021execsum.pdf (accessed February 4, 2025).

57. Heinbuch, S. (2024). Overcoming KYC banking barriers: A lesson from Mexico. *Atlantafed*. Available at: www.atlantafed.org/blogs/ta

ke-on-payments/2024/01/08/overcoming-kyc-banking-barriers–les
son-from-mexico (accessed February 4, 2025).
58. Maryland Today Staff (2023). UMD analysis: Millions of Americans
don't have ID required to vote. *MarylandToday*, April 13. Available at:
https://today.umd.edu/umd-analysis-millions-of-americans-dont-h
ave-id-required-to-vote (accessed February 4, 2025).
59. Heinbuch, S. (2024). Overcoming KYC banking barriers: A lesson
from Mexico. *Atlantafed*. Available at: www.atlantafed.org/blogs/ta
ke-on-payments/2024/01/08/overcoming-kyc-banking-barriers–les
son-from-mexico (accessed February 4, 2025).
60. IDNYC (2025). Banks and credit unions. Available at: www.nyc
.gov/site/idnyc/benefits/banks-and-credit-unions.page (accessed
February 4, 2025).
61. Nakamoto, S. (2009). Banks. *Satoshi Nakamoto Institute*, February 11.
Available at: https://satoshi.nakamotoinstitute.org/quotes/banks/
(accessed February 4, 2025).
62. Nakamoto, S. (2009). Trusted third parties. Satoshi Nakamoto
Institute, February 11. Available at: https://satoshi.nakamotoinsti
tute.org/quotes/trusted-third-parties/ (accessed February 4, 2025).
63. Maheshwari, R. (2023). What are crypto exchanges and how do they
work. *Forbes Advisor India*, June 30. Available at: www.forbes.com/a
dvisor/in/investing/cryptocurrency/what-is-a-crypto-exchange/
(accessed February 4, 2025).
64. Young, S. D. (2024). Amount of Bitcoin and Ether on exchanges reach
record multi-year lows. *Unchained*, June 3. Available at: https://unchai
nedcrypto.com/amount-of-bitcoin-and-ether-on-exchanges-reach-rec
ord-multi-year-lows/ (accessed February 4, 2025).
65. Chainanalysis Team. (2023). The Chainanalysis guide to on-chain
user segmentation for crypto exchanges. *Chainalysis*, June 22.
Available at: www.chainalysis.com/blog/crypto-exchanges-on-chai
n-user-segmentation-guide/ (accessed February 4, 2025).
66. Huddleston, T. (2020). Millennials trust the postal service more
than Amazon. *CNBC*, January 24. Available at: www.cnbc.com/202
0/01/24/millennials-trust-usps-more-than-amazon-morning-con
sult-study.html (accessed February 4, 2025).
67. Pollard, M. S. and Davis, L. M. (2021). Decline in trust in the Centers
for Disease Control and Prevention during the COVID-19

pandemic. *RAND*, April 5. Available at: www.rand.org/pubs/resear ch_reports/RRA308-12.html#fn2 (accessed February 4, 2025).

68. Postalfacts. (2021). Postal money orders. *Postal Facts*, March 4. Available at: https://facts.usps.com/306930-money-orders/ (accessed February 4, 2025).

69. Anson, J., Berthaud, A., Klapper, L., et al. (2013). Financial inclusion and the role of the post office. *World Bank*, October 1. Available at: https://documents.worldbank.org/en/publication/docu ments-reports/documentdetail/680321468163464611/financial-in clusion-and-the-role-of-the-post-office (accessed February 4, 2025).

70. Anson, J., Berthaud, A., Klapper, L., et al. (2013). Financial inclusion and the role of the post office. *World Bank*, October 1. Available at: https://documents.worldbank.org/en/publication/ documents-reports/documentdetail/680321468163464611/finan cial-inclusion-and-the-role-of-the-post-office (accessed February 4, 2025).

71. Anson, J., Berthaud, A., Klapper, L., et al. (2013). Financial inclusion and the role of the post office. *World Bank*, October 1. Available at: https://documents.worldbank.org/en/publication/ documents-reports/documentdetail/680321468163464611/finan cial-inclusion-and-the-role-of-the-post-office (accessed February 4, 2025).

72. Anson, J., Berthaud, A., Klapper, L., et al. (2013). Financial inclusion and the role of the post office. *World Bank*, October 1. Available at: https://documents.worldbank.org/en/publication/docu ments-reports/documentdetail/680321468163464611/financial-in clusion-and-the-role-of-the-post-office (accessed February 4, 2025).

73. Bustillos, M. (2013). The Bitcoin boom. *The New Yorker*, April. Available at: www.newyorker.com/tech/annals-of-technology/the-bitcoin-boom (accessed February 4, 2025).

74. Bustillos, M. (2013). The Bitcoin boom. *The New Yorker*, April. Available at: www.newyorker.com/tech/annals-of-technology/the-bitcoin-boom (accessed February 4, 2025).

75. Greenberg, A. (2024). How a 27-year-old codebreaker busted the myth of Bitcoin's anonymity. *Wired*, January 17. Available at: www.w ired.com/story/27-year-old-codebreaker-busted-myth-bitcoins-ano nymity/ (accessed February 4, 2025).

76. Nakamoto, S. (2008). Privacy. *Satoshi Nakamoto Institute*, October 31. Available at: https://satoshi.nakamotoinstitute.org/quotes/priv acy/ (accessed February 4, 2025).
77. Greenberg, A. (2024). How a 27-year-old codebreaker busted the myth of Bitcoin's anonymity. *Wired*, January 17. Available at: www.w ired.com/story/27-year-old-codebreaker-busted-myth-bitcoins-ano nymity/ (accessed February 4, 2025).
78. Meiklejohn, S., Pomarole, M., Jordan, G., et al. (2013). A fistful of Bitcoins: Characterizing payments among men with no names. *IMC'13, Proceedings of the 2013 Conference on Internet Measurement Conference*. New York, NY: Association for Computing Machinery, pp. 127–40.
79. Chainanalysis Team (2024). How to use Blockchain intelligence to investigate crypto crime. *Chainanalysis*, May 9. Available at: www.ch ainalysis.com/blog/investigate-crypto-crime-blockchain-intelli gence/ (accessed February 4, 2025).
80. Crypto Investigations (2024). *Chainanalysis*, July. Available at: www.ch ainalysis.com/solution/crypto-investigations/ (accessed February 4, 2025).
81. Coinbase (2023). Our approach to preventing illicit activity in crypto. Available at: www.coinbase.com/blog/our-approach-to-pre venting-illicit-activity-in-crypto (accessed February 4, 2025).
82. Deslandes, N. (2024). Navigating the line between crypto surveil- lance and privacy protection. *TechInformed*, May 10. Available at: https://techinformed.com/navigating-the-line-between-crypto-sur veillance-and-privacy-protection/ (accessed February 4, 2025).
83. CoinMarketCap (2024). Bitcoin. Available at: https://coinmarket cap.com/currencies/bitcoin/ (accessed February 4, 2025).
84. *The Economist* (2015). The trust machine. October 31. Available at: www.economist.com/leaders/2015/10/31/the-trust-machine (accessed February 4, 2025).
85. Levy, K. E. (2017). View of book-smart, not street-smart: Blockchain-based smart contracts and the social workings of law. *Engaging Science, Technology and Society* 3(1): 1–15.
86. Levy, K. E. (2017). View of book-smart, not street-smart: Blockchain-based smart contracts and the social workings of law.

Engaging Science, Technology and Society 3(1): 1–15 (emphasis in original).

87. Prisco, G. (2015). Slock.it to introduce smart locks linked to smart Ethereum contracts, decentralize the sharing economy. *Bitcoin Magazine – Bitcoin News, Articles and Expert Insights*, November 5. Available at: https://bitcoinmagazine.com/technical/slock-it-to-in troduce-smart-locks-linked-to-smart-ethereum-contracts-decentral ize-the-sharing-economy-1446746719 (accessed February 4, 2025).

88. Dale, B. (2023). Car-sharing service tokenizes Teslas to share revenue. *Axios*, June 29. Available at: www.axios.com/2023/06/29/car-sharing-tokenization-tesla-eloop (accessed February 4, 2025).

89. Yadlos, L. (2024). ELOOP introduces RWA tokenization platform on peaq for real-world assets. *Blockster*. Available at: https://block ster.com/eloop-introduces-rwa-tokenization-platform-on-peaq-for-r eal-world-assets (accessed February 4, 2025).

90. Yadlos, L. (2024). ELOOP introduces RWA tokenization platform on peaq for real-world assets. *Blockster*. Available at: https://block ster.com/eloop-introduces-rwa-tokenization-platform-on-peaq-for-r eal-world-assets (accessed February 4, 2025).

91. Westerheide, C. (2024). Viennese EV sharer Eloop faces insolvency. *Electrive*, April 30. Available at: www.electrive.com/2024/04/30/vien nese-ev-sharer-eloop-faces-insolvency/ (accessed February 4, 2025).

92. Securities and Exchange Commission (2017). Report of Investigation Pursuant to Section 21(a) of the Securities Exchange Act of 1934: The DAO. Available at: www.sec.gov/files/litigation/i nvestreport/34-81207.pdf (accessed February 4, 2025).

93. Securities and Exchange Commission (2017). Report of Investigation Pursuant to Section 21(a) of the Securities Exchange Act of 1934: The DAO. Available at: www.sec.gov/files/litigation/i nvestreport/34-81207.pdf (accessed February 4, 2025).

94. Statement of CFTC Division of Enforcement Director Ian McGinley on the Ooki DAO Litigation Victory (2023). *CFTC*, June 9. Available at: www.cftc.gov/PressRoom/PressReleases/871 5-23 (accessed February 4, 2025).

95. Decentralized Autonomous Organization Supplement (n.d.). Wyoming Secretary of State Chuck Gray. Available at: https://sos.wyo

.gov/Forms/WyoBiz/DAO_Supplement.pdf (accessed February 4, 2025).

96. Salvo, M. D. (2021). SEC halts token registration for first legally recognized DAO. *Decrypt*, November 10. Available at: https://decry pt.co/85781/sec-halts-token-registration-wyoming-first-dao (accessed February 4, 2025).

97. Salvo, M. D. (2021). SEC halts token registration for first legally recognized DAO. *Decrypt*, November 10. Available at: https://decry pt.co/85781/sec-halts-token-registration-wyoming-first-dao (accessed February 4, 2025).

98. Ongweso, E., Jr. (2021). Crypto investors buy 40 acres of land in Wyoming to build Blockchain city. *VICE*, November 3. Available at: www.vice.com/en/article/crypto-investors-buy-40-acres-of-land-in-wyoming-to-build-blockchain-city/ (accessed February 4, 2025).

99. Jean, R. (2023). Wyoming's first digital land buy wasn't story's historic wagon box inn, it was CityDAO near Yellowstone. *Cowboy State Daily*, May 14. Available at: https://cowboystatedaily.com/2023/05/14/wy omings-first-digital-land-buy-wasnt-storys-historic-wagon-box-inn-it-wa s-citydao-near-yellowstone/ (accessed February 4, 2025).

100. Ongweso, E., Jr. (2022). People building "Blockchain city" in Wyoming scammed by hackers. *VICE*, January 13. Available at: www .vice.com/en/article/people-building-blockchain-city-in-wyoming-sc ammed-by-hackers (accessed February 4, 2025).

101. Interview recording at 1:00–3:05 on August 19, 2024.

102. Interview recording at 6:10 on August 19, 2024.

103. Interview recording at 5:50 on August 19, 2024.

104. Interview recording at 6:50 on August 19, 2024.

105. Komolafe, O. (2023). Joseph Lubin net worth: Co-founding Ethereum for billions. *Inside Bitcoins*, July 31. Available at: https:// insidebitcoins.com/bitcoin-investors/joseph-lubin-net-worth (accessed February 4, 2025).

106. Interview recording at 6:50 on August 19, 2024.

107. Interview recording at 7:45 on August 19, 2024.

108. Interview recording at 10:14 on August 19, 2024.

109. Interview recording at 9:20 on August 19, 2024.

CHAPTER 4: HOME SECURITY UPGRADES

1. Ongweso, E., Jr. (2022). Ring cameras are going to get more people killed. *Vice Media*, October 24. Available at: www.vice.com/en/art icle/ring-cameras-are-going-to-get-more-people-killed/ (accessed February 4, 2025).

2. Campbell, J. (2022). Florida man and son arrested for allegedly shooting at woman sitting in her car they believed was a burglar, sheriff says. *CNN*, October 19. Available at: www.cnn.com/2022/ 10/19/us/florida-ring-doorbell-shooting/index.html (accessed February 4, 2025).

3. Ongweso, E., Jr. (2022). Ring cameras are going to get more people killed. *Vice Media*, October 24. Available at: www.vice.com/en/art icle/ring-cameras-are-going-to-get-more-people-killed/ (accessed February 4, 2025).

4. Pope, A. R. Improvement in electro-magnetic alarms, US Patent 9,802, June 21, 1853.

5. Hilgers, L. (2021). A brief history of the invention of the home security alarm. *Smithsonian Magazine*, March. Available at: www.smithsonian mag.com/innovation/history-home-security-alarm-180977002/ (accessed February 4, 2025).

6. Bishop, T. (2019). Shark Tank's billion-dollar blunder: How startup Ring went from TV rejection to Amazon acquisition. *Geek Wire*. Available at: www.geekwire.com/2019/shark-tanks-billion-dollar-bl under-startup-ring-went-tv-rejection-amazon-acquisition/ (accessed February 4, 2025).

7. *Business Wire* (2022). Strategy analytics: Amazon's Ring remained atop the video doorbell market in 2021. June 22. Available at: www.business wire.com/news/home/20220622005023/en/Strategy-Analytics-Amaz ons-Ring-Remained-atop-the-Video-Doorbell-Market-in-2021 (accessed February 4, 2025).

8. Vo, T. L. (2023). Amazon's "neighborhood watch" might be turning police officers into "Reddit moderators." *Pulitzer Center*, October 11. Available at: https://pulitzercenter.org/stories/amazons-neighbor hood-watch-might-be-turning-police-officers-reddit-moderators (accessed February 4, 2025).

9. Gibbs, S. (2018). Amazon buys video doorbell firm Ring for over $1bn. *The Guardian,* February 28. Available at: www.theguardian.co m/technology/2018/feb/28/amazon-buys-video-doorbell-ring-smar t-home-delivery (accessed February 4, 2025).

10. West, E. (2019) Amazon: surveillance as a service. *Surveillance and Society* 17(1/2): 27–33.

11. Garfinkle, A. (2023). Amazon has sold more than 500 million Alexa-enabled devices, drops 4 new Echo products. *Yahoo!Finance.* Available at: https://finance.yahoo.com/news/amazon-has-sold-more-than-50 0-million-alexa-enabled-devices-drops-4-new-echo-products-1400138 08.html (accessed February 4, 2025).

12. Chin, J. and Lin, L. (2022). *Surveillance State: Inside China's Quest to Launch a New Era of Social Control.* New York, NY: St. Martin's Press.

13. Ekins, E. and Gygi. J. (2023). Nearly a third of Gen Z favors the government installing surveillance cameras in homes. *Cato Institute,* June 1. Available at: www.cato.org/blog/nearly-third-gen-z-favors-ho me-government-surveillance-cameras-1 (accessed February 4, 2025).

14. Ng, A. (2022). Amazon gave Ring videos to police without owners' permission. *Politico,* July 13. Available at: politico.com/news/2022/07/ 13/amazon-gave-ring-videos-to-police-without-owners-permission-0004 5513#:~:text=Amazon%20currently%20has%20agreements%20to,sen d%20alerts%20and%20request%20videos (accessed February 4, 2025).

15. Ng, A. (2022). Amazon gave Ring videos to police without owners' permission. *Politico,* July 13. Available at: politico.com/news/2022/07/ 13/amazon-gave-ring-videos-to-police-without-owners-permission-0004 5513#:~:text=Amazon%20currently%20has%20agreements%20to,sen d%20alerts%20and%20request%20videos (accessed February 4, 2025).

16. Cameron, D. (2019). Everything cops say about Amazon's Ring is scripted or approved by Ring. *Gizmodo,* July 30. Available at: https:// gizmodo.com/everything-cops-say-about-amazons-ring-is-scripted-or-a-1836812538 (accessed February 4, 2025).

17. Cameron, D. (2019). Everything cops say about Amazon's Ring is scripted or approved by Ring. *Gizmodo,* July 30. Available at: https:// gizmodo.com/everything-cops-say-about-amazons-ring-is-scripted-or-a-1836812538 (accessed February 4, 2025).

18. Cameron, D. (2019). Everything cops say about Amazon's Ring is scripted or approved by Ring. *Gizmodo,* July 30. Available at: https://

gizmodo.com/everything-cops-say-about-amazons-ring-is-scripted-or-a-1836812538 (accessed February 4, 2025).

19. Stanley, J. (2019). Should you buy a Ring doorbell camera? *ACLU*. Available at: www.aclu.org/news/privacy-technology/should-you-bu y-ring-doorbell-camera (accessed February 4, 2025).

20. Haskins, C. (2019). Amazon is coaching cops on how to obtain surveillance footage without a warrant. *Vice Media*, August 5. Available at: www.vice.com/en/article/amazon-is-coaching-cops-on-how-to-obtain-surveillance-footage-without-a-warrant/ (accessed February 4, 2025).

21. Ng, A. (2023). The privacy loophole in your doorbell. *Politico*, March 7. Available at: www.politico.com/news/2023/03/07/priv acy-loophole-ring-doorbell-00084979 (accessed February 4, 2025).

22. Farivar, C. (2020). Cute videos, but little evidence: Police say Amazon Ring isn't much of a crime fighter. *NBC News*, February 2015. Available at: www.nbcnews.com/news/all/cute-videos-little-evidence-police-say-amazon-ring-isn-t-n1136026 (accessed February 4, 2025).

23. Stickle, B., Hicks, M., Stickle, A., et al. (2019). Porch pirates: Examining unattended package theft through crime script analysis. *Criminal Justice Studies* 33(2): 79–95, 90.

24. Harris, M. (2018). Video doorbell firm Ring says its devices slash crime – but the evidence looks flimsy. *MIT Technology Review*, October 19. Available at: www.technologyreview.com/2018/10/19/103922/video-doorbell-firm-ring-says-its-devices-slash-crimebut-the-e vidence-looks-flimsy/ (accessed February 4, 2025).

25. Harris, M. (2018). Video doorbell firm Ring says its devices slash crime – but the evidence looks flimsy. *MIT Technology Review*, October 19. Available at: www.technologyreview.com/2018/10/19/103922/video-doorbell-firm-ring-says-its-devices-slash-crimebut-the-e vidence-looks-flimsy/ (accessed February 4, 2025).

26. Farivar, C. (2020). Cute videos, but little evidence: Police say Amazon Ring isn't much of a crime fighter. *NBC News*, February 2015. Available at: www.nbcnews.com/news/all/cute-videos-little-evidence-police-say-amazon-ring-isn-t-n1136026 (accessed February 4, 2025).

27. Farivar, C. (2020). Cute videos, but little evidence: Police say Amazon Ring isn't much of a crime fighter. *NBC News*, February 2015. Available at: www.nbcnews.com/news/all/cute-videos-little-evi

dence-police-say-amazon-ring-isn-t-n1136026 (accessed February 4, 2025).

28. Farivar, C. (2020). Cute videos, but little evidence: Police say Amazon Ring isn't much of a crime fighter. *NBC News*, February 2015. Available at: www.nbcnews.com/news/all/cute-videos-little-evidence-police-say-amazon-ring-isn-t-n1136026 (accessed February 4, 2025).

29. Ng, A. (2020). Ring's work with police lacks solid evidence of reducing crime. *CNET*, March 19. Available at: www.cnet.com/home/security/features/rings-work-with-police-lacks-solid-evidence-of-reducing-crime/ (accessed February 4, 2025).

30. Farivar, C. (2020). Cute videos, but little evidence: Police say Amazon Ring isn't much of a crime fighter. *NBC News*, February 2015. Available at: www.nbcnews.com/news/all/cute-videos-little-evidence-police-say-amazon-ring-isn-t-n1136026 (accessed February 4, 2025).

31. Farivar, C. (2020). Cute videos, but little evidence: Police say Amazon Ring isn't much of a crime fighter. *NBC News*, February 2015. Available at: www.nbcnews.com/news/all/cute-videos-little-evidence-police-say-amazon-ring-isn-t-n1136026 (accessed February 4, 2025).

32. Vo, L. T. (2023). Amazon's "neighborhood watch" might be turning police officers into "Reddit moderators." *Pulitzer Center*, October 11. Available at: https://pulitzercenter.org/stories/amazons-neighborhood-watch-might-be-turning-police-officers-reddit-moderators (accessed February 4, 2025).

33. Vo, L. T. (2023). Accidental spies: Amazon Ring owners may be unknowingly emailing police. *The Markup*, October 11. Available at: https://themarkup.org/neighborhood-watch/2023/10/11/accidental-spies-amazon-ring-owners-may-be-unknowingly-emailing-police (accessed February 4, 2025).

34. Harwell, D. (2020). Ring and Nest helped normalize American surveillance and turned us into a nation of voyeurs. *The Washington Post*, February 18. Available at: www.washingtonpost.com/technology/2020/02/18/ring-nest-surveillance-doorbell-camera/ (accessed February 4, 2025).

35. Harwell, D. (2020). Ring and Nest helped normalize American surveillance and turned us into a nation of voyeurs. *The Washington Post*, February 18. Available at: www.washingtonpost.com/technology/2020/

02/18/ring-nest-surveillance-doorbell-camera/ (accessed February 4, 2025).

36. Vo, L. T. (2023). Accidental spies: Amazon Ring owners may be unknowingly emailing police. *The Markup*, October 11. Available at: https://themarkup.org/neighborhood-watch/2023/10/11/acciden tal-spies-amazon-ring-owners-may-be-unknowingly-emailing-police (accessed February 4, 2025).

37. Ross, M. (2016). Nextdoor: When a neighborhood website turns unneighborly. *The Mercury News*, August 12. Available at: www.mercur ynews.com/2015/09/01/nextdoor-when-a-neighborhood-website-tu rns-unneighborly/ (accessed February 4, 2025).

38. Kaste, M. (2019). Doorbell cameras are popular, but should we be sharing the videos online? *NPR News*, December 2. www.npr.org/20 19/12/02/784225316/doorbell-cameras-are-popular-but-should-we-be-sharing-the-videos-online (accessed February 4, 2025).

39. Read, M. (2020). I got a Ring doorbell camera. It scared the hell out of me. *Intelligencer*, February 13. Available at: https://nymag.com/in telligencer/2020/02/what-its-like-to-own-an-amazon-ring-doorbell-c amera.html (accessed February 4, 2025).

40. Read, M. (2020). I got a Ring doorbell camera. It scared the hell out of me. *Intelligencer*, February 13. Available at: https://nymag.com/in telligencer/2020/02/what-its-like-to-own-an-amazon-ring-doorbell-c amera.html (accessed February 4, 2025).

41. Haskins, C. (2019). Amazon's home security company is turning everyone into cops. *Vice Media*, February 7. Available at: www.vice.co m/en/article/amazons-home-security-company-is-turning-everyone-into-cops/ (accessed February 4, 2025).

42. Vo, L. T. (2023). Accidental spies: Amazon Ring owners may be unknowingly emailing police. *The Markup*, October 11. Available at: https://themarkup.org/neighborhood-watch/2023/10/11/acciden tal-spies-amazon-ring-owners-may-be-unknowingly-emailing-police (accessed February 4, 2025).

43. Ring (Updated in 2024). Neighbors by Ring community guidelines. Available at: https://ring.com/support/articles/q2p3w/Neighbors-by-Ring-Community-Guidelines (accessed February 4, 2025).

44. Ring (Updated in 2024). Neighbors by Ring community guidelines. Available at: https://ring.com/support/articles/q2p3w/Neighbors-by-Ring-Community-Guidelines (accessed February 4, 2025).
45. NYU School of Law. Ring & Neighbors Public Safety Service: A Civil Rights & Civil Liberties Audit. Policing Project at NYU School of Law. Available at: www.policingproject.org/ring (accessed February 4, 2025).
46. Vo, L. T. (2023). Accidental spies: Amazon Ring owners may be unknowingly emailing police. *The Markup*, October 11. Available at: https://themarkup.org/neighborhood-watch/2023/10/11/accidental-spies-amazon-ring-owners-may-be-unknowingly-emailing-police (accessed February 4, 2025).
47. McKinnon, A. and Tallam, D. (2003). Unattended delivery to the home: An assessment of the security implications. *International Journal of Retail & Distribution Management* 31(1): 30–41; Lagorio, A. and Pinto, R. (2020). The parcel locker location issues: An overview of factors affecting their location. International Conference on Information Systems, Logistics and Supply Chain. Austin, TX.
48. Tseloni, A., Thompson, R., Grove, L., et al. (2017). The effectiveness of burglary security devices. *Security Journal* 30(2): 646–64.

CHAPTER 5: THE FAILED PROMISE OF COVID INNOVATION

1. MPH Online staff. Outbreak: 10 of the worst pandemics in history. *MPH Online*. Available at: www.mphonline.org/worst-pandemics-in-history/ (accessed February 4, 2025).
2. Bourla, A. and Graybill, S. (2022). *Moonshot: Inside Pfizer's Nine-Month Race to Make the Impossible Possible*. New York, NY: Harper Audio.
3. Samuel, S. (2020). The UK is about to start deliberately infecting volunteers with Covid-19 to test vaccines. *Vox*, February 19. Available at: www.vox.com/future-perfect/2020/11/17/21540773/covid-19-vaccine-human-challenge-trial-ethics (accessed February 4, 2025).
4. Beyrer, C. (2021). The long history of mRNA vaccines. *Johns Hopkins Bloomberg School of Public Health*. Available at: https://publichealth.jhu.edu/2021/the-long-history-of-mrna-vaccines (accessed February 4, 2025).

5. Dolgin, E. (2021). The tangled history of mRNA vaccines. *Nature News*, September 14. Available at: www.nature.com/articles/d41586-021-02483-w (accessed February 4, 2025).

6. Schlake, T., Thess, A., Fotin-Mieczek, M., et al. (2012). Developing mRNA-vaccine technologies. *RNA Biology*. Available at: https://pmc.ncbi.nlm.nih.gov/articles/PMC3597572/ (accessed February 4, 2025).

7. NYS ENX: What you need to know. Department of Health. Available at: https://coronavirus.health.ny.gov/nys-enx-what-you-need-know (accessed February 4, 2025).

8. Ungku, F. (2020). Singapore launches contact tracing mobile app to track coronavirus infections. *Reuters*, March 20. Available at: www.reuters.com/article/us-health-coronavirus-singapore-technolo/singapore-launches-contact-tracing-mobile-app-to-track-coronavirus-infections-idUSKBN2171ZQ/ (accessed February 4, 2025).

9. Illmer, A. (2021). Singapore reveals Covid privacy data available to police. *BBC News*, January 5. Available at: www.bbc.com/news/world-asia-55541001 (accessed February 4, 2025).

10. Landau, N., Kubovich, Y., and Breiner, J. (2020). Israeli coronavirus surveillance explained: Who's tracking you and what happens with the data. *Haaretz*, March 18. Available at: www.haaretz.com/israel-news/2020-03-18/ty-article/.premium/israeli-coronavirus-surveillance-whos-tracking-you-and-what-happens-with-the-data/0000017f-e487-d7b2-a77f-e7873bc80000 (accessed February 4, 2025).

11. TOI Staff (2020). Phone tracking sends thousands to isolation, but many say system makes mistakes. *Times of Israel*, July 6. Available at: www.timesofisrael.com/phone-tracking-sends-thousands-to-isolation-but-many-say-system-makes-mistakes/ (accessed February 4, 2025).

12. NYS ENX: What you need to know. Department of Health. Available at: https://coronavirus.health.ny.gov/nys-enx-what-you-need-know (accessed February 4, 2025).

13. Deffenbaugh, R. (2020). State Covid tracing app slow to gain acceptance. *Crains New York*, November 30. Available at: www.crainsnewyork.com/technology/state-covid-tracing-app-slow-gain-acceptance (accessed February 4, 2025).

14. Wetsman, N. (2020). Contact tracing apps promised big and didn't deliver. *The Verge*, December 11. Available at: www.theverge.com/22

168473/coronavirus-contact-tracing-apps-exposure-notification-covi d-google-apple (accessed February 4, 2025).

15. Ladyzhets, B. (2021). We investigated whether digital contact tracing actually worked in the US. *MIT Technology Review*, June 16. Available at: www.technologyreview.com/2021/06/16/1026255/us-digital-contact-tracing-exposure-notification-analysis/ (accessed February 4, 2025).

16. *BBC News* (2022). Australia Covid: Contact tracing app branded expensive "failure." August 10. Available at: www.bbc.com/news/wo rld-australia-62496322 (accessed February 4, 2025).

17. Molla, A. and Karanasios, S. (2022). Why did this $21 million COVID-tracing app fail? *Fast Company*, August 16. Available at: www.fastcom pany.com/90779160/why-did-this-21-million-covid-tracing-app-fail (accessed February 4, 2025).

18. Dehaye, P. O. (2020). Inferring distance from Bluetooth signal strength: a deep dive. *Medium*, May 19. Available at: https://mediu m.com/personaldata-io/inferring-distance-from-bluetooth-signal-str ength-a-deep-dive-fe7badc2bb6d (accessed February 4, 2025).

19. Bluetooth Low Energy: Android Open Source Project. Available at: https://source.android.com/docs/core/connect/bluetooth/ble (accessed February 4, 2025).

20. de Blasio, B. and Menin, J. (2015). New York City Mobile Services Study. Consumer Affairs, November. Available at: www.nyc.gov/asset s/dca/MobileServicesStudy/Research-Brief.pdf (accessed February 4, 2025).

21. Wetsman, N. (2021). Android bug exposed COVID-19 contact tracing logs to preinstalled apps. *The Verge*, April 27. Available at: www .theverge.com/2021/4/27/22405425/android-google-contact-tra cing-bug-privacy (accessed February 4, 2025).

22. Lazar, K. (2021). Massachusetts is spending $130 million to identify people exposed to Covid-19, but some question if money is well spent. *The Boston Globe*, March 29, Available at: www.bostonglobe.com/202 1/03/28/metro/massachusetts-is-spending-130-million-identify-peo ple-exposed-covid-19-some-question-if-money-is-well-spent/ (accessed February 4, 2025).

23. Lazar, K. (2021). Nearly $160 million later, the state's COVID-19 contact tracing program is ending. *The Boston Globe*, December 16, Available at: www.bostonglobe.com/2021/12/16/metro/nearly-160-

million-later-states-covid-19-contact-tracing-program-is-ending/ (accessed February 4, 2025).

24. Lazar, K. (2021). Nearly $160 million later, the state's COVID-19 contact tracing program is ending. *The Boston Globe*, December 16. Available at: www.bostonglobe.com/2021/12/16/metro/nearly-160-million-later-states-covid-19-contact-tracing-program-is-ending/ (accessed February 4, 2025).

25. Lafraniere, S. (2022). "Very harmful" lack of data blunts U.S. response to outbreaks. *The New York Times*, September 20. Available at: www.nytimes.com/2022/09/20/us/politics/covid-data-outbreaks.html (accessed February 4, 2025).

26. Lafraniere, S. (2022). "Very harmful" lack of data blunts U.S. response to outbreaks. *The New York Times*, September 20. Available at: www.nytimes.com/2022/09/20/us/politics/covid-data-outbreaks.html (accessed February 4, 2025).

27. Pettypiece, S. (2022). Democrats detail effects of early pandemic failures in new Senate report. *NBC News*, December 8. Available at: www.nbcnews.com/news/amp/rcna60453 (accessed February 4, 2025).

28. US Coronavirus Vaccine Tracker. *USA Facts*, updated May 10, 2024. Available at https://usafacts.org/visualizations/covid-vaccine-tracker-states/ (accessed February 4, 2025).

29. Milligan, S. (2021). How Vermont is winning the COVID vaccination war. *US News*, November 11. Available at: www.usnews.com/news/best-states/articles/2021-11-11/vermonts-key-to-high-covid-19-vaccination-rates (accessed February 4, 2025).

30. Singh-Kurtz, S. (2021). Catching up with NYC's "vaccine daddy." *The Cut*, April 2. Available at: www.thecut.com/2021/04/a-date-with-nycs-vaccine-daddy-huge-ma-turbovax.html (accessed February 4, 2025).

31. Frishberg, H. (2021). Man who got thousands of NYers vaccinated finally gets his own shot. *NY Post*, April 6. Available at https://nypost.com/2021/04/06/man-who-got-thousands-vaccinated-finally-gets-vaxxed-himself/ (accessed February 4, 2025).

32. Honan, K. (2021). "Vax daddy" gives politics a shot: Pandemic hero runs for Queens state assembly seat. *The City*, December 12. Available at: www.thecity.nyc/politics/2021/12/12/22831522/vax-daddy-hug

e-ma-runs-for-queens-assembly-after-turbovax (accessed February 4, 2025).

33. Some of this discussion is adapted from: Selinger, E. (2020). The public is being misled by pandemic technology that won't keep them safe. *Medium*, May 22. Available at: https://onezero.medium.com/t he-public-is-being-misled-by-pandemic-technology-that-wont-keep-th em-safe-1966ed740a87 (accessed February 4, 2025).

34. Gee, G. (2022). Schools spent millions on faulty COVID scanners. *The Daily Beast*, August 5. Available at: www.thedailybeast.com/us-schools-spent-millions-of-dollars-on-faulty-covid-scanners-and-cameras/ (accessed February 4, 2025).

35. Gee, G. (2022). Schools spent millions on faulty COVID scanners. *The Daily Beast*, August 5. Available at: www.thedailybeast.com/us-schools-spent-millions-of-dollars-on-faulty-covid-scanners-and-cameras/ (accessed February 4, 2025).

36. Guariglia, M. and Quintin, C. (2020). Thermal imaging cameras are still dangerous dragnet surveillance cameras. *Electronic Frontier Foundation*, April 7. Available at: www.eff.org/deeplinks/2020/04/t hermal-imaging-cameras-are-still-dangerous-dragnet-surveillance-ca meras (accessed February 4, 2025).

37. Glaser, A. (2020). "Fever detection" cameras to fight coronavirus? Experts say they don't work. *NBC News*, March 27. Available at: www .nbcnews.com/tech/security/fever-detection-cameras-fight-corona virus-experts-say-they-don-t-n1170791 (accessed February 4, 2025).

38. Gee, G. (2022). Schools spent millions on faulty COVID scanners. *The Daily Beast*, August 5. Available at: www.thedailybeast.com/us-schools-spent-millions-of-dollars-on-faulty-covid-scanners-and-cameras/ (accessed February 4, 2025).

39. Harwell, D. (2020). Thermal scanners are the latest technology being deployed to detect the coronavirus. but they don't really work. *The Washington Post*, May 5. Available at: www.washingtonpost.com/technol ogy/2020/05/11/thermal-scanners-are-latest-technology-being-deplo yed-detect-coronavirus-they-dont-really-work/ (accessed February 4, 2025).

40. Honovich, J. (2020). Beware of Feevr. *IPVM*, April 14. Available at: https://ipvm.com/reports/feevr2 (accessed February 4, 2025).

41. Gee, G. (2022). Schools spent millions on faulty COVID scanners. *The Daily Beast*, August 5. Available at: www.thedailybeast.com/us-schools-spent-millions-of-dollars-on-faulty-covid-scanners-and-cameras/ (accessed February 4, 2025).

42. Gee, G. (2022). Schools spent millions on faulty COVID scanners. *The Daily Beast*, August 5. Available at: www.thedailybeast.com/us-schools-spent-millions-of-dollars-on-faulty-covid-scanners-and-cameras/ (accessed February 4, 2025).

43. Schneier, B. (2023). *Beyond Fear*. Göttingen: Copernicus Books.

44. Schneier, B. (2020). Don't fear the TSA cutting airport security. Be glad that they're talking about it. *Schneier on Security*, September 7. Available at: www.schneier.com/blog/archives/2018/08/dont_fear_the_t.html (accessed February 4, 2025).

45. Schneier, B. (2020). Don't fear the TSA cutting airport security. Be glad that they're talking about it. *Schneier on Security*, September 7. Available at: www.schneier.com/blog/archives/2018/08/dont_fear_the_t.html (accessed February 4, 2025).

46. Swire, P. (2020). Security, privacy and the coronavirus: Lessons from 9/11. *Lawfare*, March 24. Available at: www.lawfaremedia.org/article/security-privacy-and-coronavirus-lessons-911 (accessed February 4, 2025).

47. Brannen, D. A. and Vance, T. (2020). Thermal imaging systems in the workplace: Panacea or problem? *JD Supra*, June 4. Available at: www.jdsupra.com/legalnews/thermal-imaging-systems-in-the-85168/ (accessed February 4, 2025).

48. Edmunds, C. (2020). Heathrow airport will trial thermal imaging facial recognition cameras, ultra-violet sanitation and contactless security measures in bid to spot passengers carrying coronavirus. *Daily Mail*, May 6. Available at: www.dailymail.co.uk/news/article-8292297/Heathrow-airport-trial-thermal-imaging-cameras-spot-passengers-carrying-coronavirus.html (accessed February 4, 2025).

49. Murphy, H. (2022). Whatever happened to those self-service passport kiosks at airports? *The New York Times*, October 5. Available at: www.nytimes.com/2022/10/05/travel/customs-kiosks-facial-recognition.html (accessed February 4, 2025).

50. Mayo Clinic Staff (2023). Herd immunity and COVID-19: What you need to know. *Johns Hopkins University: Mayo Clinic*, November 4. Available at: www.mayoclinic.org/diseases-conditions/corona

virus/in-depth/herd-immunity-and-coronavirus/art-20486808 (accessed February 4, 2025).

51. Sun Kyong, L., Juhyung, S., Seulki, J., et al. (2022). Misinformation of COVID-19 vaccines and vaccine hesitancy. *Nature: Scientific Reports* 12(1): article 13681.

52. Clayton, J., Humell, A., Pervaiz, S., et al. (2021). The good, the bad, & the invasive: The impact of vaccine registries, day passes, & passports. Surveillance Technology Oversight Project, June 2. Available at: www.stopspying.org/vaccineapps (accessed February 4, 2025).

53. Governor Cuomo announces launch of Excelsior Pass to help fast-track reopening of businesses and entertainment venues statewide. *New York State Governor Office*, March 26, 2021. Available at: www.governor.ny.gov/news/governor-cuomo-announces-launch-excelsior-pass-help-fast-track-reopening-businesses-and (accessed February 4, 2025).

54. Governor Cuomo announces launch of Excelsior Pass to help fast-track reopening of businesses and entertainment venues statewide. *New York State Governor Office*, March 26, 2021. Available at: www.governor.ny.gov/news/governor-cuomo-announces-launch-excelsior-pass-help-fast-track-reopening-businesses-and (accessed February 4, 2025).

55. New York politicians support "vaccine passport." *New York Daily News*, August 8, 2021, Available at: www.nydailynews.com/2021/04/08/new-york-politicians-voice-support-vaccine-passport-system-with-some-reservations/ (accessed February 4, 2025).

56. McKinley, J., Ferré-Sadurní, L., Rubinstein, D., et al. (2020). How a feud between Cuomo and de Blasio led to a chaotic virus crackdown. *The New York Times*, October 12. Available at: www.nytimes.com/2020/10/12/nyregion/cuomo-coronavirus-orthodox-shutdown.html (accessed February 4, 2025).

57. Transcript: Mayor de Blasio holds media availability. *The Official Website of the City of New York*, August 2, 2021. Available at: www1.nyc.gov/office-of-the-mayor/news/536-21/transcript-mayor-de-blasio-holds-media-availability (accessed February 4, 2025).

58. Transcript: Mayor de Blasio holds media availability. *The Official Website of the City of New York*, August 2, 2021. Available at: www1.nyc

.gov/office-of-the-mayor/news/536-21/transcript-mayor-de-blasio-h
olds-media-availability (accessed February 4, 2025).

59. Otterman, S. (2021). Here's how you can show proof of vaccination in
New York City. *The New York Times*, August 4. Available at: www.nyti
mes.com/2021/08/04/nyregion/nyc-vaccine-pass-answers.html
(accessed February 4, 2025).

60. Otterman, S. (2021). New York's "Excelsior Pass" could cost up to
$27 million. *The New York Times*, August 19. Available at: www.nytimes
.com/2021/08/19/nyregion/new-york-excelsior-pass-cost.html
(accessed February 4, 2025).

61. Facher, L. (2021). Resistance from health experts and business
owners could doom "vaccine passports" even before they launch.
Stat News, April 1. Available at: www.statnews.com/2021/04/01/resist
ance-vaccine-passports/ (accessed February 4, 2025).

62. Spisak, B. (2021). Vaccination certificates won't end lockdown.
Prosocial approaches will. *Stat*, March 31. Available at: www.stat
news.com/2021/03/31/vaccination-certificates-wont-end-lockdown-
prosocial-approaches-will/ (accessed February 4, 2025).

63. Chowdhury, R. (2021). We tried out the Excelsior Pass, New York's
state vaccine passport. *MIT Technology Review*, July 6. Available at: www
.technologyreview.com/2021/07/06/1027770/vaccine-passport-ne
w-york-excelsior-pass/ (accessed February 4, 2025).

64. Chowdhury, R. (2021). We tried out the Excelsior Pass, New York's
state vaccine passport. *MIT Technology Review*, July 6. Available at: www
.technologyreview.com/2021/07/06/1027770/vaccine-passport-ne
w-york-excelsior-pass/ (accessed February 4, 2025).

65. Fox Cahn, A. (2021). You call this a vaccine passport? *New York Daily
News*, August 10. Available at: www.nydailynews.com/opinion/ny-op
ed-you-call-this-a-vaccine-passport-20210810-bqxd5bxgjfd6zm3iizqm
zlfsse-story.html (accessed February 4, 2025).

66. Governor Hochul announces nearly 11 million Excelsior Passes
issued to date, reminds New Yorkers to retrieve their Excelsior
Pass Plus. *New York State Governor's Office*, June 30, 2022. Available
at: www.governor.ny.gov/news/governor-hochul-announces-nearl
y-11-million-excelsior-passes-issued-date-reminds-new-yorkers
(accessed February 4, 2025).

67. Ashford, G. (2022). Ready to "undo damage," some N.Y.C. restaurants cheer the lifting of an indoor vaccine mandate. *The New York Times*, March 6. Available at: www.nytimes.com/2022/03/07/nyregion/nyc-indoor-dining-vaccine-mandate.html (accessed February 4, 2025).
68. https://time.com/6320076/american-poverty-levels-state-by-state/
69. https://evictionlab.org/eviction-tracking/
70. https://www.nelp.org/faq-unemployment-anchors/
71. https://home.treasury.gov/policy-issues/coronavirus/assistance-for-small-businesses/paycheck-protection-program
72. https://nlihc.org/sites/default/files/Overview-of-National-Eviction-Moratorium.pdf
73. https://hcr.ny.gov/system/files/documents/2023/01/fact-sheet-20-11-2020.pdf

CHAPTER 6: MOVING FAST AND BREAKING SCHOOLS WITH REMOTE PROCTORING

1. National Center for Education Statistics (2023). Fast facts: Distance learning. Available at: https://nces.ed.gov/fastfacts/display.asp?id=80 (accessed February 4, 2025).
2. Hess, A. (2020). How coronavirus dramatically changed college for over 14 million students. *CNBC*, March 26. Available at: www.cnbc.com/2020/03/26/how-coronavirus-changed-college-for-over-14-million-students.html (accessed February 4, 2025).
3. See: McGurran, B. (2020). COVID-19 and college, here's what the fall will look like. *Forbes*, August 19. Available at: www.forbes.com/sites/advisor/2020/08/19/covid-19-and-college-heres-what-the-fall-will-look-like/#2e06de153ec9 (accessed February 4, 2025); Bwog Staff (2020). Columbia and Barnard announce entirely online fall 2020. Bwog – Columbia Student News (blog). Available at: https://bwog.com/2020/08/columbia-and-barnard-announce-entirely-online-fall-2020/ (accessed February 4, 2025).
4. Online Education Statistics. Education Data. Available at: https://web.archive.org/web/20210702153901/https://educationdata.org/online-education-statistics/ (accessed February 4, 2025).
5. Education Intelligence Unit (2020). $74B online degree market in 2025, up from $36B in 2019. *Holon IQ*. Available at: www.holoniq.co

m/notes/74b-online-degree-market-in-2025-up-from-36b-in-2019 (accessed February 4, 2025); see also Singer, N. (2015). Online test-takers feel anti-cheating software's uneasy glare. *The New York Times*, April 15. Available at: www.nytimes.com/2015/04/06/technology/ online-test-takers-feel-anti-cheating-softwares-uneasy-glare.html (accessed February 4, 2025).

6. NBC New York (2020). NJ schools to shut down Wednesday; see tri-state closures here. Blog. March 8. Available at: www.nbcnewyork.co m/news/local/coronavirus-closures-here-are-the-schools-closed/23 17622/ (accessed February 4, 2025).

7. Education Week (2020). School districts' reopening plans: A snap-shot. Available at: www.edweek.org/leadership/school-districts-reop ening-plans-a-snapshot/2020/07 (accessed February 4, 2025); see also Fishbane, L. and Tomer, A. (2020). As classes move online during COVID-19, what are disconnected students to do? Brookings (blog). Available at: www.brookings.edu/blog/the-avenue/2020/03 /20/as-classes-move-online-during-covid-19-what-are-disconnected-st udents-to-do/ (accessed February 4, 2025).

8. Education Week (2020). Map: Coronavirus and school closures in 2019–2020. Available at: www.edweek.org/leadership/map-corona virus-and-school-closures-in-2019-2020/2020/03 (accessed February 4, 2025).

9. Flaherty, C. (2020). Big proctor. *Inside Higher Ed*, May 10. Available at: www.insidehighered.com/news/2020/05/11/online-proctoring-sur ging-during-covid-19 (accessed February 4, 2025).

10. Grajek, S. (2023). EDUCAUSE COVID-19 QuickPoll results: Grading and proctoring. *Educause*, April 10. Available at: https://er.educause .edu/blogs/2020/4/educause-covid-19-quickpoll-results-grading-an d-proctoring (accessed February 4, 2025).

11. Goldberg, E. (2020). Bar and medical exam delays keep graduates in limbo. *The New York Times*, September 4. Available at: www.nytimes.co m/2020/09/04/us/bar-exam-coronavirus.html (accessed February 4, 2025).

12. Hubler, S. (2020). Keeping online testing honest? Or an Orwellian overreach? *The New York Times*, May 20. Available at: www.nytimes.co m/2020/05/10/us/online-testing-cheating-universities-coronavirus .html (accessed February 4, 2025).

13. Singer, N. (2015). Online test-takers feel anti-cheating software's uneasy glare. *The New York Times*, April 15. Available at: www.nytime s.com/2015/04/06/technology/online-test-takers-feel-anti-cheat ing-softwares-uneasy-glare.html (accessed February 4, 2025).
14. Harwell, D. (2020). Mass school closures in the wake of the corona-virus are driving a new wave of student surveillance. *The Washington Post*, April 1. Available at: www.washingtonpost.com/technology/20 20/04/01/online-proctoring-college-exams-coronavirus/ (accessed February 4, 2025).
15. ProctorU. Online proctoring: Test-taker resource center. Available at: www.proctoru.com/live-plus-resource-center#how (accessed February 4, 2025).
16. See: ExamSoft (2021). Privacy policy. Available at: https://examsoft .com/privacy-policy/ (accessed February 4, 2025) (records kept as long as ExamSoft have an "ongoing business need" and when that is over, "either delete or anonymize/de-identify it or, if this is not possible (for example, because the data has been stored in backup archives), then ExamSoft will securely store the personal data and isolate it from any further processing until deletion is possible"); Meazure Learning (2023). Privacy Policy. Blog. Available at: www.m eazurelearning.com/privacy-policy (accessed February 4, 2025).
17. Kelley, J. (2022). Federal judge: Invasive online proctoring "room scans" are unconstitutional. *Electronic Frontier Foundation*, August 25. Available at: www.eff.org/deeplinks/2022/08/federal-judge-inva sive-online-proctoring-room-scans-are-also-unconstitutional (accessed February 4, 2025).
18. Harwell, D. (2020). Mass school closures in the wake of the corona-virus are driving a new wave of student surveillance. *The Washington Post*, April 1. Available at: www.washingtonpost.com/technology/2 020/04/01/online-proctoring-college-exams-coronavirus/ (accessed February 4, 2025).
19. Harwell, D. (2020). Mass school closures in the wake of the corona-virus are driving a new wave of student surveillance. *The Washington Post*, April 1. Available at: www.washingtonpost.com/technology/20 20/04/01/online-proctoring-college-exams-coronavirus/ (accessed February 4, 2025).

20. Harwell, D. (2020). Mass school closures in the wake of the corona-virus are driving a new wave of student surveillance. *The Washington Post*, April 1. Available at: www.washingtonpost.com/technology/20 20/04/01/online-proctoring-college-exams-coronavirus/ (accessed February 4, 2025).

21. Bowman, E. (2022). Scanning students' rooms during remote tests is unconstitutional, judge rules. *NPR*, August 26. Available at: www.npr.org/2022/08/25/1119337956/test-proctoring-room-scans-unconsti tutional-cleveland-state-university (accessed February 4, 2025).

22. Overton County News (2023). NC student reported to police for toy gun. Available at: www.overtoncountynews.com/schools/nc-student-reported-to-police-for-toy-gun/article_a252709e-8b86-11ed-a5ca-a3c c35101ee3.html (accessed February 4, 2025).

23. Verificient Technologies (2021). Privacy policy. Available at: https://verificient.com/privacy-policy/.

24. PSI Exams (2023). Privacy policy. Available at: www.psiexams.com/l egal/privacy-policy/ (accessed February 4, 2025).

25. American Federation of Teachers (2023). Protecting our students and their families. Available at: www.aft.org/sites/default/files/med ia/2018/plylertoolkit_sanctuary-safezone.pdf (accessed February 4, 2025).

26. Legal Defense Fund (2018). Case: School to prison pipeline. Blog. Available at: www.naacpldf.org/case-issue/school-prison-pipeline/ (accessed February 4, 2025).

27. Harwell, D. (2020). Mass school closures in the wake of the corona-virus are driving a new wave of student surveillance. *The Washington Post*, April 1. Available at: www.washingtonpost.com/technology/20 20/04/01/online-proctoring-college-exams-coronavirus/ (accessed February 4, 2025).

28. Germain, T. (2020). Poor security at Proctortrack online proctoring. *Consumer Reports*, December 10. Available at: www.consumerreports .org/digital-security/poor-security-at-online-proctoring-company-pr octortrack-may-have-put-student-data-at-risk-a8711230545/ (accessed February 4, 2025).

29. Chin, M. (2020). Exam anxiety: How remote test-proctoring is creep-ing students out. *The Verge*, April 29. Available at: www.theverge.com/

2020/4/29/21232777/examity-remote-test-proctoring-online-class-e
ducation (accessed February 4, 2025).

30. Examity. Product privacy policy. Available at: www.examity.com/prod
uct-privacy-policy/ (accessed February 4, 2025).

31. Lawson, S. (2023). Are schools forcing students to install spyware
that invades their privacy as a result of the coronavirus lockdown?
Forbes, April 24. Available at: www.forbes.com/sites/seanlawson/20
20/04/24/are-schools-forcing-students-to-install-spyware-that-inva
des-their-privacy-as-a-result-of-the-coronavirus-lockdown/
(accessed February 4, 2025).

32. Honorlock privacy commitment. Available at: https://spcollege.hos
ted.panopto.com/Panopto/Pages/Viewer.aspx?id=934907d1-df02-4
8ab-81d7-adac00fea60d (accessed February 4, 2025) (explaining that
Honorlock stores student data for 12 months and sometimes longer).

33. ProctorU. Privacy, security, and data retention/how ProctorU uses
test-taker data. Available at: https://support.proctoru.com/hc/en-u
s/articles/24762436608781-Privacy-Security-and-Data-Retention-Ho
w-ProctorU-Uses-Test-taker-Data (accessed February 4, 2025).

34. Harwell, D. (2020). Mass school closures in the wake of the coronavirus are driving a new wave of student surveillance. *The Washington
Post*, April 1. Available at: www.washingtonpost.com/technology/20
20/04/01/online-proctoring-college-exams-coronavirus/ (accessed
February 4, 2025).

35. Chin, M. (2020). Exam anxiety: How remote test-proctoring is creep-
ing students out. *The Verge*, April 29. Available at: www.theverge.com/
2020/4/29/21232777/examity-remote-test-proctoring-online-class-e
ducation (accessed February 4, 2025).

36. @nicole.rzepka (2020). TikTok. Available at: www.tiktok.com/@nicol
e.rzepka/video/6805574351845477637 (accessed February 4, 2025).

37. @xsofiapereirax (2023). College kids know #WhatsYourStuf #ima-
nexpert #PINK2020 #fyp #proctoru. TikTok. Available at: www.tik
tok.com/@xsofiacristinax/video/6783467502874742021 (accessed
February 4, 2025).

38. @kiahkramer (2020). TikTok. Available at: www.tiktok.com/@kiahk
ramer/video/6791158098791828742 (accessed February 4, 2025).

39. American Test Anxieties Association (2020). Test anxiety. Available
at: https://web.archive.org/web/20200812055202/http://amtaa.or

g/ (accessed February 4, 2025); Thomas, C., Cassady, J. C., and Finch, H. (2018). Identifying severity standards on the cognitive test anxiety scale: Cut score determination using latent class and cluster analysis. *Journal of Psychoeducational Assessment* 36(5): 492–508.

40. Change.org (2023). Sign the petition: Stop use of Proctortrack in online courses. Available at: www.change.org/p/rutgers-university-sto p-use-of-proctortrack-in-online-courses (accessed February 4, 2025); Feathers, T. (2021). Schools are abandoning invasive proctoring software after student backlash. *Vice* (blog), February 26. Available at: www .vice.com/en/article/7k9ag4/schools-are-abandoning-invasive-proc toring-software-after-student-backlash (accessed February 4, 2025).

41. Office of Special Education and Rehabilitative Services, US Department of Education (2000). A guide to the individualized education program. Available at: www2.ed.gov/parents/needs/speced/ iepguide/iepguide.pdf (accessed February 4, 2025).

42. See Protection & Advocacy for People with Disabilities Inc. (2018). Fact sheet: The rights of college student with disabilities. Available at: www.pandasc.org/wp-content/uploads/2018/07/ADA-504-College-Students-7-18-1.pdf (accessed February 4, 2025).

43. Grajek, S. (2020). EDUCAUSE COVID-19 QuickPoll results: Grading and proctoring. EDUCAUSE Review. Available at: https://er.edu cause.edu/blogs/2020/4/educause-covid-19-quickpoll-results-grad ing-and-proctoring (accessed February 4, 2025).

44. Singer, N. (2015). Online test-takers feel anti-cheating software's uneasy glare. *The New York Times*, April 15. Available at: www.nytime s.com/2015/04/06/technology/online-test-takers-feel-anti-cheat ing-softwares-uneasy-glare.html (accessed February 4, 2025).

45. Harwell, D. (2020). Mass school closures in the wake of the coronavirus are driving a new wave of student surveillance. *The Washington Post*, April 1. Available at: www.washingtonpost.com/technology/20 20/04/01/online-proctoring-college-exams-coronavirus/ (accessed February 4, 2025); Abrams, L. (2023). ProctorU confirms data breach after database leaked online. *BleepingComputer*, August 9. Available at: www.bleepingcomputer.com/news/security/proctoru-confirms-dat a-breach-after-database-leaked-online/ (accessed February 4, 2025) (ProctorU has already professed to one breach in which 440,000 user

profiles were leaked, including names, addresses, phone numbers, affiliated organizations, and more).

46. Flaherty, C. (2020). Big proctor. *Inside Higher Ed*, May 10. Available at: www.insidehighered.com/news/2020/05/11/online-proctoring-sur ging-during-covid-19 (accessed February 4, 2025).

47. Verificient Technologies (2019). How do I prepare my testing environment? Available at: https://verificient.freshdesk.com/support/so lutions/articles/1000165250-how-do-i-prepare-my-testing-environ ment (accessed February 4, 2025).

48. Swauger, S. (2020). Our bodies encoded: Algorithmic test proctoring in higher education. *Hybrid Pedagogy*, April 2. Available at: https://h ybridpedagogy.org/our-bodies-encoded-algorithmic-test-proctoring-in-higher-education/ (accessed February 4, 2025).

49. Flaherty, C. (2020). Big proctor. *Inside Higher Ed*, May 10. Available at: www.insidehighered.com/news/2020/05/11/online-proctoring-sur ging-during-covid-19 (accessed February 4, 2025).

50. Flaherty, C. (2020). Big proctor. *Inside Higher Ed*, May 10. Available at: www.insidehighered.com/news/2020/05/11/online-proctoring-sur ging-during-covid-19 (accessed February 4, 2025).

51. Flaherty, C. (2020). Big proctor. *Inside Higher Ed*, May 10. Available at: www.insidehighered.com/news/2020/05/11/online-proctoring-sur ging-during-covid-19 (accessed February 4, 2025).

52. Flaherty, C. (2020). Big proctor. *Inside Higher Ed*, May 10. Available at: www.insidehighered.com/news/2020/05/11/online-proctoring-sur ging-during-covid-19 (accessed February 4, 2025).

53. Swauger, S. (2020). Our bodies encoded: Algorithmic test proctoring in higher education. *Hybrid Pedagogy*, April 2. Available at: https:// hybridpedagogy.org/our-bodies-encoded-algorithmic-test-proctoring-in-higher-education/ (accessed February 4, 2025).

54. Patrice, J. (2020). Bar examiners ask applicants to kindly stop being diabetic for a couple days. *Above the Law*, September 3. Available at: https://abovethelaw.com/2020/09/bar-examiners-ask-applicants-to-ki ndly-stop-being-diabetic-for-a-couple-days/ (accessed February 4, 2025).

55. Flaherty, C. (2020). Big proctor. *Inside Higher Ed*, May 10. Available at: www.insidehighered.com/news/2020/05/11/online-proctor ing-surging-during-covid-19 (accessed February 4, 2025); Patil, A. and Bromwich, J. (2020). How it feels when software watches you

take tests. *The New York Times*, September 29. Available at: www.nyti
mes.com/2020/09/29/style/testing-schools-proctorio.html
(accessed February 4, 2025).

56. Flaherty, C. (2020). Big proctor. *Inside Higher Ed*, May 10. Available at:
www.insidehighered.com/news/2020/05/11/online-proctoring-sur
ging-during-covid-19 (accessed February 4, 2025) ("Twenty-six percent of institutions said they were using products that didn't meet
their accessibility standards. Respondus was by far the most widely
used product").

57. Harwell, D. (2020). Mass school closures in the wake of the coronavirus
are driving a new wave of student surveillance. *The Washington Post*,
April 1. Available at: www.washingtonpost.com/technology/2020/04/
01/online-proctoring-college-exams-coronavirus/ (accessed February 4,
2025).

58. OpulentBag (2019). Professor has accused me of cheating. Reddit
Comment, *R/College*, April 7. Available at: www.reddit.com/r/col
lege/comments/bajjum/professor_has_accused_me_of_cheating/e
kbxw48/ (accessed February 4, 2025).

59. Hubler, S. (2020). Keeping online testing honest? Or an Orwellian
overreach? *The New York Times*, May 20. Available at: www.nytimes.co
m/2020/05/10/us/online-testing-cheating-universities-coronavirus
.html (accessed February 4, 2025).

60. Crockford, K. (2020). How is face recognition surveillance technology
racist? News & Commentary. American Civil Liberties Union (blog).
Available at: www.aclu.org/news/privacy-technology/how-is-face-rec
ognition-surveillance-technology-racist (accessed February 4, 2025).

61. Heilweil, R. (2020). Paranoia about cheating is making online education terrible for everyone. *Vox*, May 4. Available at: www.vox.com/re
code/2020/5/4/21241062/schools-cheating-proctorio-artificial-inte
lligence (accessed February 4, 2025); Khan, A. [@uhreeb] (2020).
The @ExamSoft software can't "recognize" me due to "poor lighting"
even though I'm sitting in a well lit room. Starting to think it has
nothing to do with lighting. Pretty sure we all predicted their facial
recognition software wouldn't work for people of color.
@DiplomaPriv4All. X (formerly Twitter), September 8. Available at:
https://twitter.com/uhreeb/status/1303139738065481728
(accessed February 4, 2025); Hudgins, V. (2020). Bar exams' facial

recognition deployment is heightening test takers' anxiety. *Legaltech News*, August 5. Available at: www.law.com/legaltechnews/2020/08/05/bar-exams-facial-recognition-deployment-is-heightening-test-take rs-anxiety/ (accessed February 4, 2025).

62. Dimeo, J. (2017). Online exam proctoring catches cheaters, raises concerns. *Inside Higher Ed*, May 9. Available at: www.insidehighered.com/digital-learning/article/2017/05/10/online-exam-proctoring-catches-cheaters-raises-concerns (accessed February 4, 2025).

63. Eckenrode, J., Ricci, M., and Klingen, A. (2016). 7 things you should know about remote proctoring. *EDUCAUSE Learning Initiative*, May 25. Available at: https://library.educause.edu/resources/2016/5/7-things-you-should-know-about-remote-proctoring.

64. UCSB Faculty Association Board (2020). Letter from UC Santa Barbara Faculty Association to Henry Yang, Chancellor and David Marshall, Executive Vice Chancellor. Available at: https://cucfa.org/wp-content/uploads/2020/03/ProctorU_2020-1.pdf (accessed February 4, 2025).

65. UCSB Faculty Association Board (2020). Letter from UC Santa Barbara Faculty Association to Henry Yang, Chancellor and David Marshall, Executive Vice Chancellor. Available at: https://cucfa.org/wp-content/uploads/2020/03/ProctorU_2020-1.pdf (accessed February 4, 2025).

66. Callahan, D. (2010). Why honor codes reduce student cheating. *HuffPost*, December 14. Available at: www.huffpost.com/entry/why-honor-codes-reduce-st_b_795898 (accessed February 4, 2025).

67. Callahan, D. (2010). Why honor codes reduce student cheating. *HuffPost*, December 14. Available at: www.huffpost.com/entry/why-honor-codes-reduce-st_b_795898 (accessed February 4, 2025).

68. Tatum, H. and Schwartz, B. (2017). Honor codes: Evidence based strategies for improving academic integrity. *Theory Into Practice*, 56(2): 129–35.

69. Callahan, D. (2010). Why honor codes reduce student cheating. *HuffPost*, December 14. Available at: www.huffpost.com/entry/why-honor-codes-reduce-st_b_795898 (accessed February 4, 2025); Tatum, H. and Schwartz, B. (2017). Honor codes: Evidence based strategies for improving academic integrity. *Theory Into Practice*, 56(2): 129–35.

70. Snyder, A. (2020). New York City schools change traditional grading system in response to Covid-19. *CNN*, April 28. Available at: www.cnn .com/2020/04/28/us/new-york-city-grading-system-change-covid-19 /index.html (accessed February 4, 2025).

71. Retta, M. (2020). How colleges are grading students during coronavirus. *NPR*, April 10. Available at: www.npr.org/2020/04/10/830622 398/how-colleges-are-grading-students-during-coronavirus (accessed February 4, 2025).

72. Wilson, P. (2020). Jefferson schools move to pass/fail during COVID-19 closure. *Daily Jefferson County Union.* Available at: www.dailyunion .com/news/covid-19/jefferson-schools-move-to-pass-fail-during-covi d-19-closure/article_b2bc2917-7a32-5ae5-aec0-830bb5de3e7d.html (accessed February 4, 2025).

73. Gonzales, A., McCrory Calarco, J., and Lynch, T. (2020). Technology problems and student achievement gaps: A validation and extension of the technology maintenance construct. *Communication Research* 47(5): 750–70.

74. Future Ready (2020). Students of color caught in the homework gap. Available at: https://futureready.org/wp-content/uploads/2020/08 /HomeworkGap_FINAL8.06.2020.pdf (accessed February 4, 2025).

75. Future Ready (2020). Students of color caught in the homework gap. Available at: https://futureready.org/wp-content/uploads/2020/08 /HomeworkGap_FINAL8.06.2020.pdf (accessed February 4, 2025).

76. National Center for Homeless Education (2020). Federal data summary school years 2015–16 through 2017–18: Education for homeless children and youth. Available at: https://nche.ed.gov/wp-content/ uploads/2020/01/Federal-Data-Summary-SY-15.16-to-17.18-Publish ed-1.30.2020.pdf (accessed February 4, 2025).

77. Turner, C. (2020). Homeless families struggle with impossible choices as school closures continue. *NPR*, October 7. Available at: www.npr.org/2020/10/07/920320592/an-impossible-choice-for-ho meless-parents-a-job-or-their-childs-education (accessed February 4, 2025).

78. MacGillis, A. (2020). The students left behind by remote learning. *The New Yorker*, September 28. Available at: www.propublica .org/article/the-students-left-behind-by-remote-learning (accessed February 4, 2025).

CHAPTER 7: UPGRADES IN THE AGE OF GENERATIVE AI

1. Guglielmo, C. (2024). AI chatbots are here to stay: Learn how they can work for you. *CNET*, January 16. Available at: www.cnet.com/tec h/computing/features/ai-chatbots-are-here-to-stay-learn-how-they-c an-work-for-you/ (accessed February 4, 2025).
2. Hu, K. (2023). ChatGPT sets record for fastest-growing user base – analyst note. *Reuters*, February 2. Available at: www.reuters.com/tech nology/chatgpt-sets-record-fastest-growing-user-base-analyst-note-20 23-02-01 (accessed February 4, 2025).
3. Novet, J. (2023). Microsoft's complex bet on OpenAI brings potential and uncertainty. *CNBC*, April 8. Available at: www.cnb c.com/2023/04/08/microsofts-complex-bet-on-openai-brings-pot ential-and-uncertainty.html#:~:text=Microsoft's%20%2413%20bil lion%20bet%20on,along%20with%20plenty%20of%20uncertaint y&text=Microsoft's%20partnership%20with%20OpenAI%20coul d,workloads%20pile%20up%20in%20Azure (accessed February 4, 2025).
4. Mehdi, Y. (2023). Reinventing search with a new AI-powered Microsoft Bing and Edge, your copilot for the web. *Microsoft*, official Microsoft blog, published February 7. Available at: https://blogs .microsoft.com/blog/2023/02/07/reinventing-search-with-a-new-ai-powered-microsoft-bing-and-edge-your-copilot-for-the-web/ (accessed February 4, 2025).
5. Heath, A. (2024). Mark Zuckerberg's new goal is creating artificial general intelligence. *The Verge*, January 18. Available at: www.the verge.com/2024/1/18/24042354/mark-zuckerberg-meta-agi-reorg-i nterview (accessed February 4, 2025).
6. Heath, A. (2024). Mark Zuckerberg's new goal is creating artificial general intelligence. *The Verge*, January 18. Available at: www.the verge.com/2024/1/18/24042354/mark-zuckerberg-meta-agi-reorg-i nterview (accessed February 4, 2025).
7. Young, L. (2023). Chatbots are trying to figure out where your shipments are. *Wall Street Journal*, August 30. Available at: www.wsj.com/ articles/chatbots-are-trying-to-figure-out-where-your-shipments-are-7 f7f9ee7 (accessed February 4, 2025).

8. Justice Practical Guide (Beta Version). *Justiça.gov.pt.* Available at: https://justica.gov.pt/en-gb/Servicos/Justice-Practical-Guide-Bet a-Version (accessed January 12, 2025).

9. Warren, T. (2023). Microsoft rebrands Bing Chat to Copilot, to better compete with ChatGPT. *The Verge*, November 15. Available at: www .theverge.com/2023/11/15/23960517/microsoft-copilot-bing-chat-rebranding-chatgpt-ai (accessed February 4, 2025).

10. Morris, M. R. (2023). Scientists' perspectives on the potential for generative AI in their fields. arXiv (preprint), Google Research. Available at: https://arxiv.org/abs/2304.01420s (accessed February 4, 2025).

11. Ohlheiser, A. W. (2023). Chatbot therapy is risky. It's also not useless. *Vox*, December 14. Available at: www.vox.com/technol ogy/2023/12/14/24000435/chatbot-therapy-risks-and-potential (accessed February 4, 2025).

12. Chow, A. R. (2023). Why people are confessing their love for AI chatbots. *TIME*. Available at: https://time.com/6257790/ai-chat bots-love/ (accessed February 4, 2025).

13. Chatterjee, M. (2023). A new kind of AI copy can fully replicate famous people. The law is powerless. *POLITICO*, December 30. Available at: www.politico.com/news/magazine/2023/12/30/ai-p sychologist-chatbot-00132682 (accessed February 4, 2025); Pearcy, A. (2023). "It was as if my father were actually texting me": Grief in the age of AI. *The Guardian*, July 18. Available at: www.the guardian.com/technology/2023/jul/18/ai-chatbots-grief-chatgpt (accessed February 4, 2025).

14. Lazar, S. (2024). Frontier AI ethics. *Aeon*. Available at: https://aeon .co/essays/can-philosophy-help-us-get-a-grip-on-the-consequences-o f-ai (accessed February 4, 2025).

15. Altman, S. (2023). Planning for AGI and beyond. *OpenAI*, February 24. Available at: www.openai.com/research/planning-for-a gi-and-beyond (accessed February 4, 2025).

16. Ahmed, Z. (2023). When will the world see AGI? Elon Musk, Sam Altman & Geoffrey Hinton make these bold predictions. *The Indian Express*, November 9. Available at: https://indianexpress.com/art

icle/technology/artificial-intelligence/when-is-agi-coming-what-tec
h-bigwigs-say-9018612/ (accessed February 4, 2025).

17. Ahmed, Z. (2023). When will the world see AGI? Elon Musk, Sam
    Altman & Geoffrey Hinton make these bold predictions. *The Indian
    Express*, November 9. Available at: https://indianexpress.com/art
    icle/technology/artificial-intelligence/when-is-agi-coming-what-tec
    h-bigwigs-say-9018612/ (accessed February 4, 2025).

18. Vanian, J. (2023). Meta's AI chief doesn't think AI super intelligence
    is coming anytime soon, and is skeptical on quantum computing.
    CNBC, December 3. Available at: www.cnbc.com/2023/12/03/meta-
    ai-chief-yann-lecun-skeptical-about-agi-quantum-computing.html
    (accessed February 4, 2025).

19. Altman, S. (2023). Planning for AGI and beyond. *OpenAI*,
    February 24. Available at: www.openai.com/research/planning-for-a
    gi-and-beyond (accessed February 4, 2025).

20. Varanasi, L. (2023). List: Here are the exams ChatGPT and GPT-4
    have passed so far. *Business Insider*, November 5. Available at: www.b
    usinessinsider.com/list-here-are-the-exams-chatgpt-has-passed-so-far-
    2023-1 (accessed February 4, 2025).

21. Bender, E. M., Gebru, T., McMillan-Major, A., et al. (2021). On the
    dangers of stochastic parrots: Can language models be too big?
    FAccT'21, *Proceedings of the 2021 ACM Conference on Fairness,
    Accountability, and Transparency*. New York, NY: Association for
    Computing Machinery, pp. 610–23.

22. Tiku, N. (2022). The Google engineer who thinks the company's AI
    has come to life. *The Washington Post*, June 11. Available at: www.was
    hingtonpost.com/technology/2022/06/11/google-ai-lamda-blake-l
    emoine/ (accessed February 4, 2025).

23. Jamal, U. (2022). An engineer who was fired from Google believes its
    AI chatbot may have a soul but says he's not interested in convincing
    the public about it. *Business Insider*. Available at: www.businessinsider
    .com/google-engineer-blake-lemoine-artificial-intelligence-chatbot-s
    entience-2022-7 (accessed February 4, 2025).

24. Leong, B. and Selinger, E. (2019). Robot eyes wide shut:
    Understanding dishonest anthropomorphism. *Proceedings of the
    Association for Computing Machinery's Conference on Fairness,*

Accountability, and Transparency. Available at: https://papers.ssrn.co
m/sol3/papers.cfm?abstract_id=3762223 (accessed February 4,
2025).

25. Rose, J. (2023). A U.S. politician is robocalling voters with an AI
chatbot named "Ashley." *Vice.* Available at: www.vice.com/en/art
icle/4a3pvw/shemaine-daniels-congress-ai-chatbot-ashley (accessed
February 4, 2025).

26. Turton, K. (2023). Meet Ashley, the world's first AI-powered political
campaign caller. *Reuters,* December 16. Available at: www.reuters.co
m/technology/meet-ashley-worlds-first-ai-powered-political-cam
paign-caller-2023-12-12/ (accessed February 4, 2025). There isn't
enough transparency to know what generative AI models power
Ashley. The company has only discussed that there are "over 20,"
and some are "proprietary" and others "open-source."

27. Rose, J. (2023). A U.S. politician is robocalling voters with an AI
chatbot named "Ashley." *Vice.* Available at: www.vice.com/en/art
icle/4a3pvw/shemaine-daniels-congress-ai-chatbot-ashley (accessed
February 4, 2025).

28. Swenson, A. (2023). Congressional candidate's voter outreach tool is
latest AI experiment ahead of 2024 elections. *AP News.* Available at:
https://apnews.com/article/ai-chatbot-voters-election-2024-pennsyl
vania-db25cede35aa258d3e44563b517cc457 (accessed February 4,
2025).

29. One of us has written about a key process for making generative AI
safer and more trustworthy: red-teaming. Selinger, E. and Leong,
B. (2024). Getting AI ready for the real world takes a terrible
human toll. *The Boston Globe,* January 11. Available at: www.boston
globe.com/2024/01/11/opinion/ai-testing-red-team-human-toll/
(accessed February 4, 2025).

30. Sharma, A. (2023). AI chatbot confesses love for user, asks him to end
his marriage. *NDTV,* February 19. Available at: www.ndtv.com/fea
ture/ai-chatbot-confesses-love-for-user-asks-him-to-end-his-marriage-
3795575 (accessed February 4, 2025).

31. El Atillah, I. (2023). Man ends his life after an AI chatbot "encouraged" him to sacrifice himself to stop climate change. *Euro News,*

March 31. Available at: www.euronews.com/2023/03/31/man-ends-his-life-after-an-ai-chatbot-encouraged-him-to-sacrifice-himself-to-stop-climate- (accessed February 4, 2025).

32. Gross, N. (2023). What ChatGPT tells us about gender: A cautionary tale about performativity and gender biases in AI. *Social Sciences* 12(8).

33. Selinger, E. and Leong, B. (2024). Getting AI ready for the real world takes a terrible human toll. *The Boston Globe*, January 11. Available at: www.bostonglobe.com/2024/01/11/opinion/ai-testing-red-team-human-toll/ (accessed February 4, 2025).

34. Selinger, E. and Leong, B. (2024). Getting AI ready for the real world takes a terrible human toll. *The Boston Globe*, January 11. Available at: www.bostonglobe.com/2024/01/11/opinion/ai-testing-red-team-human-toll/ (accessed February 4, 2025).

35. Kleinman, Z. (2024). Why Google's "woke" AI problem won't be an easy fix. *BBC News*, February 28. Available at: www.bbc.com/news/technology-68412620 (accessed February 4, 2025).

36. Turton, K. (2023). Meet Ashley, the world's first AI-powered political campaign caller. *Reuters*, December 16. Available at: www.reuters.com/technology/meet-ashley-worlds-first-ai-powered-political-campaign-caller-2023-12-12/ (accessed February 4, 2025).

37. Belanger, A. (2024). Air Canada must honor refund policy invented by airline's chatbot. *ArsTechnica*, February 16. Available at: https://arstechnica.com/tech-policy/2024/02/air-canada-must-honor-refund-policy-invented-by-airlines-chatbot/ (accessed February 4, 2025).

38. Vanian, J. (2023). Meta's AI chief doesn't think AI super intelligence is coming anytime soon, and is skeptical on quantum computing. *CNBC*, December 3. Available at: www.cnbc.com/2023/12/03/meta-ai-chief-yann-lecun-skeptical-about-agi-quantum-computing.html (accessed February 4, 2025).

39. Tamayo-Sarver, J. (2023). I'm an ER doctor. Here's how I'm already using ChatGPT to help treat patients. *Fast Company*. www.fastcompany.com/90895618/how-a-doctor-uses-chat-gpt-to-treat-patients (accessed February 4, 2025).

40. Tamayo-Sarver, J. (2023). I'm an ER doctor. Here's how I'm already using ChatGPT to help treat patients. *Fast Company*. www.fastcom

pany.com/90895618/how-a-doctor-uses-chat-gpt-to-treat-patients (accessed February 4, 2025).

41. Kolata, G. (2023). When doctors use a chatbot to improve their bedside manner. *The New York Times*, June 12. Available at: www.nyti mes.com/2023/06/12/health/doctors-chatgpt-artificial-intelli gence.html (accessed February 4, 2025).

42. Srivastava, R. (2023). I am an oncologist: Can ChatGPT help me deliver bad news to a patient? *The Guardian*, June 21. Available at: https://amp.theguardian.com/commentisfree/2023/jun/21/i-am-an-oncologist-can-chatgpt-help-me-deliver-bad-news-to-a-patient (accessed February 4, 2025).

43. Srivastava, R. (2023). I am an oncologist: Can ChatGPT help me deliver bad news to a patient? *The Guardian*. Available at: https://amp.theguardian.com/commentisfree/2023/jun/21/i-am-an-onc ologist-can-chatgpt-help-me-deliver-bad-news-to-a-patient (accessed February 4, 2025).

44. Tulane University School of Public Health and Tropical Medicine (2022). The impact of hospital staff shortages in health care. *Tulane University*. Available at: https://publichealth.tulane.edu/blog/hos pital-staff-shortages/ (accessed February 4, 2025).

45. Derksen, F., Bensing, J., Kuiper, S., et al. (2015). Empathy: What does it mean for GPs? A qualitative study. *Family Practice* 32(1): 94–100; Derksen, F., Olde Hartman, T. C., van Dijk, A., et al. (2017). Consequences of the presence and absence of empathy during consultations in primary care: A focus group study with patients. *Patient Education and Counseling* 100(5): 987–93.

46. Squier, R. W. (1990). A model of empathic understanding and adherence to treatment regimens in practitioner–patient relationships. *Social Science & Medicine* 30(3): 325–39; Steinhausen, S., Ommen, O., Thum, S., et al. (2014). Physician empathy and subjective evaluation of medical treatment outcome in trauma surgery patients. *Patient Education and Counseling* 95(1): 53–60.

47. Leopardi, E. and Gilligan, C. (2021). Doctors are trained to be kind and empathetic, but a hidden curriculum makes them forget on the job. *The Conversation*, December 13. Available at: https://theconver sation.com/doctors-are-trained-to-be-kind-and-empathetic-but-a-h

idden-curriculum-makes-them-forget-on-the-job-171942 (accessed February 4, 2025).

48. Leopardi, E. and Gilligan, C. (2021). Doctors are trained to be kind and empathetic, but a hidden curriculum makes them forget on the job. *The Conversation*, December 13. Available at: https://theconver sation.com/doctors-are-trained-to-be-kind-and-empathetic-but-a-h idden-curriculum-makes-them-forget-on-the-job-171942 (accessed February 4, 2025).

49. Inzlicht, M., Cameron, C. D., D'Cruz, J., et al. (2024). In praise of empathic AI. *Trends in Cognitive Sciences* 28(2): 89–91.

50. Inzlicht, M., Cameron, C. D., D'Cruz, J., et al. (2024). In praise of empathic AI. *Trends in Cognitive Sciences*, 28(2): 89–91.

51. Ayers, J. W., Poliak, A., Dredze, M., et al. (2023). Comparing physician and artificial intelligence chatbot responses to patient questions posted to a public social media forum. *JAMA Internal Medicine* 183(6): 589–96.

52. Ayers, J. W., Poliak, A., Dredze, M., et al. (2023). Comparing physician and artificial intelligence chatbot responses to patient questions posted to a public social media forum. *JAMA Internal Medicine* 183(6): 589–96.

53. Ayers, J. W., Poliak, A., Dredze, M., et al. (2023). Comparing physician and artificial intelligence chatbot responses to patient questions posted to a public social media forum. *JAMA Internal Medicine* 183(6): 589–96.

54. To be clear, we are not recommending patients should use current versions of generative AI to get answers to medical questions. However, it is worth noting what one study that compared physician and ChatGPT responses found. Nov, O., Singh, N., and Mann, D. (2023). Putting ChatGPT's medical advice to the (Turing) test: Survey study. *JMIR Medical Education* 10(9): article e46939.

55. Human empathy has three main components. Imagine a doctor entering a waiting room and seeing a patient pulling at their hair while looking down at the floor right before a procedure. At a mere glance, the physician can tell the patient is upset. That's "cognitive empathy," our ability to identify someone else's emotions. When doctors internalize someone else's feelings, like some of a patient's worry, they experience "emotional empathy." Finally, if doctors feel

moved to help patients, maybe say something reassuring to provide comfort, they experience "motivational empathy." Generative AI lacks emotional and motivational empathy. And it can only demonstrate limited abilities associated with cognitive empathy. Given these limits, the technology can't care about patients and their families. All systems like ChatGPT can do is mimic empathetic expressions. Montemayor, C., Halpern, J., and Fairweather, A. (2022). In principle obstacles for empathic AI: Why we can't replace human empathy in healthcare. *AI & Society*, 37(4): 1353–9. For related arguments about the limits of AI and empathy, see Perry, A. (2023). AI will never convey the essence of human empathy. *Nature Human Behaviour* 7(11): 1808–9. For a study of the abilities related to cognitive empathy conducted with the earlier ChatGPT3, see Sorin, V., Brin, D., Barash, Y., et al. (2024). Large language models (LLMs) and empathy: Systematic review. *Journal of Medical Internet Research* 11(26): article e52597.

56. Although this is merely an illusion of care, we should keep two things in mind. First, we're recommending that doctors use the technology, not that patients interact with it directly. Hence, physicians retain the guiding intention, which is to provide quality care. Second, there is evidence that people can receive benefits from mere simulations of empathy. See Inzlicht, M., Cameron, D., D'Cruz, J., et al. (2024). In praise of empathic AI. *Trends in Cognitive Sciences* 28(2): 89–91.

57. The Associated Press (2023). Ex-Trump lawyer Michael Cohen says he unwittingly sent AI-generated fake legal cases to his attorney. *US News*, September 29. Available at: www.usnews.com/article/michael-cohen-donald-trump-artificial-intelligence-777ace9cc34aa0e56398f d47a1d6b420 (accessed February 4, 2025).

58. Frischmann, B. and Benesch, S. (2023). Friction-in-design: Regulation as 21st century time, place, and manner restriction. *Yale Journal of Law and Technology* 25: 376–447.

59. This could involve a policy-shift. Currently, patients may be interacting with AI-infused scheduling programs and giving consent for that practice without even realizing it because the terms are buried deep in user-agreements.

60. Another notable limitation of the study is that it didn't examine whether salient demographic differences among physicians, like

differences in personality types, cultural backgrounds, sex, and gender, could influence their evaluations of what ChatGPT and doctors wrote.

61. Kanter, G. P. and Packel, E. A. (2023). Health care privacy risks of AI chatbots. *JAMA* 330(4): 311–12.
62. Han, E., Yin, D., and Zhang, H. (2022). Chatbot empathy in customer service: When it works and when it backfires. *SIGHCI 2022 Proceedings*. Available at: https://aisel.aisnet.org/sighci2022/1/ (accessed February 4, 2025).
63. For more on normalization, see Selinger, E. and Rhee, J. (2021). Normalizing surveillance. *Northern European Journal of Philosophy* 22(1): 49–74; Hartzog, W., Selinger, E., and Gunawan, J. (2024). Privacy nicks: A normalizing theory of surveillance law. *Washington University Law Review* 101(3): 717–89.
64. Sharma, A., Lin, I. W., Miner, A. S., et al. (2023). Human–AI collaboration enables more empathic conversations in text-based peer-to-peer mental health support. *Nature Machine Intelligence* 5(1): 1–12.

CHAPTER 8: UPGRADING HIRING

1. Demopoulos, A. (2024). The job applicants shut out by AI: "The interviewer sounded like Siri." *The Guardian*, March 6. Available at: www.theguardian.com/technology/2024/mar/06/ai-interviews-job-applications (accessed February 4, 2025).
2. Melendez, S. (2024). Your next job interview could be with a bot. *Fast Company*, February 26. Available at: www.fastcompany.com/9103634 2/your-next-job-interview-could-be-with-a-bot (accessed February 4, 2025).
3. Resume Builder (2023). 4 in 10 companies will be using AI interview by 2024. June 5. Available at: www.resumebuilder.com/4-in-10-companies-will-be-using-ai-interviews-by-2024/ (accessed February 4, 2025).
4. Abril, D. (2023). Your next job interview could be judged by AI. Here's how to prepare. *The Washington Post*, March 28. Available at: www.washingtonpost.com/technology/2023/03/27/ai-assessed-job-interview/ (accessed February 4, 2025).

5. Matei, A. (2023). Why job searches suck right now. *Business Insider*. Available at: www.businessinsider.com/ai-chatgpt-hiring-ghost-inter views-job-search-weird-labor-market-2023–5 (accessed February 4, 2025).

6. Ortiz, S. (2024). AI could conduct your next job interview – meet Braintrust Air. *ZDNET*, April 29. Available at: www.zdnet.com/art icle/ai-could-conduct-your-next-job-interview-meet-braintrust-air/ (accessed February 4, 2025).

7. Resume Builder (2023). 4 in 10 companies will be using AI interview by 2024. June 5. Available at: www.resumebuilder.com/4-in-10-com panies-will-be-using-ai-interviews-by-2024/ (accessed February 4, 2025).

8. Raine, L., Anderson, M., McClain, C., et al. (2023). AI in hiring and evaluating workers: What Americans think. *Pew Research Center*, April 20. Available at: www.pewresearch.org/internet/2023/04/20/ ai-in-hiring-and-evaluating-workers-what-americans-think/ (accessed February 4, 2025).

9. Ryssdal, K. and Terenzio, S. (2024). For some job seekers, AI-powered "resume spammers" are a good fit. *Marketplace*, March 28. Available at: www.marketplace.org/2024/03/28/for-some-job-seekers-ai-powere d-resume-spammers-are-a-good-fit/ (accessed February 4, 2025).

10. Riccardi, G. (2024). Before AI takes your job, it's taking your job application. *Quartz*, January 24. Available at: www.qz.com/hr-soft ware-ai-algorithms-bias-1851190372 (accessed February 4, 2025).

11. Ellis, L. (2024). "You're fighting with AI": Bots are breaking the hiring process. *The Wall Street Journal*, May 10. Available at: www.wsj.com/lif estyle/careers/ai-job-application-685f29f7?st=6d0dzpsdf2nv4lj&re flink=desktopwebshare_permalink (accessed February 4, 2025).

12. Lobel, O. (2022). *The Equality Machine: Harnessing Digital Technology for a Brighter, More Inclusive Future*. New York, NY: PublicAffairs.

13. Matei, A. (2023). Why job searches suck right now. *Business Insider*. Available at: www.businessinsider.com/ai-chatgpt-hiring-ghost-inter views-job-search-weird-labor-market-2023–5 (accessed February 4, 2025).

14. Schellmann, H. (2024). *The Algorithm: How AI Decides Who Gets Hired, Monitored, Promoted, and Fired and Why We Need to Fight Back Now*. Boston, MA: De Capo Press.

15. Selinger, E. (2024). Keeping humans in the loop: On Hilke Schellmann's "The Algorithm." *Los Angeles Review of Books*, May 31. Available at: www.lareviewofbooks.org/article/keeping-humans-in-t he-loop-on-hilke-schellmanns-the-algorithm/ (accessed February 4, 2025).

16. Selinger, E. (2024). Keeping humans in the loop: On Hilke Schellmann's "The Algorithm." *Los Angeles Review of Books*, May 31. Available at: www.lareviewofbooks.org/article/keeping-humans-in-t he-loop-on-hilke-schellmanns-the-algorithm/ (accessed February 4, 2025).

17. Harwell, D. (2019). A face-scanning algorithm increasingly decides whether you deserve the job. *The Washington Post*, November 6. Available at: www.washingtonpost.com/technology/2019/10/22/ai-hiring-face-scanning-algorithm-increasingly-decides-whether-you-des erve-job/ (accessed February 4, 2025).

18. Harwell, D. (2019). A face-scanning algorithm increasingly decides whether you deserve the job. *The Washington Post*, November 6. Available at: www.washingtonpost.com/technology/2019/10/22/ai-hiring-face-scanning-algorithm-increasingly-decides-whether-you-des erve-job/ (accessed February 4, 2025).

19. Fischer, S. (2013). About face: Emotions and facial expressions may not be related. *Boston Magazine*, June 25. Available at: www.bostonma gazine.com/news/2013/06/25/emotions-facial-expressions-not-rela ted/ (accessed February 4, 2025).

20. Stark, L. and Hutson, J. (2022). Physiognomic artificial intelligence. *Fordham Intellectual Property, Media & Entertainment Law Journal* 32(4): 922–78.

21. Selinger, E. (2022). Is digital privacy overrated? *The Boston Globe*, November 24. Available at: www.bostonglobe.com/2022/11/24/opi nion/is-digital-privacy-overrated/ (accessed February 4, 2025).

22. Artificial Intelligence Video Interview Act. 820 ILCS 42/1 (2020).

23. Labor and Employment – Use of Facial Recognition Services – Prohibition. MD Labor and Employment Code § 3–717 (2024).

24. Muller, J. (2022). Your next job interview could be with a robot. *Axios*, February 16. Available at: www.axios.com/2022/02/16/automated-j ob-interviews (accessed February 4, 2025).

25. Muller, J. (2022). Your next job interview could be with a robot. *Axios*, February 16. Available at: www.axios.com/2022/02/16/automated-j ob-interviews (accessed February 4, 2025).

26. Jaser, Z. (2021). Automated job interviews and the implications for young jobseekers. *Policy@Sussex*. Available at: blogs.sussex.ac.uk/pol icy-engagement/files/2021/10/Automated-job-interviews-and-the-i mplications-for-young-jobseekers.pdf (accessed February 4, 2025).

27. Jaser, Z. (2021). Automated job interviews and the implications for young jobseekers. *Policy@Sussex*. Available at: blogs.sussex.ac.uk/pol icy-engagement/files/2021/10/Automated-job-interviews-and-the-i mplications-for-young-jobseekers.pdf (accessed February 4, 2025).

28. *The Washington Post* (2023). How to ace your next AI job interview. Online video clip. March. Available at: www.youtube.com/watch?v= olFefP5ivDM (accessed February 4, 2025).

29. Jaser, Z. (2021). Automated job interviews and the implications for young jobseekers. *Policy@Sussex*. Available at: blogs.sussex.ac.uk/pol icy-engagement/files/2021/10/Automated-job-interviews-and-the-i mplications-for-young-jobseekers.pdf (accessed February 4, 2025).

30. HR.com (accessed December 2024). About us. Website. Available at: www.hr.com/en/about_us/ (accessed February 4, 2025).

31. Oracle and HR.com (2019). *The 2019 State of Artificial Intelligence in Talen Acquisition*. HR Research Institute. Available at: www.oracle.co m/a/ocom/docs/artificial-intelligence-in-talent-acquisition.pdf?elq TrackId=%201279a8827f3d4548ae3f966beeeef458&elqai d=83148&elqat=2 (accessed February 4, 2025).

32. Ansari, A. @aliniikk (2024). Excited to introduce the world's first AI interviewer, gpt-vetting. X (formerly Twitter), April 12. Available at: https://x.com/aliniikk/status/1778796486194823514?s=51 (accessed February 4, 2025).

33. Bender, E. M. (2024). Resisting dehumanization in the age of "AI." *Current Directions in Psychological Science* 33(2). Available at: https://j ournals.sagepub.com/doi/10.1177/09637214231217286 (accessed June 10, 2025).

34. McAdams, A. (2024). Byte-Sized case study: Newhire.ai. *Byte-Sized*. Available at: www.bytesizedethics.io/p/byte-sized-case-study-newhireai (accessed February 4, 2025).

35. McAdams, A. (2024). Byte-Sized case study: Newhire.ai. *Byte-Sized.* Available at: www.bytesizedethics.io/p/byte-sized-case-study-newhireai (accessed February 4, 2025).

36. By focusing on the dehumanizing aspects of being interviewed by an AI avatar, we're taking a different approach to the problem of dehumanization than is expressed in the only peer-reviewed research article that has been published on dehumanization, AI, and hiring (Fritts, M. and Cabrera, F. (2021). AI recruitment algorithms and the dehumanization problem. *Ethics & Information Technology* 23: 791–801). Its authors argue that none of the typical definitions applies. As a more contextually appropriate alternative, they propose that AI dehumanizes the hiring process by "importing artificial values" into a domain that historically has been guided by human judgment and human values – values and judgment that are exceptionally difficult, maybe even impossible, to quantify. To illustrate, they give the hypothetical example of a ballet dancer who is denied an opportunity to perform for human judges, but is told not to worry because a highly sophisticated AI with "millions of points of data on the remaining contenders" will determine who gets a coveted spot in the New York City Ballet. You might think the authors would conclude by saying that the AI unfairly recommends another dancer, but they chose a more interesting ending. They contend the dancer might justifiably feel disappointed if she gets selected. Why is this? They claim it's because the dehumanizing process analyzed data points, not a whole person. This example focuses on the potentially flawed assessment of the intangible aspects of artistic performance. It suggests that an AI might focus solely on technical aspects of artistry (say, how high a leg moves or how quickly a position changes), but fail to perceive whether a dancer moves well but mechanically and lacks the "it" factor that captivates human audiences. While it is a significant risk that an AI could use the wrong standard to assess candidates during an interview, this concern doesn't apply to every field AI can judge. By contrast, our position focuses on an interview process with universal applicability.

CHAPTER 9: CYBERSECURITY: THE LAND OF THE TRUE UPGRADERS

1. Vijayan, J. (2023). Majority of ransomware attacks last year exploited old bugs. *Dark Reading*, February 20. Available at: www.darkreading.com/cyberattacks-data-breaches/dozens-of-vulns-in-ransomware-attacks-offer-adversaries-full-kill-chain (accessed February 4, 2025).
2. US Department of Commerce, National Institute of Standards and Technology, Joint Task Force (2020). *Security and Privacy Controls for Information Systems and Organizations.* NIST Special Publication 800-53, Revision 5. Available at: https://doi.org/10.6028/NIST.SP.800-53r5 (accessed February 4, 2025).
3. Levin, D. (2018). Machine learning: A belt and suspenders approach. *ReversingLabs Blog*, December 13. Available at: www.reversinglabs.com/blog/machine-learning-a-belt-and-suspenders-approach (accessed February 4, 2025).
4. Ross, R. and McEvilley, M. (2022). *Engineering Trustworthy Secure Systems.* NIST Special Publication 800-160, Revision 1: p. 97. Available at: https://doi.org/10.6028/NIST.SP.800-160v1r1 (accessed February 4, 2025).
5. Yaffe-Bellany, D. (2024). Bitcoin hits a milestone: $100,000. *The New York Times*, December 4. Available at: www.nytimes.com/2024/12/04/technology/bitcoin-price-record.html (accessed February 4, 2025).
6. Safire, W. (1999). The way we live now: 2.21.99 – on language; need not to know. *The New York Times*, February 21. Available at: www.nytimes.com/1999/02/21/magazine/the-way-we-live-now-2.21.99-on-language-need-not-to-know.html (accessed February 4, 2025).
7. Goldberg, S. (1995). Groves and the scientists: Compartmentalization and the building of the bomb. *Physics Today* 48(8): 38–43.
8. Rose, S., Borchet, O., Mitchell, S., et al. (2020). *Zero Trust Architecture.* NIST Special Publication 800-207. Available at: https://doi.org/10.6028/NIST.SP.800-207 (accessed February 4, 2025).
9. IEEE Digital Privacy (2024). What is privacy-by-design and why it's important? Available at: https://digitalprivacy.ieee.org/publications/topics/what-is-privacy-by-design-and-why-it-s-important (accessed February 4, 2025).

10. Porcedda, M. G. (2018). "Privacy by design" in EU law, in: Medina, M., Mitrakas, A., Rannenberg, K., et al. (eds.), *Privacy Technologies and Policy*, APF 2018. Lecture Notes in Computer Science, vol. 11079, p. 92.

11. Porcedda, M. G. (2018). "Privacy by design" in EU law, in: Medina, M., Mitrakas, A., Rannenberg, K., et al. (eds.), *Privacy Technologies and Policy*, APF 2018. Lecture Notes in Computer Science, vol. 11079, p. 177.

12. DeMers, J. (2020). 5 fears you'll need to conquer before starting a business. *Medium*, November 9. Available at: https://jaysonde mers.medium.com/5-fears-youll-need-to-conquer-before-starting-a-b usiness-49a9a1fc8113 (accessed February 4, 2025).

13. US Department of Commerce, National Institute of Standards and Technology, Joint Task Force (2018). *Risk Management Framework for Information Systems and Organizations*, NIST Special Publication 800–37, Revision 2. Available at: https://doi.org/10.6028/NIST.SP.800-3 7r2 (accessed February 4, 2025).

14. US Department of Commerce, National Institute of Standards and Technology, Joint Task Force (2018). *Risk Management Framework for Information Systems and Organizations*, NIST Special Publication 800–37, Revision 2, p. 29. Available at: https://doi.org/10.6028/NIST.S P.800-37r2 (accessed February 4, 2025).

15. Schneier, B. (2003). *Beyond Fear: Thinking Sensibly about Security*. New York, NY: Copernicus Books.

16. Odlyzko, A. (2019). Cybersecurity is not very important. *Ubiquity* 2019(2): 1–23.

17. Kurutz, S. (2024). Welcome to scam world. *The New York Times*, April 21. Available at: www.nytimes.com/2024/04/21/style/scams-i dentity-theft.html (accessed February 4, 2025).

18. AAG (2024). The latest 2024 phishing statistics. April 1. Available at: https://aag-it.com/the-latest-phishing-statistics (accessed February 4, 2025).

19. Palatty, N. J. (2024). 90+ cyber crime statistics 2024: Cost, industries & trends. *Astra Security Blog*, February 6. Available at: www.getastra.com/ blog/security-audit/cyber-crime-statistics (accessed February 4, 2025).

20. Gartner.com (2023). Gartner unveils top eight cybersecurity predictions for 2023–2024. Press release. March 28. Available at: www.gart

ner.com/en/newsroom/press-releases/2023-03-28-gartner-unveils-t op-8-cybersecurity-predictions-for-2023-2024 (accessed February 4, 2025).

21. Gartner.com (2023). Gartner unveils top eight cybersecurity predictions for 2023–2024. Press release. March 28. Available at: www.gart ner.com/en/newsroom/press-releases/2023-03-28-gartner-unveils-t op-8-cybersecurity-predictions-for-2023-2024 (accessed February 4, 2025).

22. Kestner, P. (2024). *The Art of Cyber Warfare: Strategic and Tactical Approaches for Attack and Defense in the Digital Age*. Wiesbaden: Springer Nature.

23. Kestner, P. (2024). *The Art of Cyber Warfare: Strategic and Tactical Approaches for Attack and Defense in the Digital Age*. Wiesbaden: Springer Nature.

CHAPTER 10: THE UPGRADER'S MINDSET

1. Chan, W. (2022). "Unexpected item": How self-checkouts failed to live up to their promise. *The Guardian*, December 17. Available at: www.theguardian.com/business/2022/dec/16/self-checkout-us-re tail-walmart (accessed February 4, 2025).

2. Bjella, B. (2023). "It overcharges your card sometimes, keep your receipt": Circle K now has "smart" self-checkouts. *Daily Dot*, August 7. Available at: www.dailydot.com/news/circle-k-smart-self-c heckout/ (accessed February 4, 2025).

3. Daye, K. (2023). Why you may never see a cashier at Wegmans again. *WYRK*, May 17. Available at: https://wyrk.com/smart-cart-wegmans/ (accessed February 4, 2025).

4. Chan, W. (2022). "Unexpected item": How self-checkouts failed to live up to their promise. *The Guardian*, December 17. Available at: www.theguardian.com/business/2022/dec/16/self-checkout-us-re tail-walmart (accessed February 4, 2025).

5. Chan, W. (2022). "Unexpected item": How self-checkouts failed to live up to their promise. *The Guardian*, December 17. Available at: www.theguardian.com/business/2022/dec/16/self-checkout-us-re tail-walmart (accessed February 4, 2025).

6. Taylor, J. (2023). Woolworths expands self-checkout AI that critics say treats "every customer as a suspect." *The Guardian*, February 18. Available at: www.theguardian.com/business/2023/feb/19/wool worths-expands-self-checkout-ai-that-critics-say-treats-every-customer-as-a-suspect (accessed February 4, 2025).
7. Cerullo, M. (2025). Walgreens says locking up products to prevent shoplifting hurts sales. *CBS News*, January 15. Available at: www.cbsne ws.com/news/walgreens-lock-product-up-sales/ (accessed February 4, 2025).
8. Bonos, L. (2024). A new loneliness cure: Apps that match you with strangers for a meal. *The Washington Post*, August 19. Available at: www .washingtonpost.com/technology/2024/08/19/social-apps-friends-st rangers/ (accessed February 4, 2025); Holtermann, C. (2024). The extremely offline joy of the boardgame club. *The New York Times*, December 17. Available at: www.nytimes.com/2024/12/17/style/boa rd-games-club.html (accessed February 4, 2025); Docter-Loeb, H. (2024). "I feel more connected with humanity": The club where phones are banned – and visitors pay for the privilege. *The Guardian*. Available at: www.theguardian.com/lifeandstyle/article/2024/may/0 8/i-feel-more-connected-with-humanity-the-club-where-phones-are-ba nned-and-visitors-pay-for-the-privilege (accessed February 4, 2025).
9. Fontananissan.com (2024). Unveiling innovation: The cutting-edge technology in the 2024 Nissan cars. January 18. Available at: www.fo ntananissan.com/2024/01/18/unveiling-innovation-the-cutting-edg e-technology-in-the-2024-nissan-cars/ (accessed February 4, 2025); Anglen, J. (2024). Driving confidence: Top 10 reasons to choose Mitsubishi at O'Brien Mitsubishi. *O'Brien Mitsubishi*. Available at: www.obrienteammits.com/driving-confidence-top-10-reasons-to-c hoose-mitsubishi-at-obrien-mitsubishi/ (accessed February 4, 2025); Toyotadirect.com (2024). Experience Toyota innovation: Shop new models. June 14. Available at: www.toyotadirect.com/bl ogs/3084/car-dealer-ohio/experience-toyota-innovation-shop-ne w-models/ (accessed February 4, 2025); Mbseattle.com (2024). The Art of Luxury: Mercedez-Benz Design Innovations in Seattle.' *Mercedes Benz of Seattle*, March 21. Available at: www.mbseattle.co m/blogs/4953/the-art-of-luxury-mercedes-benz-design-innov ations-in-seattle (accessed February 4, 2025).

10. Diaz, J. (2022). Cars need their buttons and knobs back. *Fast Company*, August 19. Available at: www.fastcompany.com/90780466/cars-need-their-buttons-and-knobs-back (accessed February 4, 2025).

11. Diaz, J. (2022). Cars need their buttons and knobs back. *Fast Company*, August 19. Available at: www.fastcompany.com/90780466/cars-need-their-buttons-and-knobs-back (accessed February 4, 2025).

12. Bestride.com (2016). Promos: Car advertisements of the late 1960s, and the technology they hyped. Available at: https://bestride.com/news/technology/car-ads-1960s (accessed February 4, 2025).

13. Adarlo, S. (2024). People buying cars hate touch screens, instead getting used cars with knobs and buttons. *The Byte*, June 15. Available at: https://futurism.com/the-byte/people-hate-touch-screens-used-cars-knobs-buttons (accessed February 4, 2025).

14. Ottley, S. (2023). Hallelujah! Hyundai vows to resist modern trend for all-digital cabins and keep using buttons and dials. *Cars Guide*, March 18. Available at: www.carsguide.com.au/car-news/hallelujah-hyundai-vows-to-resist-modern-trend-for-all-digital-cabins-and-keep-using. (accessed February 4, 2025).

15. Kadish, A. and Fox Cahn, A. (2020). Schoolyard surveillance: The rise of K-12 contact tracing technologies. Surveillance Technology Oversight Project. Available at: https://static1.squarespace.com/static/5c1bfc7eee175995a4ceb638/t/5f4f9a38021aa5454e09eb7d/1599052345129/schoolyard+surveillance+FINAL.pdf (accessed February 4, 2025).

16. Keierleber, M. (2020). As COVID creeps into schools, surveillance tech follows. The 74, December 2. Available at: www.the74million.org/article/as-covid-creeps-into-schools-surveillance-tech-follows/ (accessed February 4, 2025).

17. *Fair Hous. Council of San Fernando Valley* v. *Roommates.Com, LLC*, 521 F.3d 1157 (9th Cir. 2008). Available at: www.eff.org/files/fairhousing-v-roommates.pdf (accessed February 4, 2025).

Acknowledgments

Our deepest thanks go to Matt Gallaway, Executive Editor at Cambridge University Press. His unwavering support and sharp feedback helped us throughout the long and ardous writing process. We owe a special debt of gratitude to Jon Cox. His keen editorial assistance helped us find the ever-elusive academic trade voice. Likewise, we're thankful for the editorial assistance Brian Bergstein, Justin Hendriks, and Michele Pridmore Brown provided on earlier writing that was integrated into this book. We also appreciate Roger Schlueter's feedback on how to clearly present some of the complex issues.

We're grateful to Tsion Agaro, Ana Sofia Harrison, Anuj Jain, Alissa Johnson, Vibha Kannan, Elena Kuran, Anne Marie Mulligan, Cyra Paladini, Samuel Shaffery, David Siffert, Jason Taper, Anya Weinstock, and so many others at S.T.O.P. for providing invaluable assistance with the preparation of the manuscript.

We're grateful to the Rochester Institute of Technology for providing essential institutional support through both a sabbatical leave and a Publication Cost grant.

Our heartfelt appreciation goes to John Mix, whose generosity and commitment to ongoing brainstorming sessions helped push our ideas forward.

We wish to thank Jesús Aguilar, Muhammad A. Ahmad, Thomas Carroll, Brenda Leong, and Carlos Montemayor for sharing their expert insights on matters related to artificial intelligence, Divya Ramee and Ashley Taylor for their wise guidance on cryptocurrency, and Joseph Jerome for sharp thoughts on the Metaverse.

It wouldn't have been possible to write about the benefits, limitations, and risks of AI without firsthand experience. And so, we acknowledge using tools like ChatGPT, Claude, and Grammarly to see what the technology could offer to the processes of brainstorming and editing.

Finally, we're indebted to Brett Frischmann, Chiara Natali, Sille Obelitz, and Søren Riis for facilitating valuable opportunities to share some of the ideas discussed here in Copenhagen and Malmö. The collegial and international discussions greatly enriched the work.

Index